GLOBAL ECONOMIC STUDIES

FINANCIAL CRISES

IDENTIFICATION, FORECASTING AND EFFECTS ON TRANSITION ECONOMIES

GLOBAL ECONOMIC STUDIES

Additional books in this series can be found on Nova's website under the Series tab.

Additional e-books in this series can be found on Nova's website under the e-book tab.

GLOBAL RECESSION - CAUSES, IMPACTS AND REMEDIES

Additional books in this series can be found on Nova's website under the Series tab.

Additional e-books in this series can be found on Nova's website under the e-book tab.

GLOBAL ECONOMIC STUDIES

FINANCIAL CRISES

IDENTIFICATION, FORECASTING AND EFFECTS ON TRANSITION ECONOMIES

COOPER A. HAWTHORNE
EDITOR

nova publishers
New York

For permission to use material from this book please contact us:
Telephone 631-231-7269; Fax 631-231-8175
Web Site: http://www.novapublishers.com

Additional color graphics may be available in the e-book version of this book.

Library of Congress Cataloging-in-Publication Data

Financial crises : identification, forecasting, and effects on transition economies / editor, Cooper A. Hawthorne.
pages cm
Includes index.
ISBN 978-1-62808-293-7 (hardcover)
1. Financial crises. I. Hawthorne, Cooper A.
HB3722.F543 2013
338.5'42--dc23

2013022840

Published by Nova Science Publishers, Inc. †New York

CONTENTS

PREFACE

In this book, the authors present topical research in the study of the identification, forecasting and effects on transition economies relating to financial crises events. Topics discussed include the relation between the financial health of local governments and the socioeconomic environment in periods of expansion and economic crisis in Spain; age differentials and the impact of the financial crisis on social relationships; what Asia and Europe did to fight the financial crisis; determinants of firm performance during and after the 2008-09 financial crisis in Europe and Central Asia; a survey of country versus industry effects in international equity returns; the Chinese economy in transition; Iceland's financial crisis; an empirical exploration of the causes of the 2008 financial crisis; the constitution of financial uncertainties during the Greek sovereign debt crisis; and the correlation and network structure of international financial markets in times of crisis.

Chapter 1 – Over the last years, several research studies have tested the influence of various elements of the economic environment on different financial aspects of public administrations. The current deep crisis in the Spanish economy has led us to research whether the relationship between the changes occurring in the economic environment and the changes in the financial health of local governments differs between periods of growth or recession. The complexity and interrelation between variables were evaluated through the multivariate statistical technique of canonical correlation on a sample representing more than 81% of all Spanish municipalities with a population of more than 1,000. The study demonstrates that, for a given population size, the iteration between variables is different when there is economic growth compared to when the economy is in recession.

Chapter 2 – In the face of the current global financial crisis, it would be informative to investigate how past crises have affected social relationships. Apart from the impact of the financial crisis on people in general, differentials in the impact across younger and older people are also possible. A household survey of 1,170 Hong Kong adults provided data for the study. The perceived impact of the financial crisis tended to affect closeness to other people, but it did not manifest a significant effect on other dimensions of social relationship. However, older people appeared to be more susceptible to the perceived financial crisis impact. The age differential was only partly attributable to age differences in living alone and not working. The impact of the financial crisis seems to be more influential on the social life of older people, partly because of their living and working arrangements. Notably, the impact of the financial crisis was less influential on one who held a working-class job. These findings imply the need for public policy to help mitigate the adverse effects of the negative impact of the financial crisis particularly on older people's social relationships.

Chapter 3 – The paper will look at the economic and financial crisis from a public policy point of view. There was a financial crisis in several countries in south-east Asia in the late nineties. Similarly, since 2008, the European Union has been challenged with its own crisis. The question of the paper is what responses have been developed in both regions at the super-national level in order to prevent or minimise future crises. First, the paper will look at the nature of the instruments developed, such as legally binding instruments or voluntary coordination instruments. In this respect, it will explore to what extent the countries are committed to sharing sovereignty. The second question is related to the geographical scope. In this part, the paper evaluates the ability of the region to engage with its broader neighbourhood. The paper focuses on the ASEAN Plus activities carried out in the Asian region in the broader sense. In Europe, the regulatory response to the European debt crisis is on two levels - on the one hand, between all 27 members of the EU and, on the other, in the narrower circle of the euro zone. The conclusion of this part underlines the trade-off between intensity and geographical scope, i.e. between shallow and wide measures in Asia, versus deep and narrow ones in Europe. Thirdly and finally, the paper evaluates the interplay between the regional and global response to the crisis. The main focus is, on the one hand, to what extent the regional initiatives inspired global governance and, on the other, how much the global decisions shaped regional governance.

Chapter 4 – The global financial crisis that hit in 2008-2009 affected firms throughout the world. Given the depth of the recession that hit Eastern Europe in late 2008 and 2009, it is not surprising that firms in the region were seriously affected by the crisis. It led to a collapse in trade, potentially affecting exporters, a collapse in domestic demand, potentially affecting all firms, and a collapse in the availability of credit, which should have affected those firms that had access before the crisis. In this paper the authors use firm-level data to look at how different types of firms were affected by the crisis. Having access to credit before the crisis does not appear to have benefitted firms during the crisis. Once the crisis was over, however, managers of firms that had access to credit before the crisis were more likely to report that their situation was improving. Given the collapse in trade, it seems plausible that export-oriented firms might have been more vulnerable than other firms. Our econometric results do not generally support this idea. At the beginning of thc crisis, export-oriented firms appear to have been affected to similar degrees as other firms. Managers of export-oriented firms did, however, report faster growth between March 2009 and March 2010 suggesting that exporters might have recovered more quickly from the crisis than other firms.

Chapter 5 – Numerous studies have sought to determine whether investors should diversify across countries and/or industries to improve their risk-return tradeoffs. The common methodological framework is to identify the country effects and industry effects embedded in cross-sectional variations in international stock returns. In general, empirical findings in the literature suggest that country effects are more important overall especially in emerging stock markets, but that the importance of industry effects has increased in the recent years and may have overtaken the dominant position of country effects in OECD countries especially in euro zone countries. It is still an open question whether geographical importance has permanently diminished on a global basis or that industry importance has increased globally. This survey aims to summarise and evaluate key studies on the relative importance of the country and industry effects in determining the cross-sectional variations in stock returns according to some key issues involved that may have contributed to the inconclusive results and also point to several directions that derived from this topic for future research.

Chapter 6 – This paper will demonstrate what China was doing, is doing and will do for its economic expansion during and after global crisis. Many thoughts and theories about Chinese economic reforms are analyzed. The road map and goal of Chinese economic growth are examined and outlined in this paper. How to keep Chinese economy fast growth is this paper's key issue which is thoroughly discussed.

Chapter 7 – The financial crisis of 2008 had different effects on countries within the same regions of the world. The Nordic countries mostly sailed through the crisis smoothly, comparatively at least compared to the rest of Europe, with Iceland being the major exception. Finland, Sweden and Norway went through a financial crisis during the late 1980s and beginning of the 1990s, with Finland and Sweden experiencing an especially severe meltdown in their financial systems. These three countries seem to have learned from that experience some twenty years ago. Iceland, still in the early 1990s bound to political and economic restrictions, entered the recent financial crisis especially vulnerable. This research shows that warnings signs leading up to crises were very similar. All of the Nordic countries were caught in an overconfident mood and structural deficiencies.

Chapter 8 – Starting with a large number of potential causes and indicators of the 2008 crisis (over sixty possible explanatory factors considered in the literature), the best econometric model for explaining the severity of the crisis is selected using a statistical methodology only guided by data via a Genetic Algorithm. Our results show that the best econometric model contains only one factor: 'percentage of bank claims in the year 2006'. Besides, this model is very robust after a sensitivity analysis is carried out. When lower penalty is considered for the introduction of factors in the model, the severity of the crisis is robustly explained by just two financial factors: 'percentage of bank claims in the year 2006', and 'percentage in GDP of Domestic Private Credit Sector in the year 2006'. Finally, in order to find out if all countries have the same behaviour during the crisis or if there are geographical differences in their response, the authors test for the presence of structural permanence of the coefficients of the main explanatory factors selected by the Genetic Algorithm. In this sense, after considering several dummy variables for different groups of countries, the existence of structural change has been rejected. Therefore, they find evidence of a uniform response on the severity of the crisis in the different countries, to changes in the factors explaining the crisis.

Chapter 9 – Building on a relatively new literature in the sociology of knowledge and science studies, this paper analyzes how financial actors minimized the uncertainties arising in the recent European sovereign debt crisis by resorting to non-linear practices of risk valuation by which they "constituted" the reality of those same financial uncertainties. Centering on the Greek sovereign debt crisis, the authors explain why credit rating agencies (CRAs), specifically Moody's, failed to recognize early signs of trouble in Greece, and displayed rating inertia before issuing multi-notch downgrades. Using ratings reports and press releases published by Moody's, the authors first show that CRAs used ratings they had already assigned to constitute the new threats they were tasked with predicting, a technique we call "backward reasoning." Second, they show that market regulators also made constitutive use of ratings' forecasting capacities to carry out their tasks of market surveillance and monitoring, forcing CRAs to anticipate the potentially destabilizing effects that further downgrades would have on Greece's borrowing costs. Such non-linear risk valuation practices created several inconsistencies in CRAs' predictions about Greece's ability to meet its financial commitment. They additionally show how these inconsistencies played out in the unfolding Greek sovereign debt crisis.

Chapter 10 – The chapter considers the correlation, volatility, and clustering structure of the benchmark indices of the main stock exchanges in the world. The importance of understanding how stock markets relate to each other, and which ones are the most connected, is of paramount importance to the study of how crises develop and propagate. They focus on the largest worldwide crisis in the last two decades, which started with the USA subprime mortgage crisis of 2008, and continued to the Credit Crisis in Europe (2009-2012). The data consists on 79 benchmark indices of stock exchanges across the world, from 2003 to 2012. They start by studying how the use of Random Matrix Theory helps identify a market mode that varies in intensity across the years, in particular in years of crises, and a structure that is typical of markets operating at different time zones. Then, the average correlation between indices and a global measure of volatility are compared, showing that in times of high volatility the international financial market indices are more correlated between themselves. They finally analyze the clustering of those indices, using tools from Network Theory. By doing so, it becomes clear that the correlations between international financial market indices depend very much on the geographical position of their markets, and on the operating times of those markets.

In: Financial Crises
Editor: Cooper A. Hawthorne

ISBN: 978-1-62808-293-7

Chapter 1

The Relation between the Financial Health of Local Governments and the Socioeconomic Environment in Periods of Expansion and Economic Crisis in Spain

Roberto Cabaleiro Casal [*] ***and Enrique J. Buch Gómez*** [†]
University of Vigo, Department of Financial Economics and Accounting,
As Lagoas Marcosende s/n, Vigo – Spain

Abstract

Over the last years, several research studies have tested the influence of various elements of the economic environment on different financial aspects of public administrations. The current deep crisis in the Spanish economy has led us to research whether the relationship between the changes occurring in the economic environment and the changes in the financial health of local governments differs between periods of growth or recession. The complexity and interrelation between variables were evaluated through the multivariate statistical technique of canonical correlation on a sample representing more than 81% of all Spanish municipalities with a population of more than 1,000. The study demonstrates that, for a given population size, the iteration between variables is different when there is economic growth compared to when the economy is in recession.

1. Introduction

The current global financial crisis in Spain is accompanied by a deep economic crisis. Consequently, the tax bases that support the financing of various public administrations have experienced a significant decline.

[*] Corresponding author: Email: rcab@uvigo.es; Tel. 0034 986 81 24 56; Fax. 0034 986 81 24 01.
[†] Email: ebuch@uvigo.es; Tel. 0034 986 81 24 70; Fax. 0034 986 81 24 01.

This has led us to investigate the relationship between the evolution of the various socioeconomic variables of the municipality, basically focusing on elements of economic activity (movements of population, unemployment, changes in the production structure) and the evolution of variables that measure the level of financial health of the municipal administration (debt, deficit, liquidity, revenues, spending structure). The analysis is performed in two different time periods, one of economic growth and the other of economic crisis, using a large sample of Spanish municipalities.

To identify the two time periods noted above (Growth - Crisis), we analyze the behavior of various macroeconomic variables in Spain. In this sense, the Bank of Spain [BDE] reports analyzing the Spanish economy indicate that the evolution of the Spanish economy during the years 2005-2008 is characterized by persistent GDP growth, with a foreign demand growth and a sustained business investment, all accompanied by a population increase and employment growth (BDE, 2006, 2007, 2008). The economic crisis in Spain began in 2008. In annual terms, the GDP grew at a rate of 1.2% in this exercise, although it fell at a rate of 0.7% in the last quarter (BDE, 2008). The GDP decline was aggravated in 2009 (-3.6%) by the contraction in domestic demand (over 6%). Although the crisis seemed to lessen in 2010 (-0.1%) and 2011 (0.7%), the continued decline in domestic demand (-3.9%) and GDP (-1.3%) in 2012 (BDE, 2013) confirms the continued strong economic crisis in Spain. An expansion-crisis cycle is reflected in the evolution of the different basic macroeconomic data shown in Figures 1 and 2.

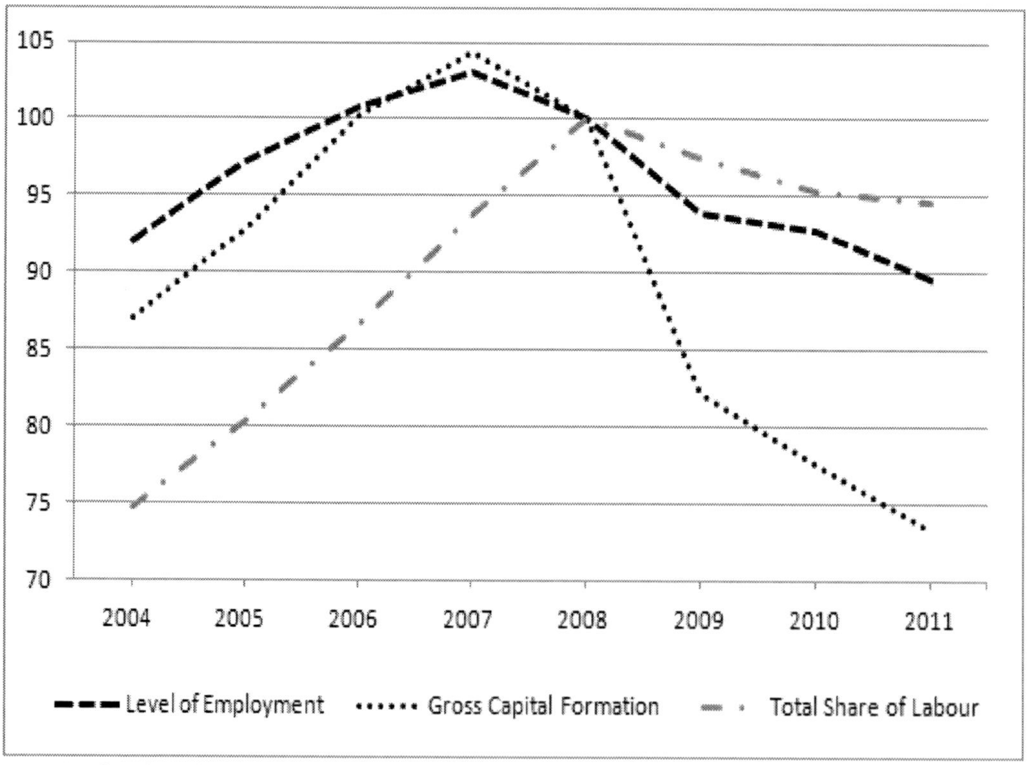

Source: National Statistics Institute.

Figure 1.

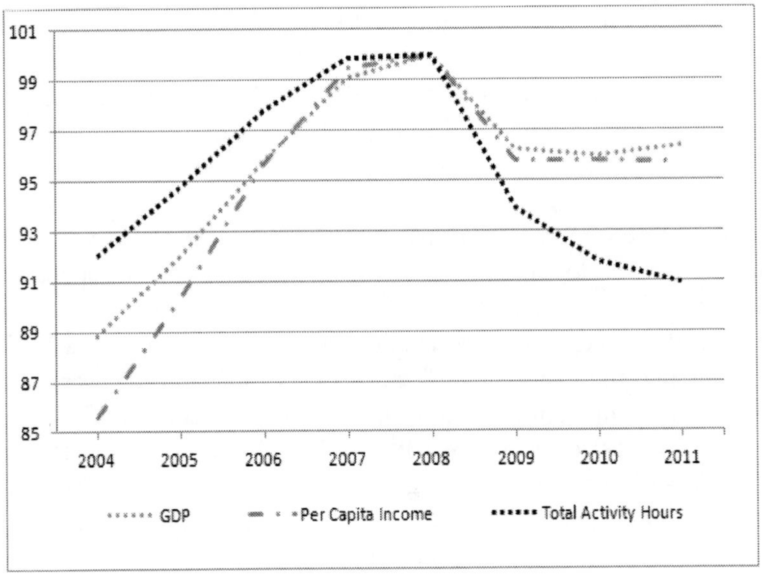

Source: National Statistics Institute.

Figure 2.

Taking the year 2008 as the turnaround point in our work, we use two time intervals, one characterized by economic growth (2005-2008) and another by the crisis (2008-2011). Taking into account these time intervals, we analyze in each of the two periods the relationship between the evolution of multiple financial indicators of the local governments and the evolution of diverse economic environment variables in their municipal geographical area, for which we will use a statistical methodology of multivariate analysis in view of the complex, multidimensional, and interdependent character that the financial health and economic environment have (Berne, 1992; Mead, 2001; Carmeli, 2007; Wang et al., 2007). This enables us to understand whether the relationship between the different aspects of the financial health of Spanish local governments and the diverse components of the economic environment in their geographical area differs between periods of growth and economic crisis.

2. Literature Review

2.1. The Financial Health of Local Governments

Knowledge of the financial health of public institutions, among which are local governments, is a constant topic today. The literature uses varied terms to analyse this issue in governments: fiscal health (Berry, 1994; Honadle and Lloyd-Jones, 1998; Ladd and Yinger, 1991; Kleine et al., 2003; Honadle, 2003; Hendrick, 2004; Carmeli, 2007), fiscal condition (Ratcliffe et al., 1990; Kloha et al., 2005a), fiscal strain (Clark and Ferguson, 1983; Morgan and England, 1983; Clark, 1994), fiscal distress (Cabill and James, 1992; Kleine et al., 2003; Kloha et al., 2005a, 2005b; Carmeli, 2007; Jones and Walker, 2007), fiscal crises (Inman, 1995; Carmeli, 2003; Honadle, 2003; Coe, 2008; Wolff, 2008), fiscal stress (Hughes and

Laverdiere, 1986; Wolman, 1992; Skidmore and Scorsone, 2011), financial condition (Lorig, 1941; Zehms, 1991; Berne, 1992; Brown, 1993, 1996; Mercer and Gilbert, 1996; Lin and Raman, 1998; Wolff and Hughes, 1998; Mead, 2001, 2006; Chaney et al., 2002; Chase and Phillips, 2004; Wang et al., 2007; Zafra et al., 2009a; Sohl et. al., 2009; Rivenbark and Roenigk, 2011), and financial health (Groves et al., 1981; Mercer and Gilbert, 1996; Zafra et al., 2009a; Cabaleiro et. al, 2012).

Referring to some of the terms previously noted, Berry (1994) defined the fiscal health of an institution as the "extent to which its financial resources exceed its spending obligations." Ratcliffe et al. (1990) used the term "fiscal condition," defining it as "the ability of a district to provide reasonable services at a reasonable tax burden on its residents." Kloha et al. (2005a, 2005b) adopted the expression "fiscal distress" and defined it as "a failure to meet standards in the areas of operating position, debt, and community needs and resources over successive years," whereas Jones and Walker (2007) referred to the same expression as "the inability to provide services at pre-existing levels." For Inman (1995), a situation of fiscal crises exists "when a city´s potential to raise revenues is insufficient to cover the city´s legally required expenditures." Financial condition was defined by Wang et al. (2007) as "the ability of an organization to timely meet its financial obligations" and by Lin and Raman (1998) as "the probability of being able to sustain the current level of services at acceptable levels of taxation." These indicate the existence of various terms, corresponding to different methodological approaches to analyze the same reality (Hendrick, 2004).

Zafra et al. (2009a) defined financial health as "the ability of the institution of meeting its debts and in turn providing acceptable levels of services." For some researchers (Honadle et al., 2004), financial condition is one of the less ambiguous terms for financial health, although the expression has been used with different connotations (Groves et al., 1981; Mead, 2001). In this sense, the Canadian Institute of Chartered Accountants [CICA] (1997) noted that the "financial health of an institution is its financial condition"; Honadle et al. (2004) also indicated that the term "financial condition" is closely linked to the concept of fiscal health.

In any case, it should be emphasized that these terms have a complex character, and they are configured by several nuances or dimensions. In this sense, Groves et al. (1981) considered four dimensions: cash solvency (the government`s capacity to generate enough cash or liquidity to pay its bills), budgetary solvency (the city`s ability to generate sufficient revenues over its normal budgetary period to meet its expenditure obligations and not incur deficits), long-run solvency (the long-run ability of a government to pay all the costs of doing business, including expenditure obligations that normally appear in each annual budget, as well as those that show up only in the years in which they must be paid), and service-level solvency (the government`s capacity to provide the level and quality of services required for the general health and welfare of a community). In addition, referring to the dimensions that the previous concepts include and applying statistical methodology to multiple indicators, Clark (1976) identified the dimensions of long- and short-run debts, expenditures, and tax efforts. Following this approach, Morgan and England (1983) distinguished three basic components. To evaluate the financial condition, Ammar et al. (2005) considered four dimensions: short-run financial condition, long-run financial condition, economic conditions, and performance. Hendrick (2004) summarized the dimensions of fiscal health as properties of the government`s environment (revenue wealth – spending needs – socioeconomic; political; and demographic features – changes in the previous), balance of fiscal structure with the environment, and properties of the government`s fiscal structure (fiscal slack – relativity of components within major structural areas – current operating conditions – future financial obligations – changes in fiscal slack; relativity of components; and current operating conditions).

Because these concepts are not directly observable, the problem arises as to the most appropriate instruments with which to measure them. There are several proposals, influenced by both the conceptual approach and the information available in each particular environment. The literature suggests considering a variety of dimensions and using some indicators. However, there has been no consensus on which dimensions and specific indicators (Wang et al., 2007). Diverse ratios and benchmarks have been used to evaluate governments' financial health, but there is no consistency in their selection, use, and application (Clark, 1976, 1994; Groves et al., 1981; Alter et. al., 1984; Zehms, 1991; Berne, 1992; Brown, 1993; Petro, 1998; Wolff and Huges, 1998; Kleine et al., 2003; Hendrick, 2004; Ammar, 2005; Kloha et al., 2005a, 2005b; Wang et al., 2007; Zafra et al., 2009a, 2009b).

The definition of terms with similar meaning (financial health, financial condition, economic condition, fiscal sustainability, financial sustainability) has also been considered by professional or normalizing institutions, such as the CICA (1997; 2009), the International City/County Management Association [ICMA] (2003), the Governmental Accounting Standards Board [GASB] (2004, 2011), the Local Government Association of South Australia [LGAs] (2006), and the Federal Accounting Standards Advisory Board [FASAB] (2009). Two of the most important contributions for its extensive application in local governments are the frameworks developed by the CICA (2009) and the ICMA (2003). Thereby, the CICA (2009) considers three dimensions: (1) sustainability (the degree to which a government can maintain its existing financial obligations both in respect of its service commitments to the public and its financial commitments to creditors, employees, and others, without increasing the relative debt or tax burden on the economy within which it operates), (2) flexibility (the degree to which a government can change its debt or tax burden on the economy within which it operates to meet its existing financial obligations both in respect of its service commitments to the public and its financial commitments to creditors, employees, and others), and (3) vulnerability (the degree to which a government is dependent on sources of funding outside its control or influence or is exposed to risks that could impair its ability to meet its existing financial obligations both with respect to its service commitments to the public and its financial commitments to creditors, employees, and others). Greenberg and Hillier (1995) also followed the analysis approach focusing on these dimensions.

Another important contribution, applied by local governments of the United States, is the Financial Trend Monitoring System (FTMS). Released by the ICMA, the FTMS is intended to serve as an internal monitoring system. The current version of the FTMS (ICMA, 2003) is adapted to the reporting requirements of Statement No. 34 (GASB, 1999) for local governments and is based on the definition and dimensions developed by Groves et al. (1981).

The GASB (2004) adopted the term "economic condition" to refer to a composite of a government's financial health and its ability and willingness to meet its financial obligations and commitments to provide services. In this sense, the GASB (2004) is assimilating financial health with financial position because it notes that economic condition includes financial position (the status of a government's asset, liability, and net asset accounts, as displayed in its basic financial statements), fiscal capacity (a government's ongoing ability and willingness to raise revenues, incur debt, and meet its financial obligations as they come due), and service capacity (a government's ongoing physical ability and willingness to supply the capital and human resources needed to meet its commitments to provide services) (Mead, 2001b; Chaney et al., 2002).

The complexity of the issue could perhaps be summarized in the Research Reports published by the GASB (Berne, 1992), which highlighted that the issue is multidimensional or multi-constituent, with complex interdependencies among its various parts, and is rooted in a government's economic environment and involves implicit as well as explicit obligations that are not necessarily reflected in cash flows or financial contracts. For these reasons, the focus is only on financial aspects in some cases (Wang et al., 2007; Rivenbark and Roenigk, 2011; Cabaleiro et al., 2012), whereas in other cases, socioeconomic aspects are also included (Sohl et. al., 2009). Wang et al. (2007) noted that considering a purely financial view of the concept would exclude socioeconomic factors from the core concept, although they can be accepted as conditioning factors.

2.2. The Economic Environment Elements as Variables that Influence the Financial Health of Municipalities

Municipal governments develop their activity in a particular physical context, and in this context lies the population that they serve. The adequate financial health of local governments, understood as an adequate financial position, is an issue of considerable importance because it facilitates compliance with the services that the institution must provide to citizens. Also, in this physical environment, economic activity is developed and configured as a basis for obtaining a significant portion of the municipal government's financial resources. It should be kept in mind that local governments use different strategies to develop their territorial space economically, practicing interjurisdictional competition through fiscal or other incentives to attract economic activity. This behavior is based on the belief (Kwon, 2006) that economic growth reduces local unemployment, strengthening the tax base and promoting a favorable business climate that increases prosperity. However, this conduct often necessitates increased outlays for public infrastructure and is accompanied by an increase in demand for public services. The relationship between the cost and benefit of this policy may result in an improvement or a worsening of the municipal financial position if the possible development does not pay all the costs of the facilities and the services extended by the local institution (Honadle, 2004). In this sense, many academics affirm that the municipal financial health and socioeconomic characteristics are interrelated (Carmeli and Cohen, 2001, Honadle et al., 2004; Wang et al., 2007). Also, the framework developed by the ICMA, the goal of which is to provide a method for monitoring the financial condition of local governments, notes that environmental factors may create demands, provide resources, or both and therefore emphasizes that these factors must be analyzed. The ICMA (2003) includes among these environmental factors the level of unemployment and business activity as aspects that are part of "community needs and resources."

Taking into account the previously mentioned theoretical foundations, several researches have examined the influence of economic environment factors on the financial aspects of public administrations, and the variables used to characterize the economic environment have been very diverse (Rubinfeld, 1987; Ladd, 1992; Clark, 1994; Smith and Edmonston, 1997;

Alesina et al., 2004; Carruthers and Úlfarsson, 2008; Hopkins, 2009; Benito et al., 2010a; 2010b; 2010c).

The population variable and its variation, justified in that they represent the whole of units that demand municipal services and are the payers of council tax, have been contrasted in several studies related to local finance (Oates, 1988; Ladd and Yinger, 1991; Cutler et al., 1993; Cox and Utt, 2004; Buettner et al., 2004; Skidmore and Scorsone, 2011; Cabaleiro et al., 2012). The impact of immigration, because it quantitatively and qualitatively modifies the population, has also been contrasted with the economic and fiscal issues of local governments (Huddle, 1993; Passel, 1994; Smith and Edmonston, 1997).

In a study about the role played by federal states in the fiscal crises experienced by local governments, Honadle (2003) considered the economic sectors, the nature of the territory, the population structure, and population movements. Kwon (2006) regarded subnational debt financing as fundamentally sensitive to subnational economic conditions and, in consequence, affirmed that economic activity factors are a key element. From a transverse perspective, Wang et al. (2007) studied the relationship between the financial condition and population (size and growth rate) and diverse economic factors; they concluded that positive and negative socioeconomic developments are associated with an improved and a deteriorated financial condition, respectively.

To develop a methodological approach for benchmarking the financial position of municipalities that have very similar profiles, Sohl et al. (2009) considered the unemployment rate as one of several variables for measuring the economic environment level. Zafra et al. (2009a, 2009b) developed another methodology to measure the financial condition of local authorities, including variables to measure the quality of the services received by the population. To create a municipal socioeconomic profile, they used the unemployment and net migration rates and the type of economic activity in the area, among other variables.

In general terms, previous studies have indicated that economic environment variables have a significant impact on the financial aspects that they considered. However, the literature has not taken into account that the relationships showing the effects that may occur between variables related to the financial position of the entity and those related to the economic environment may differ between periods of growth and economic crisis. This has led us to the following hypothesis:

Hypothesis: The relationship between the financial health of local governments and their economic environment is different between periods of growth and economic crisis.

3. The Relation between the Financial Health of Local Governments and the Socioeconomic Environment in Periods of Expansion and Economic Crisis in Spain

3.1. Data

The data used in this study to assess the financial situation of Spanish local governments were obtained from the databases *Settlement of the Local Budgets for the years 2005, 2008, and 2011* (Ministry of Economy and Finance [MEH], 2013a) and *Municipal Debt Volume for 2008 and 2011* (MEH, 2013b). The debt data for 2005 were calculated by a retrospective method from the debt of each municipality in 2008 and using information from the change in financial debt of the budget settlements for the years 2005-2008. Data on *Population* and *Immigration* were extracted from the National Statistics Institute [INE] (2013). The representative data on economic activity were extracted from the Spain Economic Yearbook of La Caixa (2006, 2009, 2012), which contains information relating to municipalities with more than 1,000 inhabitants. This therefore limited the study to municipalities with a population exceeding 1,000.

In the studied years, there were more than 3,200 municipalities in Spain with more than 1,000 inhabitants, and their aggregate population represented more than 95% of the total population of the country. After crossing all the databases used in the work and eliminating outliers, the sample of municipalities used was higher than 2,600 entities in all years. This sample represents more than 81% of all Spanish municipalities with more than 1,000 inhabitants.

3.2. Methodology

The complexity of municipal financial analysis "requires that a mosaic of indicators be employed to account for the multitude of internal and external financial factors that comprise any given community's financial profile" (Sohl et al., 2009). For coherence, to assess the different aspects of the comprehensive financial situation of Spanish municipalities, we will use as basis a set of indicators (Table 1) that reflects, in general, the dimensions that provide both the frameworks developed by professional institutions (ICMA, 2003; CICA 1997, 2009) and some concepts used in diverse researches (Zehms, 1991; Berne, 1992; Brown, 1993; Honadle et al., 2004; Hendrick, 2004; Mead, 2001, 2006; Kloha et al., 2005a; Wang et al., 2007; Zafra et al., 2009a; Rivenbark and Roenigk, 2011, Cabaleiro et al., 2012).

According to the literature that has confirmed the existence of different effects of economic environment variables on various aspects of the financial situation of public institutions, the economic environment will be measured through a set of variables related to the population (Ladd and Yinger, 1991; Cutler et al., 1993; Passel, 1994; Smith and Edmonston, 1997; Wang, 2007; Bastida et al., 2009; Benito et al., 2010a; Guillamón et al., 2011; Cabaleiro et al., 2012), unemployment, and business activity (Honadle, 2003; Sohl et al., 2009; Zafra et al., 2009a, Benito et al., 2010b; 2010c) in the geographical area of the municipality. Table 2 shows the variables used.

In performing this analysis, we cannot ignore that in Spain, article 26 of the law that regulates the basic operations of municipalities (*Ley 7/1985, de 2 de Abril, Reguladora de las Bases de Régimen Local*) (LRBRL) establishes the levels of services to be met by municipalities by population criteria. In this sense, the population segments established by this law are: less than 5,000 inhabitants; between 5,000 and 20,000 inhabitants; and more than 50,000 inhabitants. The service levels established in the law affect the amount of financial resources, as well as the structure and financial management of the institution. To avoid any possible distortion that could result from a joint analysis that does not consider these constraints, we segmented the sample of municipalities according to the above population segments to allow an analysis on homogeneous groups of municipalities.

Table 1. Financial indicators

Dimension	Ind.	Concept	Ratio	Description
Short-run solvency	FI1	Refined short-term solvency	CCE+AR-DAR-EF / OO	Refined short-term solvency: Cash and Cash Equivalents (CCE) plus accounts receivable (AR), less doubtful accounts receivable (DAR) and excess funds to finance expenditures earmarked funding (EF), divided by the outstanding obligations (OO) at year end.
	FI2	Quick ratio	CCE / OO	Quick Ratio: Cash and Cash Equivalents (CCE) divided by outstanding obligations (OO) at year end.
Long-run solvency	FI3	Sustainability/Long-run solvency	Long-term debt / TNBR	Long-term debt in relation to the total net budgetary revenues (TNBR)
Budgetary solvency	FI4	Sustainability/Current budget balance	NBR Ch(1). 1 to 5 / NBO Ch.1 to 4	Net current budgetary revenues divided by net budget obligations (NBO) from current expenditures
	FI5	Sustainability/Primary budget balance	NBR Ch. 1 a 5 / NBO Ch.1 to 4 and 9	Net current budgetary revenues divided by budget obligations from non-financial current expenditures, minus debt service.
	FI6	Flexibility/ Coverage	NBO Ch. 3 and 9 / NBR Ch.1 to 5	Debt service (interest and principal) divided by net current budgetary revenues
	FI7	Size / Revenues	Total NBR / Pop.	Total net budgetary revenues per inhabitant.
	FI8	Current Independence	NBR Ch 1 to 3 / NBO Ch 1 to 4	Direct and indirect taxes and fees divided by net budget obligations from current expenditures.
	FI9	Gross Independence	NBR Ch. 4 and 7 / Total NBR	Current and capital transfers divided by total net budgetary revenues

Table 1. Continued

Dimension		Ind.	Concept	Ratio	Description
Spending structure	Expenditure by nature	FI10	Investment effort	NBO Ch. 6 and 7 / Total NBR	Net budget obligations from capital expenditures, capital transfers and capital grants divided by total net budgetary revenues.
		FI11	Salaries of political staff expenses	NBO Ch. 1, art. 1 / NBO Ch.1 to 4	Expenses on salaries of governing bodies and management staff divided by net budget obligations from current expenditures
		FI12	Other personnel expenses	(NBO (Ch. 1 - Ch. 1, art. 1) / NBO Ch.1 to 4	Total salaries expenses minus expenses on salaries of governing bodies and management staff divided by net budget obligations from current expenditures
		FI13	Acquisition of goods and services	NBO Ch. 2 / NBO Ch.1 to 4	Obligations from expenditures on purchasing goods and contracting services divided by net budget obligations from current expenditures.
	Spending policies	FI14	Safety and security	Politic.Expend[2]. 13 / Total NBO	Obligations from expenditures on civil protection, public safety, vehicle traffic, and fire protection in relation to net budget obligations from total expenditures.
		FI15	Real state and urban planning	Politic.Expend.. 15 / Total NBO	Obligations from expenditures on housing development and urban planning protection in relation to net budget obligations from total expenditures.
		FI16	Community welfare	Politic.Expend. 16 / Total NBO	Obligations from community welfare spending (Water supply, sewerage and wastewater treatment, municipal waste collection, street cleaning, cemeteries, street lighting) protection in relation to net budget obligations from total expenditures.
		FI17	Environmental protection	Politic.Expend. 17 / Total NBO	Obligations from expenditures on environmental protection in relation to net budget obligations from total expenditures.
		FI18	Social services	Area[3] Expend. 2 / Total NBO	Obligations from expenditure on social services agency and promoting employment protection in relation to net budget obligations from total expenditures.

Dimension	Ind.	Concept	Ratio	Description
	FI19	Preferential public service	Area Expend. 3 / Total NBO	Obligations from expenditure on preferential public service (Health, education, culture and sport) pin relation to net budget obligations from total expenditures.
	FI20	Economic activity	Area Expend. 4 / Total NBO	Obligations from expenditure on promotion of economic activity in relation to net budget obligations from total expenditures.
	FI21	Total costs associated with the political management	Politic.Expend. 91 / Total NBO	Obligations from expenditure on political governing in relation to net budget obligations from total expenditures.
	FI22	General services	Politic.Expend. 92 / Total NBO	Obligations from expenditure on general services (administrative staff and expenses) protection in relation to net budget obligations from total expenditures.

(1): Chapter of the economic classification of the budgets in Spain

(2): Policy of expenditure on the Planning Programing Budgeting System in Spain

(3): Area of expenditure on the Planning Programing Budgeting System in Spain

Table 2. Indicators of economic environment

Indicator	Denomination	Description
EI1	Population	Number of inhabitants registered in the municipality
EI2	Immigrants	Number of not Spanish inhabitants registered in the municipality
EI3	Unemployment	Number of unemployed registered in the Public Employment Service in relation to the potentially active population (16 to 64).
EI4	Youth Unemployment	Number of unemployed registered in the Public Employment Service in relation to the potentially active population (16 to 24).
EI5	Industry	Number of industrial activities that are subject to tax on economic activities (IAE). The number of industrial activities is practically equivalent to the number of industrial establishments in each municipality.
EI6	Construction	Number of construction activities that are subject to tax on economic activities (IAE). The number of construction activities is practically equivalent to the number of construction establishments in each municipality.
EI7	Wholesale trade	Number of activities in wholesale trade that are subject to tax on economic activities (IAE), which are a good approximation of the number of merchant wholesale establishments in each municipality.
EI8	Retail activities	Number of retail activities that are subject to tax on economic activities (IAE). For statistical purposes, the number of retail activities is an approach to commercial premises (a commercial establishment may have one or more activities or commercial licenses).

It must be highlighted that the different aspects or dimensions that make up the financial health of any institution have multiple relationships (Berne, 1992). Consequently, this requires a comprehensive (Cabaleiro et al., 2012) analysis that jointly addresses all these aspects or financial nuances. Similarly, in the economic environment, interactions also occur between various demographic, economic, and structural factors.

The underlying problem leads us to the need to find an appropriate instrument with which to address this situation. We found information on a large group of variables that can be further classified into two subgroups; within each of these subgroups, there can also be a certain degree of correlation between variables. Removing variables to avoid loss of degrees of freedom in the models of efficiency can lead to loss of important information related to the eliminated variables. Furthermore, if there are correlations within a set of many explanatory variables, the estimated regression model for each separately endogenous variable leads to problems of inaccuracy in the estimators. For this reason, the results of individual contrasts of significance should be treated with extreme caution. This is because the correlation between the various explanatory variables causes significant sensibility in the estimations when small changes occur in the sample obtained, resulting in scarcely robust and reliable models. The application of statistical models of reduction of dimensions seeking a smaller number of uncorrelated variables would be recommended a priori when the number of correlated variables is high and it is difficult to determine which variables are the determinants of the variability. However, this has a disadvantage in that it cannot guarantee that the new variables would retain the explanatory power of the original variables that attempt to explain the variability. Furthermore, performing a factor analysis on each of the two sets of variables (dependents - explanatory) ensures intra-group noncorrelation but does not guarantee a high correlation between the two sets of variables.

The previous arguments have led us to use canonical correlation analysis, which is recommended when the number of both dependents and explanatory variables is high and there are correlations between the variables in each group.

Because the objective of this analysis is to determine whether the relationship between changes in the economic environment and changes in the financial position of Spanish municipalities is different in growth or economic crisis, it is necessary to incorporate the dynamic dimension at work.

In line with this argument and taking 2008 as the turning point (see Figures 1 and 2), we proceed to estimate the changes in the financial variables of the municipalities and in the economic environment variables identified in the previous sections during periods of expansion (2005-2008) and economic crisis (2008-2011). The variations are calculated according to the following expressions:

$$VFI_{ijt} = \frac{FI_{ijt} - FI_{ijt-1}}{FI_{ijt-1}} \qquad VEI_{kjt} = \frac{EI_{kjt} - EI_{kjt-1}}{EI_{kjt-1}};$$

VFI_{ijt}: Change in financial indicator i of the municipality j in the interval (t, t−1)

FI_{ijt}: Value of financial indicator i of the municipality j in the year t

FI_{ijt-1}: Value of financial indicator i of the municipality j in the year t-1

VEI_{kjt}: Change in economic environment indicator k of the municipality j in the interval (t, t−1)

EI_{kjt}: Value of economic environment indicator k of the municipality j in the year t

EI_{kjt-1}: Value of economic environment indicator k of the municipality j in the year t-1

t: Final year interval

$t-1$: Initial year interval

Consequently, the analysis model that we will use is based on the estimation of the vectors that best combine all the changes in the financial position of municipalities and are most correlated with the vectors that best combine all the changes in the economic environment; their correlation is maximized as follows:

$$V_{jt} = \sum_{i=1}^{22} \alpha_{ijt} VFI_{it}$$

$$W_{jt} = \sum_{k=1}^{8} \beta_{kjt} VEI_{kt}$$

$$MaxCorr(V_{jt}, W_{jt})$$

The application of this process in the two time intervals, 2005-2008 and 2008-2011, will allow us to observe from a comprehensive perspective any differences in the behavior of the financial variables in relation to the economic environment variables in both periods of growth and of economic crisis.

3.3. Analysis of Results

We calculated the values of all indicators, and on this basis, computed their variations in each of the intervals and in each of the population segments previously identified. The observation of scatterplots between the financial variables and the economic environment variables has shown us that we can consider it appropriate to analyze the association using a linear model, rejecting any other type of relationship (exponential, logarithmic, quadratic, etc.).

A first approach to the relationship between changes in economic variables and in financial position can be read in cross-correlation matrices. In the period of economic growth (2005-2008), this matrix[1] indicates a priori that, for the first three population segments (municipalities with less than 50,000 inhabitants), the change in the total independence indicator of municipalities (VFI9) is most affected by changes in economic environment variables. Those variations in municipal population (VEI1) and unemployment (VEI3) that carry a positive sign have greater correlation. This seems to indicate a concern among regional and national institutions to increase transfers when populations and unemployment grow. This is consistent with the insufficiency of own financial resources for the management of municipal responsibilities that managers have been manifesting during recent years.

In addition, and in general for municipalities of any size, the changes in population (VEI1) and unemployment (VEI3, VEI4) variables are negatively correlated with the variation in the total local government revenue per capita (VFI7). That is, the per capita budget revenues decrease when the population or unemployment increases. This seems to complement and corroborate the financial insufficiency of local governments indicated previously. It must be emphasized that in times of economic expansion, this financial insufficiency is also manifested in a negative correlation with the variation in the current independence indicator (VFI8), which is much more pronounced in the most populated municipalities (over 50,000 inhabitants).

During the period of economic crisis (2008-2011), the degree of relationship between the evolution of the financial position of local governments and the evolution of the economic environment is different. In smaller municipalities, the correlation between the economic environment evolution and the changes in the overall financial position of local governments is generally very low. In medium-sized municipalities, we detected a significant level of correlation between the variation that occurs in the sustainability/primary budget balance indicator (VFI5) and that in the economic environment. This segment also shows a sensible positive correlation between population change (VEI1) and the variation in the sustainability/current budget balance indicator (VFI4), as well as a negative correlation between the change in retail trade (VEI8) and the evolution of this financial aspect. In larger municipalities, the economic variables with the greatest influence on the municipal financial

[1] The cross-correlation tables can be obtained requested from the authors via through their e-mail.

situation are the variation in activities related to construction (VEI6) and population change (VEI1). This effect basically influences the sustainability of local finances, showing the accumulation of current and primary deficits (VFI4 and VFI5).

After this preliminary reading, we applied the analysis model of canonical correlation between the set of variables that provide a comprehensive view of the changes in the financial position of municipalities and the set of indicators of changes in the economic environment into the municipal geographical area and in each population segment.

The independence test indicates that during the period of economic growth, only the first two pairs of canonical variables have significant correlations ($p < 0.001$) (Table 3) for municipalities with less than 50,000 inhabitants. In particular, the first pair of variables, which accounts for $18.6/(18.6 + 2.9 + 2.4 + 2.1 + 1.6 + 1.0 + 0.9 + 0.5) = 62.03\%$ of the variability, reaches a correlation level of 0.431 in very small municipalities (population of less than 5,000). In municipalities with a population between 5,000 and 20,000, as well as in those with between 20,000 and 50,000 inhabitants, the first two pairs of canonical variables are significant, explaining 52.07% and 30.05% of the data variability and reaching correlation levels of 0.435 and 0.575, respectively. The evidence shows a correlation between changes in the economic environment and in the financial position in municipalities with a population of less than 50,000 during times of economic expansion, although the explained variability decreases as the municipalities increase in population size.

A different behavior is observed in the crisis period. The independence test shows the existence of more pairs of canonical variables that have significant correlations ($p < 0.1$) (Table 3) and for all population segments. For municipalities with less than 5,000 inhabitants, only the first pair of variables has a significant correlation ($p < 0.01$), accounting for 61.70% of the variability and reaching a correlation level of 0.418. In each of the remaining population segments, there are two pairs of significant canonical vectors. The first pair explains 40.29%, 23.79%, and 28.63% of the data variability for municipalities with a population between 5,000 and 20,000 inhabitants, between 20,000 and 50,000 inhabitants, and more than 50,000 inhabitants, respectively; the respective correlation levels are 0.421, 0.515, and 0.702 ($p < 0.01$). The second pair explains 20.32%, 19.73%, and 19.75% of the variability for the above-mentioned municipalities, respectively, with a correlation level of 0.299 ($p < 0.01$), 0.469 ($p < 0.05$), and 0.583 ($p < 0.1$). This seems to indicate a stronger relationship between changes in the economic environment and those in the financial position of municipalities in times of crisis compared to periods of economic growth, and such relationship is more remarkable in the most populated municipalities.

An internal reading of pairs of canonical vectors that are significantly correlated (Table 4) indicates that in the period of economic growth (2005-2008), the canonical loads in each of these vectors (V1, W1) show that, basically, the variations in population (VEI1) and unemployment (VEI3 and VEI4) indicators, in this order of importance, seem to be more associated with the changes in total vulnerability (VFI9), current vulnerability (VFI8), and per capita budget revenues (VFI7) in municipalities with less than 5.000 inhabitants. The analysis of the cross-loadings for the financial set allows us to observe that the total vulnerability (VFI9) and per capita budget revenue (VFI7) variables are more correlated with the economic environment vector, in this order for municipalities with less than 5,000 inhabitants and in reverse order for municipalities with a bigger population.

Table 3. Canonical Correlation Analysis

Municipalities less than 5000 inh.													
Interval of expansion (2005-2008)							Interval of crisis (2008-2011)						
Canonical Correlations			Test that remaining correlations are zero				Canonical Correlations			Test that remaining correlations are zero			
$P^{(*)}$	λ	Corr.	Wilk's	Chi-SQ	DF	Sig.	$P^{(*)}$	λ	Corr.	Wilk's	Chi-SQ	DF	Sig.
1	.186	.431	.726	468.749	176.000	.000	1	.175	.418	.739	451.457	176.000	.000
2	.029	.17	.891	168.342	147.000	.110	2	.034	.184	.896	163.843	147.000	.162
3	.024	.156	.918	125.493	120.000	.347	3	.025	.158	.928	112.534	120.000	.673
4	.021	.144	.941	89.514	95.000	.640	4	.021	.144	.951	74.839	95.000	.937
5	.016	.125	.961	58.643	72.000	.872	5	.012	.108	.971	43.368	72.000	.997
6	.010	.101	.976	35.393	51.000	.953	6	.011	.103	.983	25.736	51.000	.999
7	.009	.095	.986	20.333	32.000	.945	7	.005	.068	.993	9.933	32.000	1.000
8	.005	.07	.995	7.152	15.000	.953	8	.002	.045	.998	3.093	15.000	1.000
Municipalities with population between 5000 and 20000 inh.													
Interval of expansion (2005-2008)							Interval of crisis (2008-2011)						
Canonical Correlations			Test that remaining correlations are zero				Canonical Correlations			Test that remaining correlations are zero			
$P^{(*)}$	λ	Corr.	Wilk's	Chi-SQ	DF	Sig.	$P^{(*)}$	λ	Corr.	Wilk's	Chi-SQ	DF	Sig.
1	.189	.435	.679	306.355	176.000	.000	1	.177	0.421	.628	353.538	176.000	.000
2	.058	.241	.837	140.705	147.000	.631	2	.089	0.299	.763	205.443	147.000	.001
3	.039	.198	.889	93.191	120.000	.967	3	.066	.257	.838	134.458	120.000	.173
4	.032	.180	.925	61.426	95.000	.997	4	.038	.196	.897	82.577	95.000	.815
5	.024	.154	.956	35.442	72.000	1.000	5	.032	.180	.933	52.920	72.000	.955
6	.011	.105	.979	16.477	51.000	1.000	6	.017	.130	.964	27.817	51.000	.997
7	.006	.077	.990	7.732	32.000	1.000	7	.015	.121	.981	14.830	32.000	.996
8	.004	.062	.996	3.080	15.000	1.000	8	.005	.070	.995	3.685	15.000	.999

Table 3. (Continued)

Municipalities with population between 20000 and 50000 inh.													
Interval of expansion (2005-2008)							Interval of crisis (2008-2011)						
P(*)	λ	Corr.	Wilk's	Chi-SQ	DF	Sig.	P(*)	λ	Corr.	Wilk's	Chi-SQ	DF	Sig.
1	.331	.575	.290	245.907	176.000	.000	1	.265	.515	.293	239.875	176.000	.001
2	.210	.458	.433	166.304	147.000	.132	2	.220	.469	.399	179.551	147.000	.035
3	.187	.433	.547	119.658	12.000	.492	3	.158	.397	.512	13.910	12.000	.234
4	.162	.402	.674	78.404	95.000	.891	4	.132	.363	.608	97.298	95.000	.415
5	.083	.288	.804	43.323	72.000	.997	5	.112	.334	.700	69.751	72.000	.553
6	.064	.253	.877	26.088	51.000	.999	6	.099	.314	.788	46.566	51.000	.650
7	.038	.194	.937	12.929	32.000	.999	7	.076	.276	.874	26.291	32.000	.751
8	.026	.162	.974	5.283	15.000	.989	8	.054	.232	.946	1.788	15.000	.767
Municipalities more than 50000 inh.													
Interval of expansion (2005-2008)							Interval of crisis (2008-2011)						
Canonical Correlations			Test that remaining correlations are zero				Canonical Correlations			Test that remaining correlations are zero			
P(*)	λ	Corr.	Wilk's	Chi-SQ	DF	Sig.	P(*)	λ	Corr.	Wilk's	Chi-SQ	DF	Sig.
1	.396	.629	.183	191.101	176.000	.207	1	.493	.702	.124	255.737	176.000	.000
2	.301	.549	.303	134.422	147.000	.763	2	.340	.583	.244	172.614	147.000	.073
3	.254	.504	.433	94.065	12.000	.962	3	.293	.541	.370	121.802	12.000	.437
4	.187	.432	.581	61.140	95.000	.997	4	.217	.466	.523	79.375	95.000	.876
5	.125	.353	.714	37.903	72.000	1.000	5	.157	.396	.669	49.322	72.000	.981
6	.084	.289	.816	22.893	51.000	1.000	6	.117	.342	.793	28.417	51.000	.996
7	.075	.274	.890	13.113	32.000	.999	7	.057	.239	.898	13.171	32.000	.999
8	.038	.195	.962	4.349	15.000	.996	8	.048	.219	.952	5.997	15.000	.980

(*) Pairs of canonical vectors

The analysis shows that in times of economic crisis, a single significant pair of canonical vectors exists in municipalities with a population of less than 5,000. For local governments that exceed this population threshold, the statistical model indicates the existence of two significant pairs of canonical variables. This means that in municipalities with this population level, the changes in the economic environment appear to be associated with financial variables across two different behaviors.

In municipalities with less than 2.000 inhabitants, the existence of the same canonical loads as those for variations of the indicators in the period of economic crisis (a single canonical pair in municipalities with less than 5,000 inhabitants; the first canonical pair in municipalities with a population between 5,000 and 2.000), in relation to the situation observed in the period of economic growth, indicates that the responses of the financial variables to the changes in the economic environment are similar in both periods. Furthermore, for municipalities with a population between 5,000 and 2.00. this pair of canonical vectors also shows the impact of changes in the economic environment on the variation that occurs in the acquisition of goods and the procurement of services in relation to the total current expenditure of the local government.

The pairs of canonical variables more correlated in municipalities that exceed the population threshold of 2.00. are giving significant weight to the variation in population (VEI1) and changes in construction (VEI6). Retail trade (VEI8) also has an important load in middle-sized municipalities (2.000 to 5.000 inhabitants). The aspects of financial position that are more affected by alterations in the economic environment variables previously identified differ between municipalities with a population between 2.000 and 5.000 inhabitants (VFI4: Current Budget Balance, VFI7: Per Capita Budget Revenues, and VFI9: Gross Independence) and those with a bigger population (VFI4: Current Budget Balance, VFI6: Flexibility, and VRI8: Current Independence).

As noted above, unlike in the period of economic expansion, second significant pairs of canonical vectors appear for municipalities with more than 5,000 inhabitants in the crisis period. In general terms, these pairs show a marked correlation between changes in unemployment and youth unemployment, together with changes in the economic activities of construction and retail trade in the local environment with certain changes in the financial position of local governments. In municipalities with a population between 5,000 and 2.000 ($p < 0.01$), these changes in the economic environment seem to be more correlated with the weight that the preferential public service expenditure represents in the total spending (VFI19), the investment effort (VFI10), the weight that the expenses of government organs represent (VFI21), and the rigidity that the debt service involves (VFI6). In medium-sized municipalities (2.000 to 5.000 inhabitants) ($P < 0.05$), these economic environment variables are primarily correlated with the change in weight that represents non-political personnel expenses (VFI12), the procurement of goods and contracting services (VFI13), and the change in cash solvency (VFI2).

In larger municipalities (more than 5.000 inhabitants), this second pair of canonical variables explains 19.15% of the data variability, and are correlated in a 58.3% ($p < 0.10$). This shows the relationship between the variables of change in the economic environment (which give relevant weight to unemployment, youth unemployment, construction activities, and immigration) and the financial variables of change of the Sustainability / Primary Budget Balance (VFI5), the weight of housing expenditures and urbanism (VFI15), the general administration expenses (VFI22), and the community welfare expenditures (VFI16).

Table 4. Canonical Loadings

	Expansion 2005-2008				Crisis 2008-2011						
	Canonical Loadings for Set-1 of significant vectors										
	Mun. < 5000	5001< Mun.< 20000	20001<Mun< 50000	Mun. > 50000	Mun. < 5001	5001<Mun.< 20000		20001<Mun.< 50000		Mun. > 50000	
	V1(***)	V1(***)	V1(***)		V1(***)	V1(***)	V2(***)	V1(***)	V2(**)	V1(***)	V2(*)
VFI1	,075	-,097	,364	-	,115	,077	,049	,084	-,203	-,326	-,089
VFI2	,017	-,165	-,053	-	,117	-,051	,256	,272	-,402	-,110	,279
VFI3	,049	-,095	-,142	-	-,130	,268	-,063	,261	,077	-,197	-,116
VFI4	,317	-,461	,379	-	-,051	,235	,155	,456	-,003	-,415	,179
VFI5	,286	-,410	,361	-	-,029	,249	,166	,217	,101	-,281	,372
VFI6	,038	-,105	,094	-	-,232	,071	-,322	,202	,033	-,321	-,310
VFI7	,479	-,760	,858	-	,507	-,365	,066	-,370	,091	,229	,324
VFI8	,324	-,498	,396	-	,251	-,068	,138	,227	-,297	-,303	,143
VFI9	-,790	,631	-,546	-	-,350	,291	-,032	,290	,184	-,090	,001
VFI10	-,005	-,067	,302	-	,032	-,143	,352	-,234	,234	,031	,314
VFI11	-,067	,040	,077	-	-,221	-,077	-,128	,030	-,018	,046	,026
VFI12	-,291	,354	-,105	-	-,318	,393	-,156	,057	-,545	,052	-,197
VFI13	,221	-,262	,221	-	,191	-,438	,078	-,170	,439	-,180	,200
VFI14	-,177	,131	,014	-	-,399	,121	,302	-,101	-,115	-,005	,065
VFI15	-,175	,122	,126	-	-,125	,013	-,151	-,018	,150	,210	,342
VFI16	-,024	,132	,004	-	-,196	,090	,141	,109	-,135	-,207	,391
VFI17	,111	-,218	,147	-	-,331	,123	,247	-,097	-,022	,189	-,137
VFI18	-,083	,042	-,127	-	,003	,096	-,164	,006	-,212	-,015	,328
VFI19	-,266	,133	-,198	-	-,109	,033	-,410	-,221	,188	,227	,012
VFI20	-,028	,124	-,129	-	-,167	,009	-,007	-,025	-,272	-,048	-,181
VVI21	-,309	,156	,028	-	-,240	,150	-,335	,280	,186	-,145	,021
VFI22	,043	-,030	-,098	-	-,199	,057	,204	,181	-,124	-,241	-,349

Table 4. (Continued)

Cross Loadings for Set-1 of significant vectors											
	Mun. < 5001	5001<Mun. < 20000	20001< Mun.< 50000	Mun. > 50000	Mun. < 5001	5001<Mun.< 20000		20001<Mun.< 50000		Mun. > 50000	
	W1$^{(***)}$	W1$^{(***)}$	W1$^{(***)}$		W1$^{(***)}$	W1$^{(***)}$	W2$^{(***)}$	W1$^{(***)}$	W2$^{(**)}$	W1$^{(***)}$	W2$^{(*)}$
VFI1	,032	-,042	,209	-	,048	,032	,015	,043	-,095	-,229	-,052
VFI2	,007	-,072	-,030	-	,049	-,022	,077	,140	-,189	-,077	,163
VFI3	,021	-,041	-,081	-	-,054	,113	-,019	,135	,036	-,138	-,067
VFI4	,136	-,200	,218	-	-,021	,099	,046	,235	-,001	-,292	,104
VFI5	,123	-,178	,207	-	-,012	,105	,049	,112	,047	-,197	,217
VFI6	,016	-,046	,054	-	-,097	,030	-,096	,104	,016	-,226	-,181
VFI7	,206	-,330	,493	-	,212	-,154	,020	-,190	,043	,161	,189
VFI8	,140	-,217	,228	-	,105	-,029	,041	,117	-,139	-,212	,084
VFI9	-,340	,274	-,314	-	-,146	,123	-,009	,150	,086	-,063	,001
VFI10	-,002	-,029	,174	-	,013	-,060	,105	-,121	,110	,022	,183
VFI11	-,029	,018	,044	-	-,093	-,032	-,038	,016	-,008	,032	,015
VFI12	-,125	,154	-,060	-	-,133	,166	-,047	,029	-,256	,037	-,115
VFI13	,095	-,114	,127	-	,080	-,184	,023	-,087	,206	-,126	,117
VFI14	-,076	,057	,008	-	-,167	,051	,090	-,052	-,054	-,003	,038
VFI15	-,075	,053	,072	-	-,052	,005	-,045	-,009	,070	,147	,200
VFI16	-,010	,057	,002	-	-,082	,038	,042	,056	-,063	-,145	,228
VFI17	,048	-,095	,085	-	-,138	,052	,074	-,050	-,010	,133	-,080
VFI18	-,036	,018	-,073	-	,001	,040	-,049	,003	-,099	-,010	,191
VFI19	-,114	,058	-,114	-	-,046	,014	-,122	-,114	,088	,160	,007
VFI20	-,012	,054	-,074	-	-,070	,004	-,002	-,013	-,127	-,034	-,106
VVI21	-,133	,068	,016	-	-,100	,063	-,100	,144	,087	-,101	,012
VFI22	,019	-,013	-,056	-	-,083	,024	,061	,093	-,058	-,169	-,204

Table 4. Canonical Loadings

Canonical Loadings for Set-2 of significant vectors											
	Mun. < 5000	5001<Mun. < 20000	20001< Mun.< 50000	Mun. > 50000	Mun. < 5001	5001<Mun.< 20000		20001<Mun.< 50000		Mun. > 50000	
	W1(***)	W1(***)	W1(***)		W1(***)	W1(***)	W2(***)	W1(***)	W2(**)	W1(***)	W2(*)
VEI1	-,965	,957	-,961	-	-,893	,882	,206	,904	-,086	-,835	-,225
VEI2	,041	,046	,019	-	-,010	,070	,487	,195	,169	-,087	,307
VEI3	-,369	,531	-,338	-	-,518	,409	-,721	-,053	,263	,145	-,695
VEI4	-,149	,439	-,200	-	-,151	,081	-,328	-,010	,752	,308	-,547
VEI5	-,055	,087	,040	-	-,190	,209	-,119	-,094	-,232	-,109	-,127
VEI6	-,012	-,129	,153	-	,053	,039	,108	-,373	,371	,545	-,318
VEI7	-,100	,183	,036	-	-,264	,005	-,045	-,358	-,109	,202	,065
VEI8	-,188	,145	-,371	-	-,094	-,232	-,526	-,510	-,327	,280	,182

*** significance at a 1%

** significance at a 5%;

*: significance at a 10%

Conclusion

From both a theoretical and a practical perspective, the economic literature indicates that economic factors related to the environment of public institutions affect the degree or level of their financial health. However, the impact of the changes that occur in this economic environment can produce corresponding changes of a different nature in the financial position of these institutions during cycles of growth and economic crisis, not only in the expected level of resources that will be available in these institutions but also in the balance of other financial magnitudes.

We have seen how different municipalities, subject to the provision of different levels of services based on their population size, show different changes in their financial position when there are variations in their close economic environment according to the economic cycle.

In Spain, the indicators that mark the financial position of smaller municipalities seem to manifest a symmetric behavior when there are alterations in their economic environment in periods of growth and economic crisis. For small municipalities, changes in population and unemployment are the variables that appear to be more correlated with alterations in their financial vulnerability, both current and investment, which appear to be directly associated with the available budgetary resources per capita.

The symmetry previously observed in smaller municipalities seems to disappear as their population size increases. That is, as these institutions become larger, more economic environment variables and their variations appear to be significantly correlated with changes in the indicators of the financial position of the municipalities. Specifically, the most remarkable changes are those in the areas of construction activities and retail trade. When municipalities exceed the population threshold of 20000. the changes in the economic environment become more closely correlated with the changes in their flexibility, budgetary imbalances, and structure of spending, and such correlation is more pronounced in municipalities with a bigger population.

This study enables us to explore how the changes in the economic environment in times of growth and economic crisis differently affect the financial health of Spanish municipalities with a given population size. Consequently, to investigate the impact that variables related to the economic environment may have on the financial health of public institutions, the economic cycle in which the research is framed should be considered.

References

Alesina, A., Baqir, R. & Hoxby, C. (2004). Political jurisdictions in heterogeneous communities. *Journal of Political Economy,* 112, 348-396.

Alter, T. R., McLaughlin, D. K., & Melniker, N. E. (1984). *Analysing Local Government Fiscal Capacity.* University Park, PA: Pennsylvania State University, Cooperative Extension Service.

Ammar, S., Duncombe, W., Jump B., & Wright R. (2005). A Financial Condition Indicator System for School Districts: A Case Study of New York, *Journal of Education Finance*, 30 (3), 231-258.

Banco de España (BDE) (2006). Informe Anual. Banco de España. Madrid: BDE.

Banco de España (BDE) (2007). Informe Anual. Banco de España. Madrid: BDE.

Banco de España (BDE) (2008). Informe Anual. Banco de España. Madrid: BDE.

Banco de España (BDE) (2013). Boletín Económico. Informe trimestral de la Economía Española. Enero, Banco de España. Madrid: BDE.

Bastida, F. J., Benito, B., & Guillamón, M. D. (2009). An Empirical Assesment of the municipal Financial Situation in Spain. *International Public Management Journal*, 12(4), 484-499.

Benito, B. and Bastida, F. J. & Guillamón, M. D. (2010a). Urban sprawl and the cost of public services: an evaluation of Spanish local governments , *Lex Localis - Journal of Local Self-Government,* 8, 245 -264.

Benito, B., Bastida, F., & Muñoz, M. J. (2010b). Factores explicativos de la presión fiscal municipal, *Revista de Contabilidad*, 13(2), 239-283.

Benito, B., Bastida, F., & García, J. A. (2010c). Explaining differences in efficiency: an application to Spanish municipalities, *Applied Economics*, 42(4), 515-528.

Berne, R. (1992). *The Relationships between Financial Reporting and the Measurement of Financial Condition*. GASB Research Report nº 18. Norwalk: GASB

Berry, F. S. (1994). Innovation in public management: the adoption of strategic planning. *Public Administration Review*, 54 (4), 322-330.

Brown, K. W. (1993). The 10-Point Test of Financial Condition: Toward an Easy-to-Use Assessment Tool for Smaller Cities. *Government Finance Review*, 9(6), 21-26.

Brown, K. W. (1996). Trends in Key Ratios Using the GFOA Financial Indicators Databases 1989-1993. *Government Finance Review*, 12(6), 30-34.

Buettner, T., Schwager, R., & Stegarescu, D. (2004). Agglomeration, Population Size, and the Cost of Providing Public Services: An Empirical Analysis for German States. *Discussion Paper No. 04-018.*ZEW - Centre for European Economic Research.

Cabaleiro, R., Buch, E. & Vaamonde, A. (2012). Developing a Method to Assessing de Municipal Financial Health. *American Review of Public Administration*, June: DOI 10.1177/0275074012451523.

Cabill, A. G., & James, J. A. (1992). Responding to Municipal Distress: An Emerging Issue for State Governments in the 1990s. *Public Administration Review,* 52 (1), 88-94 .

Canadian Institute of Chartered Accountants (CICA). (1997). *Research Report. Indicators of Government Financial Condition*. Toronto, Canada: CICA.

Carmeli, A. (2003). Introduction: Fiscal and Financial Crises of Local Governments. *International Journal of Public Administration*, 26 (13), 1423-1430 .

Carmeli, A. (2007). The Effect of Fiscal Conditions of Local Government Authorities on Their Economic Development. *Economic Development Quarterly*, 21(1), 91-98.

Carmeli A., & Cohen A. (2001). The financial crisis of the local authorities in Israel: A resource-based analysis. *Public Administration,* 79 (4), 893-913.

Carruthers, J. I., & Úlfarsson G. F. (2008). Does `Smart Growth' Matter to Public Finance?, *Urban Studies,* 45, 1791-1823.

Chaney, B. A., Mead, D. M., & Shermann, K. R., (2002). The New Governmental Financial Reporting Model: What It Means for Analyzing Governmental Financial Condition. *The Journal of Government Financial Management*, 51(1), 26-31.

Chase, B. W., & Phillips, R. H. (2004). GASB 34 and government financial condition: an analytical toolbox. *Government Finance Review*, 20(2), 26-31.

Clark, T. N. (1976). Fiscal Management of American Cities: Funds Flow Indicators. *Journal of Accounting Research,* 15(Sup.), 54-94.

Clark, T. N. (1994). Municipal Fiscal Strain: Indicators and Causes. *Government Finance Review,* 10 (3), 27 - 29

Clark, T. N., Ferguson, L. C.(1983). City money: Political processes, fiscal strain, and retrenchment. New York: Columbia University Press.

Coe, C. K. (2008). Preventing Local Government Fiscal Crises: Emerging Best Practices. Public Administration Review 68 (4), 759-767.

Cox, W., & Utt, J. (2004). *The Costs of Sprawl Reconsidered: What the Data Really Show.* Backgrounder 1770: The Heritage Foundation.

Cutler, D. M., Elmendorf, D. W., & Zeckhauser, R. J. (1993). Demographic Characteristics and the Public Bundle. *NBER Working Paper Series* W4283.

Federal Accounting Standards Advisory Board (FASAB). (2009). *Reporting Comprehensive Long-Term Fiscal Projections for the U.S. Government.* Washington, DC: FASAB.

Governmental Accounting Standards Board (GASB) (1999). *Statement nº 34, Basic Financial Statements—and Managements Discussion and Analysis—for State and Local Governments.* Norwalk, CT: GASB.

Governmental Accounting Standards Board (GASB) (2004). *Statement nº 44. Economic Condition Reporting: The Statistical Section an amendment of NCGA Statement 1.* Norwalk, CT: GASB.

Governmental Accounting Standards Board (GASB) (2011). *Preliminary Views. Economic Condition Reporting: Financial Projections.* Norwalk, CT: GASB.

Greenberg, J. & D. Hillier. (1995). Indicators of financial condition for governments. *5th Conference of Comparative International Governmental Accounting Research.* Paris-Amy.

Guillamón, M.D., Benito, B., & Bastida F. (2011). Evaluation of local government debt in Spain. *Spanish Journal of finance and Accounting*, 150 (XL), 251-285.

Groves, S. M., Godsey, W. M., & Shulman, M. A. (1981). Financial Indicators for Local Government. *Public Budgeting and Finance*, 1(2), 5-19.

Hendrick, R. (2004). Assessing and Measuring the Fiscal Heath of Local Governments. *Urban Affaires Review*, 40(1), 78-114.

Honadle, B. W. (2003). The States′ Role in U.S. Local Government Fiscal Crises: A Theoretical Model and Results of a National Survey. *International Journal of Public Administration*, 26(13), 1431-1472.

Honadle, B. W., Costa, J.M, & Cigler, B.A. (2004). *Fiscal Heath for Local Governments.* San Diego, California: Elsevier Academic Press.

Honadle, B. W., & Lloyd-Jones, M. (1998). Analyzing Rural Local Governments Financial Condition: An Exploratory Application of Three Tools. *Public Budgeting and Finance*, 18(2), 69-86.

Hopkins, D. J. (2009). The Diversity Discount: When Increasing Ethnic and Racial Diversity Prevents Tax Increases . *The Journal of Politics,* 71, 160-177.

Huddle, D. (1993). *The net national costs of immigration.* Washington, DC: Carrying Capacity Network.

Hughes, J. W., & Laverdiere, R. (1986). Comparative Local Government Financial Analyses. *Public Budgeting & Finance*, 6(4), 23-33.

Inman, R.P. (1995). How to have a fiscal crisis: lessons from Philadelphia. Fiscal problems of cities. *AEA Papers and Proceedings*, 85 (2), 378-83.

International City/County Management Association (ICMA) (2003). *Evaluating financial condition, A Handbook for Local Government.* Washington D.C.: ICMA.

Jones, S., & Walker, G. (2007). Explanators of Local Government Distress. *Abacus,* 63 (3), 396-418.

Kleine, R., Kloha, P., & Weissert, C. (2003). Monitoring local government fiscal health: Michigan's new 10 points scale of fiscal distress. *Government Finance Review,* 19(3), 18-23

Kloha, P., Weissert, C. S., & Kleine, R. (2005a). Someone to Watch Over me: State Monitoring of Local Fiscal Conditions. *The American Review of Public Administration,* 35(3), 236-255.

Kloha, P., C. S. Weissert & R. Kleine. (2005b). Developing and Testing a Composite Model to Predict Local Fiscal Distress. *Public Administration Review ,* 65(3), 313-323.

Kwon O. (2006) Local decision-making on capital spending in US cities. *International Review of Public Administration,* 10(2),37-48

La Caixa (2006). *Spain Economic Yearbook 2005. Municipal Database* http://www.anuarieco.lacaixa.comunicacions.com , Accessed January, 2013

La Caixa (2009). *Spain Economic Yearbook 2008. Municipal Database* http://www.anuarieco.lacaixa.comunicacions.com , Accessed January, 2013

La Caixa (2012). *Spain Economic Yearbook 2011. Municipal Database* http://www.anuarieco.lacaixa.comunicacions.com , Accessed January, 2013

Ladd, H. F. (1992). Population growth, density, and the costs of providing public services. *Urban Studies,* 29, 273–295.

Ladd, H. F., & Yinger, J. (1991). *America's ailing cities: Fiscal health and design of urban policy.* Baltimore, MD: John Hopkins University Press.

Lin, W., & Raman, K. K. (1998). The housing value-relevance of governmental accounting information. *Journal of Accounting and Public Policy*, 17 (2), 91-118

Local Government Association of South Australia (LGAs). 2006. *Information Paper 9, Local Government Financial Indicators.* (http://www.lga.sa.gov.au/webdata/resources/ files/Financial_Sustainability_Info_Paper_9_Local_Government_Financial_Indicators.pd f), Accessed: May 2011.

Lorig, A. N. (1941). Determining the Current Financial Position of a City. *Accounting Review,* 16(1), 41-49.

Mead, D. M. (2001). *An Analyst's Guide to Government Financial Statements*. Norwalk, CT: GASB.

Mead D. M. (2006). A manageable system of economic condition analysis for governments. In: Howard A. Frank (Ed), Public Financial Management. New York: Taylor & Francis.

Mercer, T., & Gilbert, M. (1996). A Financial Condition Index for Nova Scotia Municipalities. *Government Finance Review*, 12(5), 36-38.

Ministry of Economy and Finance (MEH) (2013a). *Settlement of the Local Budgets.* Years 2005, 2008, and 2011 (Virtual Office for financial coordination with Local Authorities). http://serviciosweb.meh.es/apps/EntidadesLocales/BDatosPL.aspx, Accessed January 2013

Ministry of Economy and Finance MEH) (2013b) Municipal Outstanding debt. *Date 31/12/2009 and 31/12/2008* (Virtual Office for financial coordination with Local

Authorities) http://www.meh.es/es-ES/Administracion%20Electronica/OVEELL/Paginas /DeudaViva.aspx, Accessed January 2013

Morgan, D. R., & England, R. E. (1983). Explaining Fiscal Stress Among Large U.S. Cities: Toward an Integrative Model. *Public Studies Review*, 3(1), 73-78.

National Statistics Institute (2013). INEBASE. (http://www.ine.es/jaxi/ menu.do? type=pcaxis& path=%2Ft20 %2Fe260&file =inebase&L=0), Accessed January 2013

Oates, W.E. (1988). On the measurement of congestion in the provision of local public goods. *Journal of Urban Economics*, 24(1), 85-94.

Passel, J. (1994). *Immigrants and taxes: A reappraisal of Huddle's 'The costs of immigrants'.* Washington, DC: The Urban Institute.

Petro, J. (1998). Fiscal Indicators Reports and Ratio Analysis: Benchmarking Ohio Municipalities and School Districts. *Government Finance Review*, 14(5), 17-21.

Ratcliffe, K., Riddle, B., & Yinger, J. (1990). The fiscal condition of school districts in Nebraska: Is Small beautiful?. *Economics of Education Review, 9 (1), 81-89.*

Rivenbark, W.C., & D. J. Roenigk. (2011). Implementation of financial condition analysis in local governments. *Public Administration Quarterly,* 35(2): 238-264.

Rubinfeld, D. (1987). The Economics of the Local Public Sector. In Auerbach, A. J. and Feldstein, M. (Eds.), *Handbook of Public Economics,* Amsterdam: North- Holland.

Skidmore, M., & Scorsone, E. (2011). Causes and consequences of fiscal stress in Michigan cites. *Regional Science and Urban Economics*, 41, 360–371.

Smith, P.S. & Edmonston, E. (1997). *The new Americans: Economic, demographic and fiscal effects of immigration*. Washington, D.C.: National Academy Press.

Sohl, S., Peddle, M.T., Thurmaier, K., Wood, C. H., & Kuhn, G. (2009). Measuring the Financial Position of Municipalities: Numbers Do Not Speak for Themselves. *Public Budgeting & Finance*, Fall, 74 – 96.

Wang, X., Dennis, L., & Tu, Y. S. (2007). Measuring Financial Condition: A Study of U.S. States. *Public Budgeting and Finance*, 27(2), 1-21.

Wolff, G.B. (2008). Fiscal Crises in the US Cities: Structural and Non-Structural Causes. *The Icfai Journal of Public Finance*, 6(1), 7-51.

Wolff, L.W., & Hughes, J. (1998). Net Available Assets as a Proxy for Financial Condition: A Model for Measuring and Reporting Resources Available to a Local Government. *Government Finance Review*, 14(3), 29-33.

Wolman, H. (1992). Urban fiscal stress. *Urban Affairs Quarterly*, 27, 470-482.

Zafra Gómez, J. L., López Hernández, A. M., & Hernández Bastida, A. (2009a). Developing a Model to Measure Financial Condition in Local Government. *The American Review of Public Administration,* 39(4), 425-449.

Zafra Gómez, J. L., López Hernández, A. M., & Hernández Bastida, A. (2009b). Developing an alert system for local governments in financial crisis. *Public Money & Management,* 29(3), 175-181.

Zehms, K. M. (1991). Proposed Financial Ratios for Use in Analysis of Municipal Annual Financial Reports. *Government Accountants Journal*, Fall, 79-85.

Reviewed by Bernardino Benito (benitobl@um.es). He is a professor of public sector accounting at the University of Murcia (Spain). He has numerous publications in national and international books and journals.

In: Financial Crises
Editor: Cooper A. Hawthorne

ISBN: 978-1-62808-293-7

Chapter 2

AGE DIFFERENTIALS IN THE IMPACT OF THE FINANCIAL CRISIS ON SOCIAL RELATIONSHIPS

Chau-kiu Cheung*
City University of Hong Kong, China

ABSTRACT

In the face of the current global financial crisis, it would be informative to investigate how past crises have affected social relationships. Apart from the impact of the financial crisis on people in general, differentials in the impact across younger and older people are also possible. A household survey of 1,170 Hong Kong adults provided data for the study. The perceived impact of the financial crisis tended to affect closeness to other people, but it did not manifest a significant effect on other dimensions of social relationship. However, older people appeared to be more susceptible to the perceived financial crisis impact. The age differential was only partly attributable to age differences in living alone and not working. The impact of the financial crisis seems to be more influential on the social life of older people, partly because of their living and working arrangements. Notably, the impact of the financial crisis was less influential on one who held a working-class job. These findings imply the need for public policy to help mitigate the adverse effects of the negative impact of the financial crisis particularly on older people's social relationships.

INTRODUCTION

A financial crisis, which means a severe turmoil in the economy, can recur at societal, national, or international level (Vasapollo 2011). The financial crisis is problematic when it afflicts individual persons in the economy, society, country, or the world (Cutler et al. 2002). That is, a crisis only becomes pathological when the individual experiences it or its impacts

* E-mail: ssjacky@cityu.edu.hk.

(Kim 2004). In the juncture, as individual experiences the financial crisis differentially, the impacts of the financial crisis also evolve differentially, just owing to pervasive differences among people (Bergmark and Palme 2003). Conceivably, one whose asset evaporates during the financial crisis would suffer palpably from the crisis. Put alternatively, as people occupy different positions in society or the economy, they necessarily experience differential impacts from the financial crisis. Such an individual difference in the experience regarding the financial crisis is the premise and focus of the present study. The study is necessary because of the paucity and enigma concerning the non-financial or social impacts of the financial crisis on the individual, as most research has spearheaded the macroscopic economic impacts of the crisis (Kim 2004; Roberts 1996). Apart from its economic impacts, the financial crisis is very likely to affect the individual's broader social life as well (Lim and Han 2003). The impact of the financial crisis on the social relationship among individuals is certainly a crucial but inadequately charted topic. Such an impact is crucial because the economic and communal aspects of the social life are tangled and inalienable (Cutler et al. 2002). Essentially, the cause of and solution to the financial crisis all rest on a bearing on social relationships (Kwon 2001). With social relationships as the focal criterion, the study sets out to unravel the impact of the financial crisis and its differentials across age or age groups. Such differentials would be a crucial entry point for understanding individual differences in the social responses to the financial crisis. The differentials are also in need of recital in view of the paucity and indeterminacy of data concerned (Charles and Carstensen 2009).

Social relationships refer to the ways of social interaction. They cover an individual's closeness, caring, receiving care from, disclosure, recourse, and contributing to other people (Barr et al. 2005; Diewald and Ludicke 2006; Keyes and Shapiro 2004; Vogel et al. 2006). Essentially, they fulfill social functions required for the maintenance and longevity of society. First, closeness or intimacy to other people is an inherent human nature signifying the meaning of human life (Meyer and Lang 2003). It is also an integral indicator of social cohesion and the equitable social relationship (Hatfield and Rapson 2012). In this respect, closeness provides the drive and channel for exchange, which is indispensable to human, social life. Second, disclosure or specifically self-disclosure is integral to closeness or intimacy (Sharabany 1994). In this way, disclosure helps constitute friendships (Turner et al. 2007). It is also crucial to alliance building by paving the road to exchange (Binder et al. 2012). For instance, disclosure helps secure care from other people, notably by informing others about one's problems (Gant et al. 1999). Third, caring is ethically valuable in human life (Fine 2007). Functionally, caring helps convey compassion, love, affection, meaning, warmth, and devotion. It necessarily deserves promotion to consolidate citizenship (Schervish and Havens 2002). Caring is also the cornerstone for the community. Fourth, receiving care is just the counterpart of caring, just as caring involves at least a pair of persons. Receiving care thus also represents the fulfillment of social life (Ganster and Victor 1988). Benefits from receiving care are myriad, notably in solving the care recipient's problems (Goodwin et al. 2001). Essentially, caring and receiving care uphold a fair exchange that meet people's needs (Molm 2006). Fifth, recourse or help seeking is often necessary in order to get needed care. Recourse is a vital means of coping and problem solving (Armstrong et al. 2005). It is pervasive because of the single person's incapability of tackling problems (Tang 2006). Such incapability, nevertheless, is just normal and recourse reflects normal or rational functioning (Oppenheimer and Heller 1984). As such, recourse is always instrumental or functional (Newman 1998). Sixth, contribution to others is also vital for social cohesion (Keyes and

Shapiro 2004). Contribution is also a marker of sociability (Chan 2009). In addition, contribution is relevant to the close relationship (Rossi 2001). In all, all such social relationships or interactions function to enrich and perpetuate social life. They are therefore of paramount concern for social research and policy (Smyth 2008).

The study of the impact of the financial crisis is viable through the identification of the perceived or experienced impact. Such perception or experience pivotally serves as the mediator to pinpoint the impact on social relationships. The pivotal mechanism concerned reflects the case that a social impact happens through the individual's perception or experience about the impact (Seligson 2005; Vanclay 2003). The perceived or experienced financial impact registers financial or economic stress when the impact is adverse (Lantz et al., 2005). Conversely, a positive financial impact perceived represents financial uplift (Maybery et al. 2006). The perceived impact of the financial crisis can then run from the lower end of financial stress to the upper end of financial uplift. Typically, financial stress is the default in view of the pervasive negative impacts of the financial impacts in terms of bankruptcy, loss, unemployment, poverty, deprivation, and indebtedness (Bergmark and Palme 2003; Hicks and Kingson 2009; Kim 2004; Roberts 1999). Despite these, the financial impact can be positive when it provides opportunities to gain by speculation and activation in financial and social aspects (Kim 2004; Lim and Han 2003). Accordingly, one can see silver lining amid any crisis. Financial stress, notably stemming from the financial crisis, is thus likely to be destructive to the individual (Leiser et al. 2010; Lupien et al. 2009; Wallenius 2006). Conversely, financial uplift is salutary to the individual (Maybery et al. 2006). In both cases, the import of finance to the person is evident, as finance provides the person with means to acquire resources for survival and flourishing (Kessler et al. 2000). At any rate, financial stress as a source of stress is of great concern because of its noxious ramifications (Lupien et al. 2009). Age difference is itself an age-old concern, as aging is prominent and irresistible in the human population. Essentially, age difference represents a crucial difference among people (Riley and Riley 1999). Age difference becomes more important as it accentuates myriad other differences through the life course (O'Rand 1996). For instance, accumulation of experience with aging would create a great difference in countless outcomes. Aging and age difference thus necessarily draw public attention toward better understanding and tackling of them. Regarding age, a notable concern is on older age, that is, being 60 years old or older. The concern is appealing in view of its implications for longevity, age stratification, retirement, and numerous social policies (Timopen 2008; van Praag and Frijtens 1999). Such older age also generate connotations about wisdom, adaptation, and integrity on the one hand and senescence, deterioration, and dependency on the other (Heinz 2002; Ranzijn 2002). Related to the concern about the aging is the growth of various elaborations about aging, such as socioemotional selectivity theory (Charles and Carstensen 2009).

Financial Impacts on Social Relationships

The impacts of the financial crisis on the person's social relationships, as suggested, operate through the person's perception or experience about the crisis, and all of these can vary from one person to another person.

In this case, the reasonable expectation is that the negative impact of the financial crisis perceived or financial stress would erode one's social relationships. Conversely, the perceived positive impact of the financial crisis or financial uplift would foster social relationships. When the high end of the perceived impact represents the positive impact, the expectation is that the perceived impact maintains a positive effect on social relationships. Simply put, the expectation represents an effect from the financial aspect to the social aspect. Such an effect in turn can embody the transfer of resources, according to resource theory (Jones 2006). Accordingly, it is the transfer of financial resources to facilitate engaging in social relationships. In this case, financial resources would serve as fuel to activate the engagement (Lennartsson 2010). Conversely, decline in financial resources due to the financial crisis is likely to defuse social relationships (Espvall and Dellgren 2008). A finer explication suggests that social relationships are of two kinds, one acquiring resources from and another sharing resources with others. Acquiring resources include recourse and receiving care, whereas sharing resources include closeness, disclosure, caring, and contribution. The former is the acquisitive social relationship and the latter is the compassionate social relationship. While resource theory explains the positive effects of resources on resource sharing through social relationships, it does not comfortably explain the positive effects on acquiring resources. Accordingly, it seems awkward to find having resources to trigger further resource acquisition.

In this case, need theory would provide a more reasonable explanation, such that resource deficiency prompts getting resources from social relationships (Chen 2006). Need theory thus expects that the positive impact of the financial crisis introduce a negative effect on acquisitive social relationships.

That is, financial stress arising from the financial crisis is likely to galvanize acquisitive social relationships. Conversely, need theory expects a negative effect of financial stress on the compassionate social relationship. This expectation concurs with that of resource theory. Hence, resource theory and need theory mainly differ in their expectations about the acquisitive social relationship. Whereas resource theory expects a positive effect of the perceived positive impact of the financial crisis, need theory envisions a negative effect of the same perception.

Existing evidence supporting the expectations of resource and need theories is the following. Closeness to others is predictable by such resources as the parental loan, secure attachment, and cohesive family (Buelow et al. 1996; Cooney and Hutchinson 1995; Kemp 2007). Nevertheless, closeness is also predictable by such needs as those arising from awareness about death (Mikulincer et al. 2003). Disclosure is predictable by such needs as those springing from depression (Rotenberg and Hamel 1988). Caring or helping is predictable by such resources as those from personal income and family income (Bjornberg and Ekbrand 2008; Hofferth et al. 1999; Straume and Odeen 2010). However, giving or contributing to others is predictable by such resources as those arising from personal income and reward power (Godoy et al. 2007; Molm 1997). Similarly, donating is predictable by such resources as personal income and family income (Bekkers 2008; Brown and Ferris 2007). The existing findings thus offer support to both resource and need theories. Some contradiction in the findings happens, and this spurs the present investigation for a clarification of the contradictory findings.

Age Effects on Social Relationships

Age represents both resources such as experience and wisdom and needs arising from physical decline (Charles and Carstensen 2009; Hess et al. 2005). Hence, age is suitable to be an indicator of both the resource and need theory of the social relationship. In terms of resource theory, age would uphold the social relationship, whereas age would attenuate the compassionate social relationship and bolster the acquisitive social relationship according to need theory. At any rate, existing research has not been certain about the impact of age on the social relationship (Charles and Carstensen 2009). On the one hand, when age represents need or resource deficiency, it appears to reduce the compassionate social relationship (Bull et al. 2004; Henry et al. 2009; von Hippel and Dunlop 2005). By contrast, when age embodies resources, it has appeared to facilitate the compassionate social relationship (Inglehart 2003). Research findings have also manifested that age reduces social support received (Degenne et al. 2004; Magliano et al. 2006). This is in line with the expectation of need theory such that age implies resource sufficiency and lowered need for social support.

Age may also make a difference in the effect of the perceived impact of the financial crisis on the social relationship. The expectation is that age augments the positive effect of the perceived positive impact, according to socioemotional selectivity theory. This theory posits that age is a crucial contributor to socioemotional selectivity, which is a motivation for adapting to the diminishing life horizon with aging (Charles and Carstensen 2009; Kliegel et al. 2007). Such an adaptive motivation would magnify the concern for the selectivity as a response to changing conditions, including stress. In the face of stress, hence, the selectivity is to reduce and simplify social relationships. As the selectivity increases with age, according to the theory, stress would generate a greater reduction in the older person's social relationship. Conversely, uplift allows the older person to maintain a greater social relationship. When the uplift is due to the financial crisis, the theory thus expects that the positive impact of the financial crisis enhance the social relationship more intensely for the older person. In other words, financial uplift is likely to increase the older person's social relationship for the older person and financial stress is likely to reduce the older person's social relationship.

Hypotheses

A recapitulation of foregoing theorizing about the person's experience about the financial crisis, the following hypotheses emerge for empirical investigation.

1 Resource theory: The financial impact (i.e., uplift vs. stress) generates a positive effect on such a compassionate social relationship as closeness, disclosure, caring, and contribution and acquisitive social relationships as recourse and receiving care.

1.1 The financial impact (i.e., uplift vs. stress) generates a more positive effect on compassionate and acquisitive social relationships with increasing age.

2 Need theory: The financial impact (i.e., uplift vs. stress) generates a negative effect on such an acquisitive social relationship as recourse and receiving care.

As required, testing of the hypotheses involve controlling for age and a number of background characteristics, which potentially affect social relationships as well as the perceived impact of the financial crisis. These additional background characteristics include gender, education, social class, marital status, religious faith, living arrangement, and volunteering experience. The characteristics are likely to be influential in view of existing research.

For instance, the female has appeared to be more caring and generous than does the male (Bekkers 2010; Fine 2007). Caring and helping are also more likely in one who is in higher social class, marriage, religious affiliation, or a larger family (Bekkers 2008; Brown and Ferris 2007; Fridberg and Kangas 2008b; Uslaner 2002). Care received is less likely when one lives in a larger family, or has lower education or lower social class (Lennertsson 2010; Viry et al. 2009). In addition, recourse is less likely in the female (Vogel et al 2006). Volunteering experience obviously is a precursor to helping (Paolicchi 1995; Wilson and Musick 1997). Similarly, religious affiliation is conducive to one's maintaining good social relationships (Skerkat and Ellison 1999). Moreover, financial strain has been higher in the female, older person, or one with lower education or in lower social class (Fridberg and Kangas 2008).

Hong Kong Context

Hong Kong has witnesses a number of financial crises during its transition toward a developed economy (Holliday 2005; Li 2012). Severe crises occurred in 1973, 1987, 1997, and 2008.

The crisis focused in this study is that in 1997, stemming from the crisis in Thailand or Southeast Asia. Without doubt, the financial crisis caused serious economic slumps and hardship in Hong Kong and many places of East Asia (Jung and Cheon 2006). Such adversity would reasonably raise awareness about the impact of the financial crisis among the population of Hong Kong.

Hence, Hong Kong is certainly not immune to the contagion of the financial crisis in other places, due to the pivotal international position of Hong Kong as a regional financial center.

Method

Data for the study came from a random-sample household survey of 1,170 adults residing in Hong Kong for the study conducted from 2006 to 2007. The random sample was available from the governmental agency of Hong Kong. Within each approached household, trained interviewers for the survey invited one resident aged 18 years or above to respond, using a random sampling procedure.

As such, the survey employed a face-to-face interview to ensure collecting adequate responses. Before the conduct of the survey, each sampled household received a letter of invitation. After the completion of the survey, each responding household then received some compensation for the time expended for the survey.

To represent the population in Hong Kong, a post-survey weighting procedure applied to weigh the sample to according to the joint distribution of age and gender in the population. After the weighting, the sampling displayed the following major characteristics: an average age of 40.8 years, women accounting for 63.1%, age schooling of 9.2 years, and non-employed people representing 47.9%. Notably, 26.7% held working-class jobs of blue-collar workers, 22.1% were holders of middle-class jobs of office workers, and 3.3% were self-employed people. Nonreligious people were slightly more numerous than were religious ones (57.1% vs. 42.9%). Over half lived with their spouses (55.9%). In contrast, only 6.0% lived alone.

MEASUREMENT

A number of rating items identified the measure of the impact of the financial crisis experienced, closeness, disclosure, caring, contributing, recourse, and receiving care in social relationships, as adapted from various sources (Bowling et al. 2003; Piquero and Sealock 2004). The items were interspersed within sections in a survey questionnaire to minimize interference due to adjacent items for the same measure.

The impact of the financial crisis experienced was a single item asking the respondent to indicate the extent of the impact of the financial crisis broken out in 1997 on the respondent using a scale running from -3 to +3. This scale represented a positive impact or uplift in the higher end and a negative impact or stress in the lower end. Thus, a higher score indicated higher financial uplift or lower financial stress. Closeness combined four items, about closeness to family, other relatives, neighbors, and friends. Each of the items generated a score on a 1-5 rating scale, with a higher score representing more closeness. The internal consistency reliability of the composite was .697.

Disclosure combined five items, about disclosure to family, other relatives, neighbors, friends, and professionals. Each of the items generated a score on a 1-5 rating scale, with a higher score representing more disclosure. The internal consistency reliability of the composite was .525. Caring combined four items, about taking care of family, other relatives, neighbors, and friends. Each of the items generated a score on a 1-5 rating scale, with a higher score representing more caring. The internal consistency reliability of the composite was .714. Contribution combined four items, about contribution to the family, profession, community organization, and the masses. Each of the items generated a score on a 1-5 rating scale, with a higher score representing more contribution. The internal consistency reliability of the composite was .539. Recourse during financial hardship combined five items, about recourse to family, other relatives, neighbors, friends, and others. Each of the items generated a score on a 1-5 rating scale, with a higher score representing more recourse. The internal consistency reliability of the composite was .538. Receiving care was a single item, as rated on a 1-5 scale. A higher score indicated receiving more care.

ANALYSIS

Linear regression analysis provided estimates in terms of standardized regression coefficients for predicting social relationships and the perceived impact of the financial crisis. In predicting functioning and close relationship, the analysis took two steps, for examining the effect of the impact of the financial crisis and age or age groups.

The interaction term was the product of socioeconomic change and borrowing money, based on their standard scores in order to circumvent the collinearity problem (Cohen et al. 2003). All the analyses and their steps included background characteristics as control variables. In addition, simple analysis of variance and correlation analysis showed the difference due to age and nexuses among social relationships.

RESULTS

Simple descriptive statistics showed that the perceived impact of the financial crisis had a negative mean (M = -0.80, see Table 1). The negative sign indicated that financial stress rather than financial uplift was likely. That is, the financial crisis tended to foment a negative impact. The perception was not significantly different between the older and younger persons (aged below 60 years). Concerning the social relationships, caring for others appeared to be the highest, on average (M = 3.30). In contrast, recourse was the lowest (M = 1.25). Disclosure is the next lowest social relationship (M = 1.75). Both recourse and disclosure were significantly lower in the older person than in the younger one (aged below 60 years). Moreover, the older person showed lower contribution than did the younger one. The six social relationships maintained significant and substantial positive interccreolations, except the correlation between closeness and recourse (see Table 2). Regression analysis of the six social relationships revealed that the perceived impact of the financial impact only displayed a significant positive effect on closeness (β = .069, see Table 3). The positive effect indicated that financial uplift raised closeness, or alternatively financial stress eroded closeness. This finding was in line with Hypothesis 1 about the compassionate social relationship. Meanwhile, the perceived impact of financial impact did not display a significant effect on the acquisitive social relationship, involving recourse and receiving care. This finding failed to support Hypothesis 2, which rests on need theory. Age manifested a significant effect only on recourse. The negative effect suggested that the older person showed less recourse during financial hardship (β = -.179, see Table 3). The significant effects of interactions between age and the perceived impact of the financial crisis unfolded the following.

First, age made the effects of the perceived impact or financial uplift on caring (β = .120), contributing (β = .160), and receiving care (β = .137) more positive (see Table 3). That is, financial stress eroded such social relationships more in the older person. Second, older age (60 years or higher) made the effects of financial uplift on disclosure (β = .087), caring (β = .095), and receiving care more positive (β = .115). That is, financial stress eroded such social relationships more in the older person. Third, age below 40 years made the effects of financial uplift on closeness (β = -.075) and contributing (β = -.097) less positive. That is, financial stress eroded such social relationships less in the younger person. All these findings were in line with Hypothesis 1.1.

Among the background characteristics, female gender introduced significant positive effects on disclosure (β = .161, see Table 3), caring (β = .123), and receiving care (β = .157). Cohabitation generated positive effects on disclosure (β = .229) and recourse (β = .183). Volunteering experience offered positive effects on disclosure (β = .066), caring (β = .094), contributing (β = .222), and receiving care (β = .064). Other significant findings were more sporadic.

Regression analysis of the perceived impact of the financial impact revealed that education (β = -.144), residency (β = -.083), and ancestor worship (β = -.090) indicated significant negative effects on the impact. That is, these characteristics raised financial stress.

Table 1. Unweighted means by age groups (*N* = 1,170)

	Scoring	Age under 60	Age 60+	All	*Eta*
Age under 40	0-1	0.49	0.00	0.39	.417
Age 40-59	0-1	0.51	0.00	0.40	.424
Age 60+	0-1	0.00	1.00	0.21	-
Living with the father	0-1	0.29	0.01	0.23	.277***
Living with the mother	0-1	0.34	0.02	0.27	.302***
Living with grandparents	0-1	0.03	0.00	0.03	.085***
Living with siblings	0-1	0.25	0.01	0.20	.242***
Living with the spouse	0-1	0.53	0.57	0.54	.038
Living with children	0-1	0.54	0.52	0.53	.013
Living with other relatives	0-1	0.02	0.01	0.02	.042
Living with friends	0-1	0.01	0.01	0.01	.004
Living with others	0-1	0.03	0.14	0.06	.194
Protestant	0-1	0.15	0.08	0.13	.086***
Catholic	0-1	0.03	0.05	0.04	.042
Buddhist	0-1	0.13	0.23	0.15	.110***
Muslim	0-1	0.00	0.00	0.00	.029
Hindu	0-1	0.00	0.00	0.00	.015
Daoist	0-1	0.01	0.02	0.01	.028
Ancestor worshipper	0-1	0.13	0.22	0.15	.111***
Confucian	0-1	0.00	0.02	0.01	.079**
Faith in another religion	0-1	0.01	0.04	0.01	.115***
Atheist	0-1	0.58	0.43	0.55	.124***
Education	1-5	2.93	1.70	2.66	.373***
Income	1-7	3.62	2.26	3.33	.320***
Residency	years	29.96	48.79	34.01	.465***
Female	0-1	0.58	0.54	0.57	.038
Married	0-1	0.57	0.67	0.59	.077**
Unmarried	0-1	0.35	0.06	0.29	.265***
Cohabited	0-1	0.01	0.00	0.01	.051

Table 1. (Continued)

	Scoring	Age under 60	Age 60+	All	Eta
Divorced	0-1	0.04	0.06	0.05	.024
Widowed	0-1	0.02	0.22	0.06	.343***
Self-employed	0-1	0.04	0.01	0.03	.060*
Middle class	0-1	0.23	0.02	0.18	.226***
Working class	0-1	0.29	0.07	0.24	.217***
Surplus class	0-1	0.44	0.90	0.55	.383***
Volunteered	0-1	0.29	0.17	0.27	.114***
Financial crisis impact (high = positive)	-3 - +3	-0.81	-0.76	-0.80	.018
Contributing to others	1-5	2.79	2.65	2.76	.088**
Closeness in social relationship	1-5	2.20	2.25	2.21	.025
Family	1-5	2.52	2.48	2.51	.014
Other relatives	1-5	2.28	2.42	2.31	.046
Neighbors	1-5	1.38	1.76	1.46	.121***
Friends	1-5	2.62	2.34	2.56	.088**
Receiving care	1-5	2.67	2.59	2.65	.042
Receiving care and respect	1-5	2.67	2.59	2.65	.042
Disclosure about discomfort	1-5	1.57	1.50	1.55	.043
Family	1-5	2.64	2.49	2.61	.054
Other relatives	1-5	1.40	1.41	1.40	.005
Neighbors	1-5	0.74	1.06	0.81	.153***
Friends	1-5	2.32	1.63	2.17	.252***
Professionals	1-5	0.74	0.93	0.78	.077**
Recourse during financial hardship	1-5	1.18	1.10	1.17	.045
Family	1-5	2.45	2.01	2.36	.135***
Other relatives	1-5	0.97	0.97	0.97	.003
Neighbors	1-5	0.34	0.51	0.37	.108**
Friends	1-5	1.12	0.84	1.07	.111
Others	1-5	0.54	0.60	0.55	.031
Caring others	1-5	3.32	3.23	3.30	.054
Family	1-5	4.20	4.01	4.16	.095
Other relatives	1-5	3.20	3.17	3.19	.013
Neighbors	1-5	2.42	2.67	2.47	.096**
Friends	1-5	3.46	3.06	3.38	.160***
Contributing to others	1-5	2.79	2.65	2.76	.088**
Family	1-5	3.95	3.69	3.89	.108***
Profession	1-5	3.07	2.46	2.94	.211***
Community organization	1-5	2.06	2.22	2.10	.066*
The masses	1-5	2.10	2.22	2.12	.055

* $p < .05$. ** $p < .01$. *** $p < .001$.

In addition, Hindu faith ($\beta = .109$) displayed a significant positive effect on the perceived impact. This finding meant that Hindu faith lowered financial stress attributed to the financial crisis. Importantly, these characteristics did not affect any of the social relationships, and they unlikely confounded the effect of the perceived impact of the financial crisis on the social relationships.

Table 2. Correlations

Correlate	Closeness	Cared	Disclosure	Recourse	Caring
Cared	.176***				
Disclosure	.202***	.344***			
Recourse	.028	.133***	.339***		
Caring	.250***	.372***	.467***	.232***	
Contributing	.132***	.198***	.221***	.137***	.350***

* $p < .05$. ** $p < .01$. *** $p < .001$.

DISCUSSION

Results offered some support to Hypotheses 1 and 1.1 concerning the effects of the perceived impact of the financial crisis on social relationships and age differentials in the effects. The support for Hypothesis 1, in terms of the positive effect of the perceived impact on closeness is supportive of the expectation of resource theory. Accordingly, financial uplift due to the financial crisis would activate closeness or conversely financial stress due to the crisis would dampen closeness. This finding suggests that deprivation of resources due to the financial crisis would weaken closeness. In addition, findings supportive of Hypothesis 1.1 reveal that age made the effects of financial uplift on social relationships more positive. This means that financial stress diminishes social relationships more in the older person. Conversely, financial stress impairs social relationships less in the younger person. These findings uphold the expectation derived from socioemotional selectivity theory. Accordingly, as age serves as the basis for socioemotional selectivity, it heightens the skimping of social relationships in response to financial stress emanating from the financial crisis. This theory rests on the need for adaptation to changing conditions with aging, particularly in view of reducing life expectancy.

In the face of financial stress, thereby, the older person is ready to be selective in and thus withdrawing from social relationships. The age differentials in the effects of financial stress or uplift are important in that they unveil differences that are not readily observable in the examination of the effect of financial stress or uplift. That is, although financial stress due to the financial crisis did not patently affect social relationships in the person in general, it was more consequential in the older person.

That is, the older person is susceptible to the financial crisis or its impact, whereas the younger one is not. The reason, owing to socioemotional selectivity theory, is that the older anticipates a shorter time horizon and thus a greater need to be responsive to the impact of the financial crisis. Moreover, resource theory provides an explanation for increasing socioemotional selectivity with aging. Accordingly, a reason for the increasing selectivity is the diminishing resources with aging.

In terms of resource theory, the perceived impact of the financial crisis only sparingly affects one's social relationship because one has sufficient resources to cope with the short-lived crisis. By contrast, only the older person, who is likely to be deficient in resources, is sensitive and susceptible to the impact of the financial crisis. This observation and interpretation are likely because the younger person is likely to replenish resources repeatedly through regular earnings and other sources of income or resources.

Table 3. Standardized regression coefficients for predicting social relationships

Predictor	Closeness	Disclosure	Caring	Contributing	Recourse	Cared
Financial crisis impact	.069*	-.005	.018	-.039	-.030	.040
Age	.011	-.067	.001	-.045	-.179*	-.034
Age 60+	.015	-.061	-.040	.053	-.004	.050
Living with the father	.001	-.011	-.020	.039	.064	.017
Living with the mother	-.026	-.045	-.072	-.052	-.030	-.050
Living with grandparents	-.018	.013	-.004	.021	.049	-.002
Living with siblings	.089	.031	.034	-.022	.081	-.009
Living with the spouse	.049	-.002	.143*	.003	.060	.057
Living with children	.077	.004	.075	.066	-.056	.045
Living with other relatives	.001	.038	.041	-.004	.017	.020
Living with friends	.052	.070*	.007	.004	.056	-.013
Living with others	.017	.022	.033	.027	.088*	-.045
Protestant	-.004	.034	-.014	.078**	.015	.044
Catholic	-.014	.029	-.050	-.019	-.010	-.018
Buddhist	.048	.025	.010	.025	.045	.054
Muslim	.013	.017	.037	.019	.094**	.023
Hindu	-.004	-.067*	-.035	-.024	-.036	-.034
Daoist	.073*	-.026	.016	.005	.025	-.001
Ancestor worshipper	-.046	.078*	.048	.044	.035	-.003
Confucian	-.041	.037	-.010	-.007	.053	-.056
Faith in another religion	-.043	.013	.056	-.086**	.048	.004
Family income	.043	-.014	.035	.051	-.050	.112**
Duration of residence	.047	.005	.007	.092*	.034	.059
Female	.002	.161***	.123***	.015	.021	.157***
Education	.026	.048	.097*	.087*	.031	.095
Cohabited	.098	.229**	-.067	.088	.183*	-.063
Married	-.025	-.001	-.007	-.012	.063	-.049
Divorced	-.004	.064	.015	.002	.154**	-.026
Self-employed	-.003	.024	.028	.099**	.031	.021

Predictor	Closeness	Disclosure	Caring	Contributing	Recourse	Cared
Middle class	-.016	.022	-.017	.206***	.034	.006
Working class	-.047	.004	-.003	.157***	.048	-.014
Having volunteering experience	.032	.066*	.094**	.222***	.014	.064*
Financial crisis impact × Age	.079	.109	.120#	.160*	-.021	.137*
Financial crisis impact × Age 60+	.014	.087*	.095*	.052	.020	.115**
Financial crisis impact × Age 40-59	.064	-.015	-.029	.062	-.061	-.058
Financial crisis impact × Age under 40	-.075#	-.057	-.051	-.097*	.047	-.040
Financial crisis impact × Living alone	.017	.043	.058#	.050#	.020	.052
Financial crisis impact × Working class	.008	-.010	-.037	-.032	-.074#	-.106**
R^2	.062	.098	.076	.165	.062	.082

* $p < .05$. ** $p < .01$. *** $p < .001$.

Table 4. Standardized regression coefficients for predicting the perceived financial crisis impact

Predictor	(1)	(2)
Age	-.056	-.008
Living with the father	-.060	-.065
Living with the mother	.054	.051
Living with grandparents	-.037	-.033
Living with siblings	-.027	-.025
Living with the spouse	-.041	-.041
Living with children	-.060	-.049
Living with other relatives	.026	.026
Living with friends	-.002	-.004
Living with others	.044	.040
Protestant	-.008	-.008
Catholic	-.052	-.053
Buddhist	-.007	-.007
Muslim	.000	.001
Hindu	.107**	.109***
Daoist	-.026	-.024
Ancestor worshipper	-.092**	-.090**
Confucian	.014	.014

Table 4. (Continued)

Predictor	(1)	(2)
Faith in another religion	-.013	-.014
Family income	-.033	-.033
Residency	-.092*	-.083*
Female	-.044	-.042
Education	-.144***	-.144***
Cohabited	-.044	-.045
Married	.037	.034
Divorced	.054	.056
Widowed	.062	.057
Self-employed	.006	.009
Middle class	.049	.046
Working class	.047	.052
Having volunteering experience	.016	.019
Age 40-59	-	-.076
Age 60+	-	-.032
R^2	.063	.065

* $p < .05$. ** $p < .01$. *** $p < .001$.

In contrast, the older person, who is unlikely to have sufficient recurrent income inflows, is running out of resources to maintain resilience to the impact of the financial crisis. This means that the financial crisis would not seriously drain resources in the ordinary or younger person to affect his or her social relationships. Echoing this is the observation that the financial crisis has not appeared to vitiate the job and employment (Parrado 2005). In contrast, the financial crisis or its impact is likely to foment a trouble in the older person, who already has limited physical, material, and social resources (Charles and Carstensen 2009). According to the resource base of socioemotional selectivity theory, resource change would be critical enough to alter the older person's social relationship (Lang et al. 2011). As such, selectivity as sensibly is an adaptive response to resource change in the older person. In this connection, resource increase concomitant with financial uplift can be fuel for activating social relationships, where resource drain attributed to financial stress can prompt the selection and thus dwindling of social relationships. Findings therefore champion and consolidate resource theory as an explanation for the social relationship, including compassionate and acquisitive ones, especially in the older person.

Meanwhile, the stressful impact of the financial crisis did not arouse the acquisitive social relationship of the person or older one particularly. The negative effect of the positive impact of the financial finding on recourse, albeit in line with the hypothesis, was not sufficient to be statistically or practically significant. Moreover, the older person received more care from others when the impact of the financial crisis was more positive. This finding just contrasts with the expectation that the older person would receive more care when the person is under stress or in need of care. The finding indicates that resources overwhelm need as a drive for the social relationship, including the acquisitive one. This is plausible because the acquisitive social relationship, as well as the compassionate social relationship, would entail resources for its building. The primacy of resources in activating social relationships has been pervasive in existing theory and evidence (Brinberg and Castell 1982; Wilson and Musick 1997). Conversely, stress is likely to impede the acquisitive social relationship (Dunkel-Schetter and Bennett 1990). Put alternatively, removing the need is conducive to the social relationship (Downie et al. 2008).

Age manifested a negative effect on recourse but not on other social relationships. This finding again supports resource based socioemotional selectivity theory, as opposed to need theory. If age is an indicator of need, need theory would expect greater social relationships with aging. The negative effect of age on recourse is at odds with need theory. In contrast, the negative effect is likely to reflect resource decline with age and this decline constrains the social relationship such as recourse. According to resource-based socioemotional selectivity theory, the older person would be more selective in using resources in maintaining social relationships, including recourse. Even though recourse can be a way of coping or problem solving, the older person is less likely to engage in such a practice (Caplan and Schooler 2007). Nevertheless, age generally makes a very difference in the social relationship. This echoes the view that one can adapt one's social relationship to one's age, thus nullifying the age effect on the social relationship (Charles and Carstensen 2009).

Other background effects on social relationships can also be explicable with respect to resource theory. First, the woman maintains a higher social relationship conceivably because of her personal resources for social relationship building, as compared with the man (Feingold 1994; Tamres et al. 2002). Second, education is conducive to the social relationship, plausibly due to the increased knowledge base concomitant with education (Bull et al. 2004). In this case, knowledge is an empowerment factor for the social relationship (Phillips 2006; Tindall and Wellman 2001). Third, the cohabited person shows a greater social relationship, probably because the person is socially vibrant, which in turn results from freedom from marital bondage (Brines and Joyner 1999). Fourth, volunteer experience facilitates the social relationship, reasonably because of skill and knowledge acquired from volunteering for fostering the social relationship (Musick and Wilson 2008). Notably, volunteering enables the incumbent to work and socialize with strangers, and this would lubricate social relationship building.

LIMITATIONS AND FURTHER RESEARCH

Limitations inherent in the study necessitate further research to corroborate and substantiate findings from the study. Notable limitations transpire from the single site of the study in Hong Kong, one-time survey, and self-report measurement. Accordingly, Hong Kong Chinese society has its distinctive features rendering the findings different from those derived from the West or the rest of the world. One obvious feature is the affluence of the metropolis in general, which may insulate the stressful impact of the financial crisis (Delang and Lung 2010). That is, when Hong Kong people are rich in financial resources, they can be immune to the agitation of the financial crisis. However, the older Hong Kong Chinese are particularly at risk for the stress of the financial crisis, because of their particularly weak financial position (Estes 2002). Their dire position stems from the lack of savings and social security insurance for aging. This means that the older Hong Kong Chinese are likely to be sensitive and susceptible to the financial crisis and its stress. Their selection as an adaptive response would therefore operate in their social relationships. Moreover, the selective response is likely to happen in view of social distrust prevailing in Hong Kong (Teets 2009). This would discourage the acquisitive social relationship as a way to gratify the need created by the financial crisis. Besides, the one-time survey and self-report measure cannot guarantee the validity of the findings to reflect the real causal mechanism revolving around the financial crisis. In this case, although the financial crisis was a past episode, perception about the impact of the financial crisis and social practice are not definite in time. Causal indeterminacy is thus a problem, particularly when the measures involved emanated from subjective judgment. Altogether, the palpable methodological limitations certainly require further research to address. Research that employs samples from socioculturally diverse sites, a panel or experimental design, and multiple sources of measurement is utterly desirable to generate rigorous findings. This is vital simply because the financial crisis is a worldly event not only plaguing a single place. Notably, objective sources of measurement through observation and alternative informants would help secure objective measurements, with guaranteed validity by using the triangulation of measures (Arminion and Hultgren 2002).

Resource theory and resource-based socioemotional selectivity theory are of crucial concern for further research to substantiate their application to the social impact of the financial crisis. First, resources need to be explicit and active factors in analysis in order to demonstrate their roles in activating social relationships and mediating the impact of the financial crisis. Herewith, the protective function of resources for diverting the impact of the financial crisis on the social relationship is a paramount thesis for further examination. This means that one devoid of resources, such as the older person, would suffer from the social relationship, and this possibility is an important research question. What is more, the influence of limited resources on socioemotional selectivity, notably in the older person, is an additional crux for further study. In this connection, socioemotional selectivity needs to play an explicit role in data analysis. Essentially, further research needs to reveal the linking mechanism underlying resource-based socioemotional selectivity theory outright (Lang et al. 2011). In case the selectivity is unconscious, it would require implicit measurement (Carmel et al. 2003).

Implications

Mitigating work is helpful to strengthen the older person's social relationship during and in the wake of the financial crisis. This is because the older person is particularly vulnerable to the alienating effect of financial stress arising from the financial crisis. In contrast, when the person has sufficient resources, he or she would not require help for sustaining the social relationship, as the relationship can be immune to the noxious impact of the financial crisis. Hence, the person's resources are of primal concern for delivering support for bolstering social integration. In this respect, encouraging the person's closeness to others would be most important in mitigating stress due to the financial crisis. With respect to resource theory, the principle of crisis intervention is to mobilize resources for the person to cope with the stress of the financial crisis (Knox and Roberts 2008).

Persons of some backgrounds are particularly in need for the mitigation against the detrimental impact of the stress of the financial crisis on social relationships. They include men, those with lower education, those with no volunteer experience, and those who are not in cohabitation. Those with lower education are also particularly in need of mitigation that relieves the stress fomented by the financial crisis. In all, people deficient in resources are the target for crisis intervention. Importantly, a large share of resources can reside in the person and they just require reactivation by the intervention (Brun and Rapp 2001).

REFERENCES

Arminio, Jan L., and Francine H. Hultgren. 2002. "Breaking out from the Shadow: The Question of Criteria in Qualitative Research." *Journal of College Student Development* 43(4):446-460.

Armstrong, Mary I., Shelley Birnie-Lefcovitch, and Michael T. Ungar. 2005. "Pathwys between Social Support, Family Well Being, Quality of Parenting, and Child Resilience: What We Know." *Journal of Child and Family Studies* 14(2):269-281.

Barr, Jeffrey A., Nambee G. Choi, Jun E. Mutchler, and Francis G. Caro. 2005. "Caregiving and Volunteering: An Private and Public Helping Behaviors Linked?" *Journal of Gerontology: Social Sciences* 60B(5):S247-S256.

Bekkers, Rene. 2008. "Straight from the Heart." *Advances in Medical Sociology* 10:197-221.

Bergmark, Ake, and Joakim Palme. 2003. "Welfare and the Unemployment Crisis: Sweden in the 1990s." *International Journal of Social Welfare* 12:108-122.

Binder, Jens F., Sam G. B. Roberts, Alistair G. Sutcliffe. 2012. "Closeness, Loneliness, Support: Core Ties and Significant Ties in Personal Communication." *Social Networks* 34:206-214.

Bjornberg, Ulla, and Hans Ekbrand. 2008. "Financial and Practical Kin Support in Sweden: Normative Guidelines and Practice." *Journal of Comparative Family Studies* 39(1): 73-95.

Bowling, Ann, Anne Fleissig, Zahava Gabriel, David Banister, Joanna Dykes, Lee Marriott Dowding, Stephen Sutton, and Oga Evans. 2003. "Let's Ask Them: A National Survey of Definitions of Quality of Life and Its Enhancement among People Aged 65 and over." *International Journal of Aging and Human Development* 56(4):269-306.

Brinberg, David, and Patricia Castell. [1982] 1993. "A Resource Exchange Theory Approach to Interpersonal Interactions: A Test of Foa's Theory." Pp.41-56 in *Resource Theory: Explorations and Applications*, edited by Uriel G. Foa, John Converse, Jr., Kjell Y. Tornblom, and Edna B. Foa. San Diego, CA: Academic Press.

Brown, Eleanor, and James M. Ferris. 2007. "Social Capital and Philanthropy: An Analysis of the Impact of Social Capital on Individual Giving and Volunteering." *Nonprofit and Voluntary Sector Quarterly* 36(1):85-99.

Brun, Carl, and Richard C. Rapp. 2001. "Strengths-based Case Management: Individuals' Perspectives of Strengths and the Case Manager Relationship." *Social Work* 46(3):278-288.

Buelow, George, Mark McClain, and Irene McIntosh. 1996. "A New Measure for an Important Construct: The Attachment and Object Relations Inventory." *Journal of Personality Assessment* 66(3):604-623.

Bull, S. Salyers, M. McFarlane, L. Lloyd, and C. Rietmeijer. 2004. "The Process of Seeking Sex Partners Online and Implications for STD/HIV Prevention." *AIDS Care* 16(8):1012-1020.

Caplan, Leslie J., and Carmi Schooler. 2003. "the Role of Fatalism, Self-Confidence, and Intellectual Resources in the Disablement Process in Older Adults." *Psychology and Aging* 18(8):551-561.

Carmel, David, Eran Dayan, Ayelet Naveh, Ori Raveh, and Gershon Ben-Shakhar. 2003. "Estimating the Validity of the Guilt Knowledge Test from Simulated Experiments: The External Validity of Mock Crime Studies." *Journal of Experimental Psychology: Applied* 9(4):261-269.

Chan, Alfred Cheung-ming. 2009. *Validation of Measurement for the Outcome of Social Capital: The Caring Index*. Hong Kong, China: Aberdeen Kai-fong Welfare Association Social Service Centre.

Charles, Susan T., and Laura L. Carstensen. 2009. "Social and Emotional Aging." *Annual Review of Psychology* 61:383-409.

Chen, Chaonan. 2006. "A Household-based Convoy and the Reciprocity of Support Exchange between Adult Children and Noncoresiding Parents." *Journal of Family Issues* 27(8):1100-1136.

Cohen, Jacob, Patricia Cohen, Stephen G. West, and Leona S. Aiken. 2003. *Applied Multiple Regression/Correlation Analysis for the Behavioral Sciences*. New York: John Wiley and Sons.

Cooney, Teresa M., and M. Katherine Hutchinson. 1995. "Surviving the Breakup? Predictors of Parent-adult Child Relations after Parental Divorce." *Family Relations* 44(2):153-161.

Cutler, David M., Felicia Knaul, Rafael Lozano, Oscar Mendez, and Beatrig Zurita. 2002. "Financial Crisis, Helth Outcomes and Ageing: Mexico in the 1980s and 1990s." *Journal of Public Economics* 84:279-303.

Degenne, Alain, Marie-Odile Lebeaux, and Yannick Lemel. 2004. "Does Social Capital Offset Social and Economic Inequalities?" Social Capital in Everyday Life." Pp.51-73 in *Creation and Returns of Social Capital: A New Research Program*, edited by Henk Flap and Beate Volker. London: Routledge.

Delang, Claudio O., and Ho Cheuk Lung. 2010. "Public Housing and Poverty Concentration in Urban Neighbourhoods: The Case of Hong Kong in the 1990s." *Urban Studies* 47(7):1391-1413.

Diewald, Martin, and Jorg Ludicke. 2006. "Community Lost or Freedom Gained? Chantes of Social Networks after 1989." Pp.191-213 in *After the Fall of the Wall: Life Courses in the Transformation of East Germany*, edited by Martin Diewald, Anne Goedicke and Karl Ulrich Mayer. Stanford, CA: Stanford University Press.

Downie, Michelle, Genevieve A. Mageau, and Richard Koestner. 2008. "What Makes for Pleasant Social Interaction? Motivational Dynamics of Interpersonal Relations." *Journal of Social Psychology* 148(5):523-534.

Dunkel-Schetter, Christine, and Tracy L. Bennett. 1990. "Differentiating the Cognitive and Behavioral Aspects of Social Support." Pp.267-296 in *Social Support: An Interactional View,* edited by Barbara R. Sarason, Irwin G. Sarason and Gregory R. Pierce. New York: John Wiley and Sons.

Espvall, Majen, and Peter Dellgren. 2008. "Can We Count on Each Other? Reciprocity and Conflicts in Financial Support in Sweden." *International Journal of Social Welfare* 19:84-94.

Estes, Richard J. 2002. "Toward a Social Development Index of Hong Kong: The Process of Community Engagement." *Social Indicators Research* 58:313-341.

Feingold, Alan. 1994. "Gender Differences in Personality: A Meta-analysis." *Psychological Bulletin* 116(3):429-456.

Fine, Michael D. 2007. *A Caring Society? Care and the Dilemmas of Human Service in the Twenty-first Century*. Houndmills, UK: Palgrave.

Fridberg, Torben, and Olli Kangas. 2008. "The Welfare State, Poverty and Social Exclusion." Pp.22-47 in *Nordic Social Attitudes in a European Perspective*, edited by Heikki Ervasti, Torben Fridberg, Mikael Hjerm, and Kristen Ringdal. Cheltenham, UK: Edward Elgar.

Ganster, Daniel, and Bart Victor. 1988. "The Impact of Social Support on Mental and Physical Health." *British Journal of Medical Psychology* 61:71-36.

Gant, Judy R., Robert J. Calsyn, and Joel Winter. 1999. "Predicting Agreement between Providers and Recipients of Social Support." *Journal of Social Behavior and Personality* 14(4):523-546.

Godoy, Ricardo, Victoria Reyes-Garcia, Tomas Huanca, William R. Leonard, Romona G. Olvera, Jonathan Bauehet, Zhao Ma, Jonathan St. John, Marisa Miodowski, Oscar Zapata Rios, Vincent Vadez, and Craig Seyfried. 2007. "The Role of Community and Individuals in the Formation of Social Capital." *Human Ecology* 35:709-721.

Goodwin, Robin, George Nizharadze, Lan Anh Nguyen Luu, Eva Kosa, and Tatiana Emelyanava. 2001. "Social Support for a Changing Europe: An Analysis of Three Post-communist Nations." *European Journal of Social Psychology* 31:379-393.

Hatfield, Elaine, and Richard L. Rapson. 2012. "Equity Theory in Close Relationships." Pp.200-217 in *Handbook of Theories of Social Psychology* (vol.2), edited by Paul A.M. Van Lange, Arie W. Kruglanski and E. Tory Higgins. London, CA: SAGE.

Heinz, Walter R. 2002. "Self-socialization and Post-Traditional Society." *Advances in Life Course Research* 7:41-64.

Henry, Julie D., William von Hippel, and Kate Baynes. 2009. "Social Inappropriateness, Executive Control, and Aging." *Psychology and Aging* 24(1):239-244.

Hess, Thomas M., Nicole L. Osowski, and Christina M. Leclerc. 2005. "Age and Experience Influences on the Complexity of Social Inferences." *Psychology and Aging* 20(3):447-459.

Hicks, Jennifer, and Eric R. Kingson. 2009. "The Economic Crisis: How Fare Older Americans?" *Generations* 33(3):6-11.

Hofferth, Sandra L., Johanne Boisjoly, and Greg J. Duncan. 1999. "The Development of Social Capital." *Rationality and Society* 11(1):79-110.

Holliday, Ian. 2005. "East Asian Social Policy in the Wake of the Financial Crisis: Farewell to Productivism." *Policy and Politics* 33(1):145-162.

Inglehart, Ronald. 2003. "Modernization and Volunteering." Pp.55-70 in *The Values of Volunteering:* Cross-cultural Perspectives, edited by Paul Dekker and Loek Halman. New York: Kluwer.

Jones, Keely S. 2006. "Giving and Volunteering as Distinct Forms of Civic Engagement: The Role of Community Integration and Personal Resources in Formal Helping." *Nonprofit and Voluntary Sector Quarterly* 35(2):249-266.

Jung, EeHwan, and Byung-you Cheon. 2006. "Economic Crisis and Changes in Employment Relations in Japan and Korea." *Asian Survey* 46(3):457-476.

Kemp, Candace L. 2007. "Grandparent-grandchild Ties: Reflections on Continuity and Change across Three Generations." *Journal of Family Issues* 28(7):855-881.

Kessler, Thomas, Amelie Mummendey, and Utta-Kristin Leisse. 2000. "The Personal-group Discrepancy: Is There a Common Information Basis for Personal and Group Judgment?" *Journal of Personality and Social Psychology* 79 (1):95-109.

Keyes, Corey L.M., and Adam D. Shapiro. 2004. "Social Well-being in the United States: A Descriptive Epidemiology." Pp.350-372 in *How Healthy Are We: A National Study of Well-being at Midlife*, edited by Orville Gilbert Brim, Carol D. Ryff and Ronald C. Kessler. Chicago, IL: University of Chicago Press.

Kim, Andrew Enungi. 2004. "The Social Perils of the Korean Financial Crisis." *Journal of Contemporary Asia* 34 (2):221-337.

Kliegel, Matthias, Theodor Jager, and Louise H. Phillips. 2007. "Emotional Development across Adulthood: Differential Age-related Emotional Reactivity and Emotion-regulation in a Negative Mood Induction Procedure." *International Journal of Aging and Human Development* 64 (3):217-244.

Knox, Karen S., and Albert R. Roberts. 2008. "The Crisis Intervention Model." Pp.249-274 in *Theoretical Perspectives for Direct Social Work Practice: A Generalist-eclectic Approach*, edited by Nick Coady and Peter Lehmann. New York: Springer.

Kwon, Soonman. 2001. "Economic Crisis and Social Policy Reform in Korea." *International Journal of Social Welfare* 10:97-106.

Lang, Frieder R., Margund K. Rohr, and Bettina Williger. 2011. "Modeling Success in Life-span Psychology: The Principles of Selection, Optimization, and Compensation." Pp.57-85 in Handbook of Life-Development, edited by Karen L. Fingerman, Cynthia A. Berg, Jacque Smith and Toni C. Antonucci. New York: Springer.

Leiser, David, Sacha Bourgeois-Gironde, and Rinat Benita. 2010. "Human Foibles or Systemic Failure: Lay Perceptions of the 2008-2009 Financial Crisis." *Journal of Socio-Economics* 39:132-141.

Lennartsson, Carin. 2010. "Need and Support: Determinants of Intra-familial Financial Transfers in Sweden." *International Journal of Social Welfare* 20:66-74.

Li, Kui-Wai. 2012. Economic Freedom: Lessons of Hong Kong. Singapore: World Scientific.

Lim, Hyun-Chin, and Joon Han. 2003. "The Social and Political Impact of Economic Crisis in South Korea: A Comparative Note." *Asian Journal of Social Science* 31(2):198-220.

Lupien, Sonia J., Bruce S. McEwen, Megan R. Gunnar, and Christine Heim. 2009. "Effects of Stress thoroughout the Lifespan on the Brain, Behavior and Cognition." *Nature Reviews: Neuroscience* 10:434-445.

Magliano, Lorenza, Andrea Fiorillo, Claudio Malangone, Corrado De Rosa, and Mario Maj. 2006. "Social Network in Long-term Diseases: A Comparative Study in Relatives of Persons with Schizophrenia and Physical Illnesses versus a Sample from the General Population." *Social Science and Medicine* 62:1392-1402.

Maybery, D.J., Jenny Jones-Ellis, Jason Neale, and Alexandra Arentz. 2006. "The Positive Event Scale: Measuring Uplift Frequency and Intensity in an Adult Sample." *Social Indicators Research* 78:61-83.

Mikulincer, Mario, Victor Florian, and Gilad Hirschberger. 2003. "The Existential Function of Close Relationships: Introducing Death into the Science of Love." *Personality and Social Psychology Review* 7(1):20-40.

Molm, Linda D. 1997. *Coercive Power in Social Exchange*. Cambridge, UK: Cambridge University Press.

Molm, Linda D. 2006. "The Social Exchange Framework." Pp.24-45 in Contemporary Social Psychological Theories, edited by Peter J. Burke. Stanford, CA: Stanford Social Sciences.

Newman, Richard S. 1998. "Students' Help Seeking during Problem Solving: Influences of Personal and Contextual Achievement Goals." *Journal of Educational Psychology* 90(4):644-658.

Neyer, Franz J., and Frieder R. Lang. 2003. "Blood Is Thicker Than Water: Kinship Orientation across Adulthood." *Journal of Personality and Social Psychology* 84 (2):310-321.

Oppenheimer, Louis, and Jan Heller. 1984. "Development of Cooperation and Help-seeking Activities: An Action Theoretical Approach." Pp.177-200 in *Development and Maintenance of Prosocial Behavior: International Perspectives on Positive Morality*, edited by Ervin Staub, David Bar-Tal, Jerzy Karylowski and Janusz Reykowski . New York: Plenum.

O'Rand, Angela M. 1996. "The Cumulative Stratification of the Life Course." Pp.188-207 in *Handbook of Aging and the Social Sciences*, edited by Robert H. Binstock and Linda K. George. San Diego, CA: Academic.

Paolino, Phillip. 1995. "Group-Salient Issues and Group Representation: Support for Women Candidates in the 1992 Senate Elections." *American Journal of Political Science* 39(2):294-313.

Parrado, Emilio A. 2005. "Globalization and the Transition to Adulthood in Mexico." Pp.327-348 in *Globalization, Uncertainty and Youth in Society*, edited by Hans-Peter Blossfeld, Erik Klijzing, Melinda Mills and Karin Kurz. London: Routledge.

Phillips, David. 2006. *Quality of Life: Concept, Policy and Practice*. London: Routledge.

Piquero, Nicole Leeper, and Miriam D. Sealock. 2004. "Gender and General Strain Theory: A Preliminary Test of Broidy and Agnew's Gender GST Hypotheses." *Justice Quarterly* 21(1):125-158.

Ranzijn, Rob. 2002. "The Potential of Older Adults to Enhance Community Quality of Life: Links between Positive Psychology and Productive Ageing." *Ageing International* 27(2):30-55.

Riley, Matilda White, and John W. Riley, Jr. 1999. "Sociological Research on Age: Legacy and Challenge." *Ageing and Society* 19:123-132.

Roberts, Marcus. 1996. *Analytical Marxism: A Critique*. London: Verso.

Rossi, Alice. 2001. "Domains and Dimensions of Social Responsibility: A Sociodemographic Profile." Pp.97-134 in *Caring and Doing for Others: Social Responsibility in the Domain of Family, Work, and Community*, edited by Alice S. Rossi. Chicago, IL: University of Chicago Press.

Rotenberg, Ken J., and Jocelyn Hamel. 1988. "Social Interaction and Depression in Elderly Individuals." *International Journal of Aging and Human Development* 27(4):305-318.

Schervish, Paul G., and John J. Havens. 2002. "The Boston Area Diary Study and the Moral Citizenship of Care." *Voluntas* 13(1):47-71.

Seligson, Mitchell. 2005. "The Measurement and Impact of Corruption Victimization: Survey Evidence from Latin America." *World Development* 34(2):381-404.

Sharabany, Ruth. 1994. "Intimate Friendship Scale: Conceptual Underpinnings, Psychometric Properties and Construct Validity." *Journal of Social and Personal Relationships* 11:449-469.

Skerkat, Darren E., and Christopher G. Ellison. 1999. "Recent Developments and Current Controversies in the Sociology of Religion." *Annual Review of Sociology* 25:363-394.

Smyth, Paul. 2008. "Closing the Gap? The Role of Wages, Welfare and Industry Policy in Promoting Social Inclusion." *Journal of Industrial Relations* 50(4):647-663.

Straume, Sivert, and Magnus Odeen. 2010. "International and Domestic Altruism: A Study among the Adult Population in Norway." *Journal of Applied Social Psychology* 40(3):618-635.

Tamres, Lisa K., Denise Janicki, and Vicki S. Helgeson. 2002. "Sex Differences in Coping Behavior: A Meta-analytic Review and an Examination of Relative Coping." *Personality and Social Psychology Review* 6(1):2-30.

Tang, Fengyan. 2006. "What Resources Are Needed for Volunteerism? A Life Course Perspective." *Journal of Applied Gerontology* 25(5):375-390.

Teets, Jessica C. 2009. "Post-earthquake Relief and Reconstruction Efforts: The Emergence of Civil Society in China?" *China Quarterly* 198:330-347.

Timopen, Virpi. 2008. *Ageing Societies: A Comparative Introduction*. Maidenhead, UK: Open University Press.

Tindall, D.B., and Barry Wellman. 2001. "Canada as Social Structure: Social Network Analysis and Canadian Sociology." *Canadian Journal of Sociology* 26(3):265-307.

Turner, Rhiannon N., Miles Hewstone, and Alberto Voci. 2007. "Reducing Explicit and Implicit Outgroup Prejudice via Direct and Extended Contact: The Mediating Role of Self-disclosure and Intergroup Anxiety." *Journal of Personality and Social Psychology* 93(3):369-388.

Uslaner, Eric M. 2002. *The Moral Foundations of Trust*. Cambridge, UK: Cambridge University Press.

van Praag, Bernard M.S., and Paul Frijtens. 1999. "The Measurement of Welfare and Well-being: The Layden Approach." Pp.413-433 in *Well-being: The Foundations of Hedonic Psychology*, edited by Daniel Kahneman, Ed Diener and Norbert Schwarz. New York: Russell Sage.

Vanclay, Frank. 2003. "Conceptual and Methodological Advances in Social Impact Assessment." Pp.1-9 in *The International Handbook of Social Impact Assessment: Conceptual and Methodological Advances*, edited by Henk A. Becker and Frank Vanclay. Cheltenham, UK: Edward Elgar.

Vasapollo, Luciano. 2012. *Crisis of Capitalism: Compendium of Applied Economics*. Leiden, Netherlands: Brill.

Viry, Gil, Vincent Kaufmann, and Eric D. Widmer. 2009. "Social Integration Faced with Commuting: More Widespread and Less Dense Support Networks." Pp.121-143 in *Mobilities and Inequality*, edited by Timo Ohnmacht, Hanja Maksim, and Marfred Max Bergman. Farnham, UK: Ashgate.

Von Hippel, William, and Sally M. Dunlop. 2005. "Aging, Inhibition, and Social Inappropriateness." *Psychology and Aging* 20(3):519-523.

Wallenius, Mariut A. 2006. "Personal Project Content and Stress: Relations to Subjective Health and Depressive Mood." *Social Indicators Research* 81:35-50.

Wilson, John, and Marc A. Musick. 1997. "Work and Volunteering: The Long Arm of the Job." *Social Forces* 76(1):251-272.

In: Financial Crises
Editor: Cooper A. Hawthorne

ISBN: 978-1-62808-293-7

Chapter 3

WHAT DID ASIA AND EUROPE DO TO FIGHT THE FINANCIAL CRISIS?

Petr Blizkovsky[*,†]
Council of the European Union, Brussels, Belgium

ABSTRACT

The paper will look at the economic and financial crisis from a public policy point of view. There was a financial crisis in several countries in south-east Asia in the late nineties. Similarly, since 2008, the European Union has been challenged with its own crisis. The question of the paper is what responses have been developed in both regions at the super-national level in order to prevent or minimise future crises.

First, the paper will look at the nature of the instruments developed, such as legally binding instruments or voluntary coordination instruments. In this respect, it will explore to what extent the countries are committed to sharing sovereignty.

The second question is related to the geographical scope. In this part, the paper evaluates the ability of the region to engage with its broader neighbourhood. The paper focuses on the ASEAN Plus activities carried out in the Asian region in the broader sense. In Europe, the regulatory response to the European debt crisis is on two levels - on the one hand, between all 27 members of the EU and, on the other, in the narrower circle of the euro zone. The conclusion of this part underlines the trade-off between intensity and geographical scope, i.e. between shallow and wide measures in Asia, versus deep and narrow ones in Europe.

Thirdly and finally, the paper evaluates the interplay between the regional and global response to the crisis. The main focus is, on the one hand, to what extent the regional initiatives inspired global governance and, on the other, how much the global decisions shaped regional governance.

Keywords: Financial crisis, Asia, European Union, ASEAN, economic governance, policy coordination

---

[*] Petr Blizkovsky is Director at the General Secretariat of the Council of the European Union. In 2011/2012 he served as EU Fellow at the Lee Kuan Yew School of Public Policy at the National University of Singapore.

[†] The opinions expressed in this article are those of the author alone.

1. Introduction

The objective of this paper[1] is to analyse the policy adjustments of Asia, focusing on ASEAN - the Association of Southeast Asian Nations (ASEAN) - and the European Union (EU) to the economic crisis. The paper looks at the cross-country reaction only and does not comment on the policy responses taken at national level only.

The paper looks at this topic from two perspectives. First, how the region reacted to its own crisis. There are two crises events to be looked at: on the Asian side the financial crisis of 1997-1998 in Southeast Asia and on the European Union's side the financial crisis of 2008 followed by its sovereign debt crisis. Secondly, the question is how the regions contributed to the global regulatory response to the global economic downturn which followed after 2008.

On the first issue, regulatory instruments used at the cross-country regional level, the paper will analyse the nature, procedures and actors of the decision taken. It will also look at geographical scope to which new measures would apply to. The paper will subsequently evaluate to what extent the financial crisis provoked a closer regional cooperation.

On the second topic, interplay between the regional and global response to the crisis, the focus will be on how Asia and Europe contributed to shape global governance in order to minimise the next financial crisis and what each region might want in future in this respect.

2. Asia and Europe: Regional Financial Crises and Regional Policy Responses

Asia and Europe have their regional grouping, such as ASEAN and EU. On the way how these regional co-operations coordinate their cross-boarder economic issues there are both several similarities as well as substantial differences. On the side of similarities, both regions entered into the integration process several decades ago. The Association of Southeast Asian Nations (ASEAN) was established in 1967, while the predecessor of the EU, the European Economic Community, 10 years before that. Both regions consist of the voluntary cooperation of several Member States of which the number has been progressively growing. In the case of ASEAN, there were five signatories in the beginning (Indonesia, Malaysia, the Philippines, Singapore and Thailand) and now there are at 10 (Brunei Darussalam, Vietnam, Lao PDR and Myanmar, and Cambodia). In the case of the EU, it grew from an initial six members to the current 27 (with Croatia joining as of 2013). Both regional co-operations contributed positively to the stability (note that there was no military conflict between any of the Members on either side) and arguably also to the economic prosperity of its Members.

On the side of differences, there is the nature and ambition of cooperation in both regions. The ASEAN region, whose welfare disparities are wider, relies on the working method of cooperation and voluntary cooperation, without sharing sovereignty. Its decision-making process relies on consensus and consultation. Dispute settlements are not subject to court ruling, and institutional intensity is low. Several authors elaborated on this, such as Tan, G., 2003, Welfens, P. J. J. et al (eds.), 2009, Caballero-Anthony, M., 2009, Lee, J. 2010 and Severino, R., C., 2010. On the EU side, regional cooperation is a legally-binding process,

[1] The paper is based on the article Petr Blizkovsky: Economic governance: What can the EU and ASEAN learn from each other after the economic crises? ASEAN Economic Bulletin (2013, in preparation)

where Treaties (currently the Treaty on the EU and the Treaty on the functioning of the EU) specify the areas and extent of sovereignty sharing, EU law has primacy over national law, the European Court of Justice is charged with judiciary responsibility and there is a strong institutional structure supporting the functioning of the EU.

A comparative overview of the economic governance in ASEAN and the EU shows that the key difference in the working method is the fact that; while the ASEAN economic governance before the crisis in the region was based on political dialogue and consultation, the EU pre-crisis economic governance was based on a set of legally-binding rules in the single market area with free circulation of production factors. This was coupled with the European Economic and Monetary Union (EMU) as of 1992. The EMU covers the obligations for macroeconomic policy coordination and the creation of the single monetary policy for the Euro Area Member States.

In the EU, the critical aspect of the functioning of the single currency area is fiscal and growth-related coordination. Fiscal coordination was ensured by the Stability and Growth Pact (SGP) which stipulates that they should aim for a budgetary position close to balance, or in surplus, over the medium-term in a period of normal economic growth. The Member States of the EU (with the exception of the United Kingdom) are also obliged to avoid an excessive deficit above 3% of GDP. In addition, Member States should have maximum 60% of government debt of GDP according to the SGP. In the pre-crisis period, the implementation of the SGP was done in a way that has been criticised for being too lax, notably due to the fact that the sanctions foreseen by the SGP and the Treaties have never been used so far. Growth-related policy coordination was implemented in a soft way via a policy recommendation foreseen in the Treaties - Broad Economic Policy Guidelines (BEPGs) - and a peer-pressure process based on political commitment (Lisbon agenda). Also the policy effectiveness here was sub-optimal if measured by the competitiveness differentiation inside the Euro Area. The shortcomings of the pre-crisis economic governance were analysed both from the governance perspective (Council of the European Union, 2010, Kirkegaad, J. F., 2011, Marzinotto, B., Sapir, A. and Wolff, G. B., 2011,) as well as from the economic side (Llewellyn, J. and Westeway, P., 2011, Schuknecht, L., Moutot, Ph., Rother, Ph. and Stark, J., 2011, Nordvig, J., 2012).

a) Regional Crises

Both regions were hit by financial and economic crises. In ASEAN, it was the financial crisis of 1997-1998, in the EU, the financial, economic and sovereign debt crisis starting in 2008.

The Asian crisis was linked to the fixed exchange peg to the US in the situation of the international free movement of capital. The crisis started in Thailand and spread to Indonesia, Malaysia, the Philippines and eventually to Hong Kong and Korea. The EU crisis of 2008 was started by the US subprime mortgage market. Via the banking crisis, it hit developed EU economies with the notable feature of triggering a sovereign debt crisis in some European Union Members, such as Greece, Portugal, Ireland, Spain and Italy in the Euro Area, and Hungary, Romania, the Baltic states and others outside the Euro Area. Subsequently, the growth of EU economies slowed down significantly, partly due to the fiscal adjustments.

The comparison of both crises has been researched extensively (IMF 1998, Rajan R. S., 2006, ASEAN Studies Centre, 2010, Henning, R. C., 2011, Blizkovsky, P., 2012, Rana, P. B., Blomenhofer, M. and Rajaratnam, S., 2013). The two crises happened in different political and economic environments, attacked economies at different stages of development, were caused by case-specific causes, had various geographical scopes and witnessed specific reactions by international institutions.

Rajan, R. S. and Gopalan S. (2011) suggest the following overview of similarities and differences of both crisis events. The commonalities lie in the fact that troubled countries:

- accumulated current account deficits of 8-9% of their respective GDP
- had open capital accounts coupled with fixed exchange rates (soft pegs to the US dollar in the case of Asian countries)
- experienced a decline in their competitiveness
- had much of their external liabilities in foreign currencies, and finally
- experienced sharp credit growth.

On the side of differences, the authors noted the following features:

- the structure of the current account deficit in Asian countries was predominantly due to investments, while in the EU countries it was due to consumption
- the Asian countries carried over a sound fiscal policy, while this was not the case in some of the Euro Area members
- the debt situation was less favourable in the respective EU countries compared to the Asian ones
- the growth rate in Asian countries prior to the crisis event was higher than in its EU peers
- the international economic situation was better in the 1997-1998 crisis
- the stressed Asian countries allowed for the depreciation of their currencies, which was not the case in the Euro Area countries
- the spill over effect via the banking sector was much stronger in the case of the EU
- the IMF reaction to both crises was different – more favourable in the EU case, in terms of speed and conditionality.

Based on the Root Cause Analysis, Rana, P. B., Blomenhofer, M. and Rajaratnam, S.(2013) conclude that the Asian financial crisis had two causes: policy mistakes (premature liberalisation of capital flow and pegged exchange rate system) and weak regulation and supervision of banks. In the EU crisis they detect roots of the crisis in unsustainable public finances, weak financial regulation and flaws in the policy designs of the economic and monetary union (absence of the lender of last resort for the monetary union).

b) Regional Policy Response

However different or similar the starting policy design and crises were, the policy response was fundamental. Both crises changed the way of regional cooperation and its economic governance. On the ASEAN side, the subject was studied amongst others by Sjoholm, F. and Tongzon, J. (2005); ASEAN Studies Centre (2009); Acharya, A. (2010); Baldwin, R. (2011); Hammilton-Hart, N., (2011); Lesher, M. and Plummer, G. (2011); Nakagawa, J. (2011); Wong, M.-H.; Shankar, R. and Toh, R. (2011) and Yeo, L. H. (2009 and 2011). Major developments consisted in the creation of the ASEAN Community and the adoption of the ASEAN Charter. On top of this, financial cooperation was strengthened in both the ASEAN and ASEAN Plus frameworks.

The ASEAN Community was established in 2007 by the Cebu Declaration with the objective of closer regional cooperation. The target date for its implementation is 2015. The process has three aspects: political and security, economic, and socio-cultural. On the economic governance side, the ASEAN Economic Community should be also operational as of 2015.

The next institutional development was the adoption of the ASEAN Charter (ASEAN Secretariat, 2008) which entered into force in 2008. It mainly provided a new legal status and institutional framework for ASEAN to become a legally-binding agreement.

The ASEAN economic governance response played a role in enhancing financial stability in the broader region. It started with a network of bilateral currency swaps in 2002. It was followed by the Chiang Mai Initiative Multilateralisation (ASEAN Plus 3, 2010). Another instrument of economic governance was the Asian Bond Markets Initiative, aimed at creating efficient and liquid bond markets in the region (see Chung, W.C. (2006), Japan Bank for International Cooperation (2011)). Also the Macroeconomic Research Office (AMRO) was created as a regional macroeconomic surveillance and crisis management unit for ASEAN Plus 3.

In the case of the EU, economic governance is undertaking multiple adjustment due to the crisis - see Begg, I., Belke, A., Dullien, S., Schwarter, D. and Vilpisaukes, R. 2011; Begg, I. 2011; Blizkovsky P., 2011 and 2012; Bishop, G. 2011; Featherstone, K., 2011 and Verhelst, S., 2011. It aims at enhancing macro-economic coordination, strengthening existing legal instruments in the fiscal area, creating new financial assistance facilities and establishing a macro-prudential body. New bodies have been created in order to strengthen the EU economic governance and especially that of the Euro Area. Importantly, separate legal and political obligations have been agreed among smaller groups of countries, be it the Euro Area or at the Euro Area Plus format.

3. Regional Economic Policy Instruments Triggered by Crisis

This chapter analyses new economic policy instruments from the perspective of their objectives, decision-making methods, enforcement and involvement of policy actors.

a) ASEAN Economic Governance

In the period after the Asian financial crisis, the regional response aimed at closer cooperation in the region. ASEAN agreed the ASEAN Charter (ASEAN Secretariat, 2008) created a framework within which ASEAN Member States can enter into substantive agreements on specific areas, such as economic integration, environmental protection and climate change, equitable development, transnational crime and security. An example of this is the ASEAN Economic Community Blueprint by 2015. The objective of the ASEAN Economic Community is to create a stable, prosperous and highly competitive ASEAN economic region in which there is a free flow of capital, economic development and reduced socio-economic disparities. The AEC plans to establish ASEAN as a single market production base and mitigate the economic diversities of the region. Specific objectives relate to the progressive liberalisation of financial services by 2015, except for those sub-sectors and modes where pre-agreed flexibilities are determined.

More specifically on economic policy objectives, in the area of the free flow of goods, ASEAN has made great strides in reducing tariff barriers. From 1 January 2010, all tariffs for products in the Common Effective Preferential Tariff Inclusion Lists of ASEAN-6 (Brunei Darussalam, Indonesia, Malaysia, Philippines, Singapore and Thailand), representing 99% of total tariff lines, have been eliminated for intra-ASEAN trade. The average tariff was down to 0.9% in 2009 from 4.4% in 2000.

In the area of the free flow of services, ASEAN Member States have so far negotiated and agreed on seven packages of commitments under the ASEAN Framework Agreement on Services. ASEAN signed and ratified the protocol implementing the fourth package of financial service commitments where Member States have made further liberalisation commitments.

In the area of the free flow of investments, the existing investment agreements, including investment guarantees, have been enhanced and consolidated into the ASEAN Comprehensive Agreement on Investment.

In the area of the free flow of capital, ASEAN endorsed in April 2009 an implementation plan to promote the development of an integrated ASEAN capital market. ASEAN has intensified its efforts in the cross-border liberalisation of products and services, mutual recognition of market professionals, common exchange linkages, and bond market developments.

The ASEAN Member States have also liberalised capital account measures to allow for greater mobility in the region. A stock-taking of capital account measures for foreign direct investment shows that the majority of ASEAN has no restrictions on inward and outward foreign investments.

In the area of the free flow of skilled labour, a greater mobility of qualified service professionals in the region is foreseen by the mutual recognition arrangements in medical services, engineering services, nursing services, architectural services and surveying qualifications. The implementation of the main objective is politically speaking on track even if with some delays and gaps in the sub-sectoral objectives (Wong, M.-H.; Shankar, R. and Toh, R., 2011).

On the decision-making method and enforcement, the new rulebook sticks to the traditional decision method of ASEAN, namely consultation and consensus (ASEAN Charter, Art. 20.1). In addition, the ASEAN Summit may decide how a specific decision can be made if consensus cannot be achieved (ASEAN Charter, Art. 20.2).

On enforcement, a case of serious breaching of the Charter can be referred to the ASEAN Summit for a decision (ASEAN Charter, Art. 20.4). The dispute settlement mechanism in specific ASEAN instruments will be established within these instruments. In the case of ASEAN economic agreements, the ASEAN Protocol on enhanced dispute settlement mechanism should be followed (ASEAN Charter, Art. 24.3).

On instruments, important developments have occurred in economic governance since the crisis. Importantly, they aim at greater financial integration with China, Japan and the Republic of Korea in the wider geographical scope of the ASEAN Plus 3 framework (ASEAN Plus 3, 2010). It comprises the following instruments:

1. The Chiang Mai Initiative Multilateralisation (CMIM)

The CMIM aims at providing financial stability in the broader region and to address short-term liquidity difficulties. It reacted to the crisis experience and evolved from a network of bilateral currency swaps started in 2002. CMIM is a currency swap facility involving 26 central banks and finance ministries of ASEAN Plus 3 countries and the Monetary Authority of Hong Kong, China. It came into effect on 24 March 2010. The total size of CMSM is US dollar 120 billion and the objective is to address balance of payment and short-liquidity difficulties. Maturity of swaps is 90 days with possible prolongation to approximately two years.

2. Asian Bond Markets Initiative (ABMI)

The aim of ABMI is to promote local currency-denominated bond markets and thus enhance macroeconomic and financial stability in the region. The participant countries are those of ASEAN Plus 3 (see above). The ABMI was endorsed at the Ministerial level in 2003. At this Ministerial Meeting in Madrid in 2008, Ministers agreed on a new ABMI Roadmap. The governance structure of the ABMI is on voluntary commitments. The working structure is based at the Ministerial level, Deputies level, ABMI Steering Group and working teams according to the policy area and chaired by individual ABMI members. The ASEAN Plus 3 Bond Market Forum (ABMF) was established in this context as a platform to standardise market practices and harmonise regulatory practice. It is on a voluntary basis.

3. Credit Guarantee and Investment Facility (CGIF)

The aim of the CGIF is to support the issuance of local currency denominated bonds in the region. It was established in 2010 (ASEAN Plus 3, 2010). It will also support the issuance of corporate bonds in the ASEAN Plus 3 region. It was organised as a trust fund of the Asian Development Bank with an initial capital of US dollar 700 million.

4. ASEAN+3 Macroeconomic Research Office (AMRO)

The AMRO is a regional macroeconomic surveillance and crisis management office. It was launched by the ministries of finance, central banks and monetary authorities of the ASEAN Plus 3 countries. It complements the CMIC by carrying out a regional surveillance function. AMRO monitors macroeconomic trends, assesses financial vulnerability and provides assistance on policy recommendations from the ASEAN Plus 3 countries to safeguard regional financial stability. AMRO is based in Singapore and has a relatively small staff of less than 20 people.

5. ASEAN+3 Macroeconomic Research Group (AMRG)

AMRG is a research-type grouping endorsed by the ASEAN Plus 3. It studies the locally-denominated trade settlements and liquidity risks in the region. Ministers mandate the research work of the AMRG.

Finally, on the creation of new actors and bodies, a distinction should be made between the general ASEAN and the financially-oriented ASEAN Plus 3. The new highest body of ASEAN is the ASEAN Summit (ASEAN Charter, Art. 7). It provides policy guidelines and takes decisions on key issues of ASEAN. It also instructs the Ministerial level. It decides by cooperation and consensus. The ASEAN Summit authorises the creation of ASEAN sectoral ministerial bodies and establishes their mandates. They work towards strengthening cooperation in their respective fields. The ASEAN coordinating Council, comprising the Foreign Ministers of ASEAN, prepares the summits and coordinates the ASEAN work. The summit and ministerial level chairmanship rotate. A Committee of Permanent Representatives to ASEAN represents the Member States on a daily basis at the preparatory level. The institutional intensity remains low even if an ASEAN Secretariat and Secretary-General were created by the ASEAN Charter. The competence and size of the General Secretariat do not go beyond the secretariat function and are without policy initiative and implementation power.

The CMIM, ABMI, CGIF, AMRO and AMRG are new actors and bodies at the ASEAN Plus 3 level. Their common feature is that they go geographically beyond ASEAN, are based on an inter-governmental agreement and aim at strengthening the financial stability in the region. The logic of all the bodies is two-fold. Firstly they provide a framework for financial assistance in stressed times (CMIM) and secondly they strengthen macroeconomic surveillance and analysis (AMRO and AMRG). In addition, they create more efficient bond markets (ABMI, CGIF). All bodies have their ownership at the Ministerial level. Institutionally the most advanced body is the CMIM. The decision-making for the amendment of the CMIM's basic-text agreement is consensus at the Ministerial Level. Executive decisions are governed by a 2/3 vote at the executive level decision-making body (deputy-level) where the voting power is based on financial contributions and agreed 'purchasing multiple'. The total voting power of China, Japan and ASEAN countries combined is 28.41% each and of Korea 14.77%. The decision making of the other bodies is based on consensus and cooperation is on a voluntary basis.

b) EU Economic Governance

The EU responded to its sovereign debt crisis by strengthening the regulatory framework in the financial service area, on fiscal rules for the EU and in the Euro Area, and on competitiveness surveillance. This effort was complemented both by the creation of financial assistance in the case of sovereign debt stress and by pro-growth measures. Importantly, the decision-making structures have been enhanced in order to make the EU economic governance more efficient.

1. New instruments

First on financial services. The EU adopted new rules in the area of banks, insurance companies and financial markets and created the European Systemic Risk Board (ESRB) too for the early identification of risks. On top of it, it prepares the progress of banking union. It will start with a Single Supervisory Mechanism (SSM) in which the European Central Bank (ECB) and national competent authorities would supervise the banks in the euro area. Member states from outside the euro area can join in if they wish so. The SSM will start supervision of banks as of March 2014, or 12 months after the entry into force of the legislation, whichever is later.

Second on fiscal rules. The EU has tightened fiscal rules by the adoption of the so-called six pack (European Union, 2011). It establishes and monitors the adjustment paths of Member States towards their medium-term budgetary objectives. Sanction rules were strengthened by, introduction of semi-automatic decision rules if fiscal rules are not respected. Also, there is the possibility to impose sanctions already in the preventive part of the Stability and Growth Pact. For the first time, the public debt level is subject to specific rules, as it is demanded the adjustment towards the medium-term objective for high-debt countries of the speed of reduction of the debt level above the 60% debt threshold by 1/20 annually. Strengthening the monitoring and reporting obligations of Euro Area Members will be done through so-called two pack rules, to be adopted in 2013.

Additionally, new fiscal policy obligations were agreed outside the EU framework by 25 countries via the Treaty on Stability, Coordination and Governance (TSCG) (see European Union, 2012). It provides for an obligation to implement nationally via constitution or framework-law the "Golden Rule", similar to the medium-term budgetary objectives with the imposed limit of a deficit of 0.5% of GDP - this being stricter than the up to 1% deficit limit stipulated in the Stability and Growth Pact until now. New sanctions can be imposed in the case of obligations not being respected.

Third, on economic coordination and pro-growth measures. As economic policy remains under national competence, the obligations for coordination within the EU have been reinforced. There is a legally binding surveillance framework for the monitoring and correction of excessive imbalances based on surveillance, alert and sanctions. The objective is to prevent potentially harmful imbalances within the EU. The European Semester was introduced as a tool for stronger community involvement in the preparation of national budgets. This combines Broad Economic Policy Guidelines and the review of the Stability or Convergence programmes in a single text for each Member State and is of a policy recommendation nature.

Europe 2020 is another instrument providing guidelines to EU Members and the EU as a whole on structural reforms. Finally, the Euro Plus Pact was agreed as the political commitment among 23 Member States to increasing competitiveness, fostering employment, reinforcing financial stability, and improving the state of public finances, especially in the pension sector. It also aims at tax coordination to the extent possible (European Council, 2011).

Fourth, on creating financial assistance. The Members of the Euro Area created several financial assistance tools to assist stressed countries. Importantly, the conditionality linked to the assistance is linked with the EU rules and EU decision-making framework. In the first stage short-term crisis resolution mechanisms were agreed, such as the Balance of Payment for Greece (BoP) and the European Financial Stability Facility (EFSF) as a company under private law and owned by the Euro Area countries. The BoP was taken over by the EFSF in 2012. At a later stage, a limited change to the Treaty on the functioning of the EU (Article 136) was agreed to allow the creation of the European Stability Mechanism: expected to enter into force in 2013. The European Stability Mechanism (ESM) is the permanent crisis resolution mechanism within the Euro Area, operational as of mid-2013 (Council of the European Union (2012).

The following Table provides an overview of newly created instruments for the economic governance of the EU.

2. Decision-making

Concerning the decision-making structures linked to the new instruments, they have been strengthened but have also become more complex. Two types of decision-making were agreed for economic governance.

First, there is a legally binding decision-making method. Inside the EU, it is based on the EU Treaties. It represents the traditional EU 'community method'. Its use was broadened in a sense that it makes fiscal decisions inside the Council of the EU easier, such as in the case of the six pack. It introduces 'reverse qualified majority' to impose sanctions for breaching fiscal rules. The qualified majority of the Council can stop the sanctions as proposed by the Commission rather than imposing them. This method was also used for macro-economic surveillance for competitiveness measures and as a basis for financial assistance to protect the Euro Area as a whole.

Outside of the EU, legally binding decision-making structures were introduced for the Euro Area/Euro Area Plus format based on inter-governmental agreements. Under this category, the European Stability Mechanism (ESM) is a primary law instrument between Euro Area Members and open to other EU Members. The EU institutions, such as the European Commission and the European Central Bank, are involved in its implementation. The voting rules are mutual agreement, qualified majority or simple majority, as specified in the Treaty. By way of derogation, an emergency voting procedure can be used where the Commission and the ECB both conclude that a failure to urgently adopt a decision to grant or implement financial assistance would threaten the economic and financial sustainability of the Euro Area. The emergency voting rule is qualified majority of 85% of the votes cast. Another example is the Treaty on Stability, Coordination and Governance (TSCG). This is a primary law instrument between 25 Members and open to other EU Members. The EU institutions, such as the European Commission, European Court of Justice and European Central Bank, are involved in its implementation. Additionally, as in the case of the TSCG, the instrument contains a clear commitment to become part of the EU structure as soon as possible. National Parliaments and the European Parliament have a defined consultancy role.

Second, there are decisions based on political commitments. In this case, the decisions are not binding and have form of recommendations. This soft way of recommendations and peer pressure is used within the EU to the Europe 2020 and European Semester. The EU institutions are involved in the implementation.

In the case of Euro Area/Euro Area Plus these are based on an inter-governmental basis. The Euro Plus Pact is represented in this case. The EU institutions are involved in the implementation (European Commission, Council and European Council).

The EU response is work in progress. The European Council (European Council (2012)) discussed four building blocks moving towards the genuine EMU. These cover an integrated budgetary framework, an integrated budgetary framework, an integrated economic framework and measures to enhance democratic legitimacy and accountability.

Table 1. New instruments in the economic governance of the European Union

Instrument	Participating Member States	Body in charge
Policy guidance Legislator/Co-legislator Co-legislator	27	European Council Council European Parliament
Risk warnings		European Systemic Risk Board (ESRB)
Policy guidance, decisions Informal meeting, guidance of the Euro Area	17	Euro Summit Eurogroup
Monetary policy		European Central Bank
European Financial Stability Facility decisions	17	European Financial Stability Facility board meeting
Assistance to Greece	16	Balance of Payment
Euro Plus Pact, open to observers	23 plus	Euro Plus Pact meeting
European Stability Mechanism decisions, open to other members Bank supervision	17 plus	European Stability Mechanism board Single Supervisory Mechanism
Binding rules on budgetary discipline	25	Treaty on Stability, Coordination and Governance in the Economic and Monetary Union

(1) Protocols 1 and 2 to the Treaties of the EU
(2) Article 13, Treaty on Stability, Coordination and Governance in the Economic and Monetary Union.

4. Impact of New Economic Governance on Regional Cooperation

The regional cooperation in ASEAN before the crisis was characterised by shallow institutions and non-legally binding structures. In the EU, the regional cooperation was institution-intensive and based on legally-binding structures of shared sovereignty. The way the regional governance developed in both regions after the crisis shows both commonalities and differentiations.

a) Assistance-Surveillance Path: Strengthening of Regional Cooperation

On commonalities, a twin 'assistance-surveillance' approach was pursued in both regions. An assistance facility was developed to mitigate future financial and economic crises, which was inexistent at the pre-crisis stage. This is coupled with the strengthening of macroeconomic surveillance to follow more closely the competitiveness development in the region. An interdependence of the intensity between assistance and surveillance can be followed in order to mitigate the financial burden of possible assistance.

In ASEAN, the assistance facility is represented by CMIM which provides a short-term security network. The surveillance is ensured in the larger sense by pro-growth measures in the area of the creation of a single market which arguably ensures the harmonisation of the competitiveness structures and contains the peer-pressure process of macro-economic surveillance. On top of this and in a narrow sense, the macro-economic developments are monitored by AMRO and studied by AMRG. Other newly created bodies, such as ABMI and CGIF, play a supportive role.

In the EU, the 'assistance-surveillance' approach is also clearly visible. In the first stage of the crisis response, the ad-hoc financial assistance, BoP, was coupled with ad-hoc macro-economic surveillance and conditionality for Greece. Later, the financial assistance to the Euro Area (the EFSF) was complemented by the pro-growth measures of the EU 2020, European semester and Euro Plus Pact and by the legally binding six pack. This staging effort was eventually complemented by the adoption of the TFEU amendment and of the TSCG and ESM treaties. In the stage under progress, the supervision of banks and ESM conditionality would be prerequisite for possible ESM interventions to the stressed banks. Finally, for the future there is an open-ended question of a stronger control of the budgetary policies coupled with fiscal capacity or some form of debt mutualisation for the Euro Area members.

The 'assistance-surveillance' overview is presented in Table 2.

Table 2. Policy response to economic crisis by ASEAN and the European Union

Region	Period	Fiscal rules	Economic policy coordination	Assistance
ASEAN	Before crisis	NA	NA	NA
	Policy response to crisis	NA	Political commitment Creation of single market plus creation of bodies (AMRO, ABMI, CGIF, AMRG)	CMIM
EU	Before crisis	Legally binding: primary and secondary law (SGP)	Policy recommendation (BEPGs, Lisbon strategy)	Only for non-Euro Area
	Policy response to crisis: phase 1	In addition: Ad-hoc conditionality for Greece	In addition: Ad-hoc conditionality for Greece New macro-economic supervision	PoB for Greece
	Policy response to crisis: phase 2	Strengthened legally-binding: primary and secondary law (six pack)	Strengthened policy recommendation (EU 2020, European Semester, Euro Plus Pact) Legally binding (macroeconomic surveillance – six pack)	EFSF for Euro Area
	Policy response to crisis: phase 3	Strengthened secondary law (two pack) In addition: New legally binding primary law (TSCG)	New legally binding primary law (TSCG)	ESM (legally binding, for Euro Area)
	Policy response to crisis: phase 4	ESM conditionality	Single Supervisory Mechanism	ESM interventions to bank possibility

b) Deep-Wide Dilemma

The policy reaction of ASEAN and EU differences relate to a 'deep-wide' pattern. The issue here is to what extent the regional policy reaction is *deep* in terms of legally binding force, enforceability and actual implementation. A related issue is the geographical scope, how wide the policy goes: does it stay within the region or does it engage 'region plus' or 'region minus' areas?

The ASEAN reaction to its economic crisis was a 'shallow-wide' one. Shallow, because not legally binding, without a specific court authority, with a soft dispute settlement scheme only, without direct democratic control of Parliaments, with consensus as a voting rule and without institutions charged with a policy mandate. These are the characteristics of the ASEAN Charter and the ASEAN Economic Community. The various new instruments as described above are based on a voluntary inter-governmental approach. However, this 'shallow' design has been somewhat deepened compared to the former ASEAN policy design. A first example is the aim of creating the single market of ASEAN with stronger monitoring and peer pressure by ASEAN peers. A second example is the CMIC, where the voting rules on the executive decisions are done by 2/3 votes. This is a notable exception to the consensus rule of ASEAN.

On the other side, the ASEAN economic governance response has been 'wider'. By engaging with three important economies of Plus 3 countries, the ASEAN policy framework has become much more relevant. Interestingly, the commonly used name for the CMIC, AMRO, ABMI, CGIF and AMRG instruments is ASEAN Plus 3 and not China Plus one as economic logic would suggest. In this sense ASEAN has managed to be a relevant actor in the larger region.

The EU story is different. The character of the crisis has notably been that of the sovereign debt crisis of the single currency area. Thus the origin of the crisis triggered the adjustment of the policy design and of its full implementation, including addressing the competitiveness differentiation in the Euro Area. The policy reaction has therefore been rather inward-looking – 'narrow' and aimed at tightening, 'deepening' the policy design. The deepening is translated by the new primary law obligation, enforceability ensured by the European Court of Justice (even in the case of the TSCG obligation), the role of the national and European Parliaments, the strengthening of the role of the European institutions such as the independent European Commission, and the easing of voting rules of the Council in defined cases as described above. This deepening effort is coupled with new political commitments going to areas outside EU competences and subject to peer pressure and monitoring by the EU. On the other side, not all the new deeper instruments are binding or applicable to all EU 27 members as presented in Table 1.

The intensity of the economic governance influences the overall cooperation in the region. Therefore, the move from shallow to wide governance arguably increases the level of integration of the region. Similarly, the wide approach on economic governance increases the impact of the region beyond its territory and thus enlarges the influence of the region.

A synthesis of the 'shallow-wide' policy reaction in both regions is provided in the table below.

Table 3. Summary of the economic policy response to the crisis in ASEAN and the European Union

Region	Period	Fiscal and economic coordination governance		Financial assistance	
		Intensity	Geographical scope	Intensity	Geographical scope
ASEAN	Before crisis	Very low	ASEAN	NA	NA
	Policy response to crisis	Low	Wider	Low	Wider
EU	Before crisis	High	EU	Low/NA(1)	EU
	Policy response to crisis	Very high	Narrowing	High	Narrow

(1) Low for the non-Euro Area, NA for the Euro Area.

5. Interplay between the Regional and Global Response

The regional policy response in Asia and in Europe has an impact on the global economic governance and vice versa (Renard, T., Bishop, S., 2012). The issue is whether there is a mutual synergy or rather an antagonistic relation.

As explained above, the key response in both regions was the establishment of the regional financial assistance mechanisms. The immediate question is: why both regions came up with the regional instrument instead of using the existing global one of the IMF? The reasons on the ASEAN side can be seen in the mistrust towards the IMF. The countries affected with the crises were not comfortable with the policy response and the conditionality linked with the assistance packages. Therefore they opted for a regional alternative which would increase their independence from the IMF.

In case of the EU and the Euro Area in particular, the regional approach has been chosen because of political considerations linked to the Economic and Monetary Union. Additionally, there is a ′stigma′ effect related to the IMF assistance, especially for the developed countries. Euro Area has nevertheless closely coordinated the assistance to its stressed economies in terms of conditionality, monitoring and sharing of financial burden.

G20 at the level of Heads of states and governments raised as a governance novelty during the crisis. The reasons for its establishment were several. It bypasses the problem of distribution of power between developed and emerging economies of the IMF and the World Bank. Its informal character makes it easier to solve an ad hoc problem with ad hoc commitments. Finally, its limited membership makes negotiations easier. On the other side, it has several shortcomings, such as lack of institutional capacity, non-binding nature of the commitments made and strong dependence on the presidency country to set out agenda. Conferring some monitoring and evaluation functions to established international institutions like IMF and OECD helps to overcome some of the limitations.

Looking at the EU, the EU and its Member States have been proactive stakeholders of global economic governance and have thus shaped the global economic rules. On the other hand, the EU has been a recipient of the global economic governance and implemented what has been decided at the global level.

Table 4. Global and EU economic governance

	Global governance		EU governance		
Issues	**Forum**	**Instrument**	**Forum**	**Instrument**	**Comment**
Macroeconomic policy	G20, G7/8	FfG[3], dialogue	EU-27 EU-17 Eurogroup, Euro Summit EU-25 EU-23	EU Treaty, SGP[4], 6 pack, 2 pack Policy guidance Treaty (TSCG)[5] Euro Plus Pact	EU coordination more advanced (normative governance) Source of inspiration for global governance
Monetary policy	G7, G20	Dialogue	EU, ECB	Single currency	Euro area governance fully harmonised
Structural policy	G8, G20	FfG, dialogue	EU-27 EU-17, Eurogroup, Euro Summit EU-25 EU-23	EU Treaty, SGP, 6 pack, 2 pack Policy guidance Treaty (TSCG) Euro Plus Pact	EU coordination more advanced (normative, coordination, peer pressure) Source of inspiration for global governance
Financial assistance	IMF	Loans	EU-27 EU-17	Loans for non-euro members EFSF[6], ESM[7], loans for euro members	Global governance source of inspiration for euro area
Financial stability	G20, G8, FSF	Risk identification	EU	EFSF - risk identification	Global governance source of inspiration for EU

3 Framework for growth
4 Stability and Growth Pact
5 Treaty on Stability, Coordination and Governance in the Economic and Monetary Union
6 European Financial Stability Facility
7 European Stability Mechanism

Table 4. (Continued)

	Global governance		EU governance		
Issues	**Forum**	**Instrument**	**Forum**	**Instrument**	**Comment**
Financial regulation	G20	Political commitment	EU	Legal obligations	Binding EU governance in line with global political commitments
Capital requirements of banks	G20 Basel process	Political commitment Rule-setting	EU	Legal obligations follow Basel process	EU governance follows global governance
Accountancy	G20 IASB	Political commitment Rule-setting	EU	Legal obligations follow IASB process	EU governance follows global governance
Tax coordination	N/A	N/A	EU EU-25	Voluntary coordination Euro Plus Pact	Soft EU coordination. Source of inspiration for global governance

There has been a mutual influence between regional and global governance. Table 4 compares the approach taken at the global and EU levels in different segments of economic governance at the regional level in the EU. In some cases, the practices of the EU could have been of interest for the global scale. Examples are in the case of macroeconomic policy within the G20 Framework for Growth and the EU instruments of budgetary surveillance, competitiveness development, structural policy and possibly tax coordination. On the other hand, the EU has taken the global governance standards as its own rules in areas such as financial assistance and financial regulations (including capital requirements for banks or accountancy standards). Similarly, the ASEAN financial mechanisms and surveillance tools benefited from the experience existing already at the global scale.

The above overview shows that paradoxically, the relation between regional and global governance is more of a cooperative character, even though is might be a product of the initial mistrust. The current practice demonstrates that closer regional cooperation in Asia and in Europe is based on similar principles and is using similar tools as the global governance for reaching objectives of economic and financial coordination. Regional instruments are fully compatible with the global mechanisms. Thus the result is that the closer regional cooperation is a useful tool of coordination which is supportive to the coordination at global level. The reactions to the crisis confirmed the known experience that cooperating in smaller group of countries facing similar challenges can benefit from the higher level of understanding and trust and this makes decisions on difficult subjects easier.

Conclusion

Economic crises hit parts of Asia and Europe within the time difference of ten years. Both crises had different roots. The crisis in Southeast Asia was mainly of an external nature, the EU crisis was mainly internally-driven. In both cases the pre-crisis policy design was at the origin of the crisis: in Asia it was the fixed exchange rate combined with free circulation of capital, in the EU it was the supranational monetary policy combined with economic policy staying at national level and subject to sub-optimal enforcement of the fiscal discipline.

Both regions reacted to its crisis forcefully. The ASEAN method relied on lower institutional intensity. The ASEAN reaction tends to be 'shallow-wide' with decision-making relying on consensus and cooperation. The new financial stability instruments have however been agreed for the ASEAN Plus format which makes it more far-reaching and relevant.

The regional reaction of the EU policy design was 'deep-narrow'. Several new binding instruments have been adopted via primary law obligations. Additionally, the EU members agreed politically and legally to cooperate deeply in new areas of economic governance, such as growth policy, competitiveness surveillance and financial assistance. On the other side, some of the new instruments are applicable to a smaller number of countries inside the EU, namely to those in the Euro Area.

One of the conclusions of the paper is that economic difficulties in the regions gave birth to closer cooperation in economic area. Regions as a institutional entities emerged stronger after the crises.

In parallel to the regional response, there was a global policy reaction. A new format of economic coordination was established, namely the G20. There was an interplay between regional and global economic governance. This resulted in ′export and import′ of policy ideas. Regions were able to influence global design. This was mainly the case of the EU, which is a natural development while the EU is well equipped in searching for compromises in coordination effort. The second conclusion of the paper is therefore that the regional policy coordination resulted in being a support for rather than a competition with the global governance.

REFERENCES

Acharya, A. (2010). Whose does matter? Agency and power in Asian regionalism. Utopia Press, Singapore, *189* ISBN, 978-981-4279-15-4.

ASEAN Plus 3 (2010). The Joint Ministerial Statement of the 13th ASEAN Plus 3 Finance Ministers' Meeting, 2 May 2010, Tashkent, Uzbekistan.

ASEAN Secretariat (2008). *The ASEAN Charter*. Jakarta, ASEAN Secretariat, January 2008, ISBN: 978-979-3494-62-7

ASEAN Studies Centre (2009). ASEAN economic community blueprint. Singapore: Institute of Southeast Asian Studies. *Asian Survey*, *42*, 3, 440–455. ISSN: 0004–4687

ASEAN Studies Centre (2010). *The global economic crisis: implications for ASEAN*. Report No. 10. ISBN 978-981-4279-41-3.

Baldwin, R. (2011). Sequencing Regionalism: Theory, European Practice and Lessons for Asia. Asian Development Bank, ADB Working Paper Series on Regional Economic Integration, No. 80, June 2011.

Begg, I. (2011). The EU's Response to the Global Financial Crisis and Sovereign Debt Crisis: Economic governance under Stress? Workshop on Leadership, Decision-making and Governance in the EU and East Asia: Crisis and Post-crisis. EU Centre in Singapore, 21-22 November 2011. Singapore.

Begg, I., Belke, A., Dullien, S., Schwarter, D. & Vilpisauskas, R. (2011). European Economic Governance. Impulses for Crisis Prevention and New Institutions. Europe in Dialogue 2011/12 Bertelsmann Stiftung. ISSN: 1868-5048.

Bishop, G. (2011). The EU Fiscal Crisis: Forcing Eurozone Political Union in 2011? Searching Finance Ltd, London, ISBN 978-1-907720-14-7, 94.

Blizkovsky, P. (2011). Economic Governance and Solidarity: A Complex Relationship. In: Lepoivre, M., Keller-Noellet, J. and Verhelst, S. (eds.), The European Union and Economic Governance, Studia Diplomatica, volume LXIV nr. *4*, Ghent: Academia Press, 105.

Blizkovsky, P. (2011a). The new economic governance of the European Union: What it is and who does what? Policy Brief Series, Issue 4, Dec.

2011, National University of Singapore, Lee Kuan Yew School of Public Policy, Singapore, 8.

Blizkovsky, P. (2012). Two Crises, Two Responses - Adjustment of Economic Governance in ASEAN and the European Union. In: Asia Eur J, DOI 10.1007/s10308-012-0312-8. Springer-Verlag.

Caballero-Anthony, M. (2009). Evolving Regional Governance in East Asia: from ASEAN to an East Asian Community. In: Thomas, N.: Governance and Regionalism in Asia, 32-6, Routledge, ISBN: 10 0-415-45699-9.

Chung, W. C. (2006). Asian Bond Markets Initiative. Japanese Representative Office. Asian Development Bank: August.

Council of the European Union (2010). Final Report by the Task Force, 21 October 2011, doc 15302/10, Brussels.

Council of the European Union (2012). Treaty Establishing the European Stability Mechanism, website of the Council of the European Union, http://www.consilium.europa.eu/policies/council-configurations/economic-and-financial-affairs/the-eurogroup.aspx?lang=en.

Euro Area (2011a). Euro Summit Statement, Brussels, 26 October 2011. http://www.consilium.europa.eu/uedocs/cms_data/docs/pressdata/en/ec/125644.pdf.

European Council (2011). Conclusions of the European Council of 24-25 March 2011. http://www.consilium.europa.eu/uedocs/cms_data/docs/ pressdata/en/ec/120296.pdf.

European Council (2011a). Statement by the Euro Area Heads of State or Government, Brussels, 9 December 2011. http://www.consilium.europa.eu/uedocs/cms_data/ docs/ pressdata/en/ec.pdf.

European Council (2012). Statement by the Euro Area Heads of State or Government, Brussels, 9 December 2011. Towards a genuine economic and monetary union. Report of the President of the European Council, in close collaboration with the President of the European Commission, President of the Eurogroup and President of the European Central Bank, 5 December 2012, http://www.consilium.europa.eu/uedocs/cms_data/ docs/ pressdata/en/ec/134069.pdf.

European Union (2011). Official Journal of the European Union, L 306, Vol. *54*, 23 November 2011, ISSN: 1977-0677, Luxembourg.

European Union (2012). Treaty on Stability, Coordination and Governance. Text signed on 2 March 2012 by the Heads of State or Government. http://european-council.europa.eu/eurozone-governance/ treaty-on-stability.

Featherstone, K. (2011). The Greek Sovereign Debt Crisis and EMU: A Failing State in a Skewed Regime. *Journal of Common Market Studies*, vol. *49*, No 2, 193-217, Oxford.

Hammilton-Hart, N. (2011). Regional Governance: East Asia after the Global Financial Crisis. Workshop on Leadership, Decision-making and Governance in the EU and East Asia: Crisis and Post-crisis. EU Centre in Singapore, 21-22 November 2011. Singapore.

Henning, R. C. (2011). Economic Crises and Institutions for Regional Economic Cooperation. ADB Working Paper Series on Regional Economic Integration, No. 81, June 2011, Asian Development Bank.

Kirkegaard, J. F. (2011). Congressional Testimony: The Euro Crisis: Origins, Current Status, and European and US Responses. In: Peterson Institute of International Economics: http://www.piie.com/publications/ testimony/kirkegaard20111027.pdf.

IMF (2008). Annual Report, (2008): International Monetary Fund, Washington D.C., USA.

Lee, J. (2010). ASEAN's unchanged Melody? The Theory and Practice of 'non-interference' in Southeast Asia. *The Pacific Review*, vol. *23*, No. 4, September 2010, 479-502.

Lesher, M. & Plummer, G. (2011). Back to Basics. Post-crisis Macroeconomic Rebalancing in ASEAN. *ASEAN Economic Bulletin*, vol. *28*, No 2 pp 160-82. ISBN 0217-4472.

Llewellyn, J. & Westeway, P. (2011). Europe will work. *Nomura Global Economics*, March 2011, 122.

Marzinotto, B., Sapir, A. & Wolff, G. B. (2011). What kind of fiscal union? Bruegel Policy Brief. Issue 2011/6, November 2011

Nakagawa, J. (2011). Multilateralism and regionalism in global economic governance: trade, investment and finance. Routledge Publ., 337 ISBN: 978-0-415-59569-8.

Nordvig, J. (2012). Currency Risk in the Eurozone: Accounting for break-up and redenomination risk, Anchor Report, G10 FX Inside. Nomura Securities International, 3 January 2012, 47.

Rajan, R. S. (2006). Crises, Private Capital Flows and Financial Instability in Emerging Asia. UNESCAP Working Paper, WP/09/06.

Rajan, R. S. & Gopalan S. (2011). Comparing the Asian and Eurozone Crises: A perspective from Asia. Policy Brief Series, Issue 5, Dec 2011, National University of Singapore, Lee Kuan Yew School of Public Policy, Singapore, 12.

Rana, P. B., Blomenhofer, M. & Rajaratnam, S. (2013). The Eurozone Crisis and Its Impact on Asia, RSIS Working Paper No. 254, 6 February 2013.

Schuknecht, L., Moutot, Ph., Rother, Ph. & Stark, J. (2011). The Stability and growth pact crisis and reform. European Central Bank, Occasional paper series, No. 129, September 2011.

Sjoholm, F. & Tongzon, J. (2005). Institutional change in Southeast Asia. Routledge, New York, 206 ISBN, 0415338719.

Tan, G. (2003). Asean Economic Development and Cooperation. Eastern Universities Press, 3rd edition, 361 ISBN, 981-210-257-4.

Verhelst, S. (2011). The Reform of European Economic Governance: towards a Sustainable Monetary Union? Egmont - The Royal Institute for International Relations, Brussels, ISBN: 978-90-382-1802-1, 62.

Volz, U. (2010). Prospects for Monetary Cooperation and Integration in the East Asia. MIT Press, ISBN: 978-0-262-01399-4, 416p.

Welfens, P. J. J. et al (eds.) (2009). EU – ASEAN: Facing Economic Globalisation. DOI 10.1007/978-3540-87389-1, Springer-Verlag Berlin Heldeberg.

Wong, M.-H., Shankar, R. & Toh, R. (2011). ASEAN Competitiveness Report 2010. Asia Competitiveness Institute, National University Singapore. ISBN, 978-981-08-8429-1.

Yeo, L. H. (2009). The Everlasting Love for Comparison: Reflections on the EU's and ASEAN's Integration. In: Kanet, R., E., ed.: The United States of Europe in a Changing World. Dodrecht, Republic of Letters Publishing, 185-205.

Yeo, L. H. (2011). Where is ASEAN Heading – Towards a Network Approach to Global Governance? In: Panorama: Insights into Asian and European Affairs. Asia and Europe moving towards a common agenda. Konrad Adenauer Stiftung, Singapore, 19-26.

In: Financial Crises
Editor: Cooper A. Hawthorne

ISBN: 978-1-62808-293-7

Chapter 4

DETERMINANTS OF FIRM PERFORMANCE DURING AND AFTER THE 2008-09 FINANCIAL CRISIS IN EUROPE AND CENTRAL ASIA

George R. G. Clarke* and Aparna Gosavi†
[1]Division of International Banking and Finance Studies,
A.R. Sanchez, Jr. School of Business, Texas A&M International University,
Laredo, Texas, US

ABSTRACT

The global financial crisis that hit in 2008-2009 affected firms throughout the world. Given the depth of the recession that hit Eastern Europe in late 2008 and 2009, it is not surprising that firms in the region were seriously affected by the crisis. It led to a collapse in trade, potentially affecting exporters, a collapse in domestic demand, potentially affecting all firms, and a collapse in the availability of credit, which should have affected those firms that had access before the crisis. In this paper we use firm-level data to look at how different types of firms were affected by the crisis. Having access to credit before the crisis does not appear to have benefitted firms during the crisis. Once the crisis was over, however, managers of firms that had access to credit before the crisis were more likely to report that their situation was improving. Given the collapse in trade, it seems plausible that export-oriented firms might have been more vulnerable than other firms. Our econometric results do not generally support this idea. At the beginning of the crisis, export-oriented firms appear to have been affected to similar degrees as other firms. Managers of export-oriented firms did, however, report faster growth between March 2009 and March 2010 suggesting that exporters might have recovered more quickly from the crisis than other firms.

* Clarke (corresponding author): Associate Professor, Division of International Banking and Finance Studies, A.R. Sanchez, Jr. School of Business, Texas A&M International University, 5201 University Boulevard, Laredo, Texas 78041. E-mail: GEORGE@GRGCLARKE.COM. The data used in this paper are from the World Bank Enterprise Surveys [Enterprise Surveys (http://www.enterprisesurveys.org), The World Bank]. Responsibility for all errors, omissions, and opinions rests solely with the authors.

† E-mail: aparnagosavi@dusty.tamiu.edu

I. Introduction

The sub-prime mortgage crisis that started in the United States in 2008 quickly developed into a full-fledged global financial and economic crisis. [8] Per capita world GDP, which grew by 2.7 percent in 2007, shrunk by 0.1 percent in 2008 and 3.4 percent in 2009 (World Bank, 2012). The problems in the financial sector and the subsequent collapse in economic growth was accompanied by an even greater collapse in world trade (Freund, 2009). Exports fell by 10.7 percent in 2009–almost three times faster than per capita growth (World Bank, 2012).

Because the financial sectors of many countries in Europe and Central Asia are highly integrated into global financial markets, the region was particularly vulnerable to the financial crisis. [9] In five of the six countries that we look at in this study—Bulgaria, Hungary, Latvia, Lithuania, and Romania—foreign banks held over 60 percent of banking sector assets before the crisis (Claessens & Van Horen, 2012). [10] Since most of these banks came from developed economies in Europe and North America, this meant that the region might have been particularly at risk during the financial crisis. If international banks ended up retrenching their operations to help support their operations in their home countries, they might withdraw support from Eastern Europe. [11] It therefore might not be surprising that Europe and Central Asia suffered from a particularly severe recession—GDP growth was slower in Europe and Central Asia in 2009 (-6.5 percent) than in any other region of the World (see Table 1).

Table 1. Per Capita GDP growth during the crisis

	2007	2008	2009	2010	2011
World	**2.7**	**0.1**	**-3.4**	**3.2**	**1.6**
High Income					
European Union	2.8	-0.2	-4.7	1.9	1.2
United States	0.9	-1.3	-4.4	2.2	1.0
Low and Middle Income					
Europe & Central Asia	7.0	3.5	-6.5	5.3	5.3
Sub-Saharan Africa	3.6	2.2	-0.3	2.6	2.1
Middle East & North Africa	4.1	2.9	1.9	2.4	
Latin America & Caribbean	4.7	3.1	-2.7	5.1	3.6
East Asia & Pacific	11.5	7.7	6.7	9.0	7.6
South Asia	7.4	2.4	5.9	7.1	5.0

Source: World Bank (2012)

[8] See Mishkin (2011) for a description of how the crisis developed from a subprime mortgage crisis in the United States to a global economic crisis. Lo (2012) and Gorton and Metrick (2012) provide literature surveys of this topic.

[9] De Hass and Van Neeltje (2012) note that cross-border lending is particularly important in this region.

[10] In the sixth country, Turkey, foreign banks held only about 14 percent of sector assets (Claessens & Van Horen, 2012).

[11] Clarke and others (2003) argue that early evidence suggest that foreign banks might be a stabilizing influence during a financial crisis. However, most of the evidence that they considered involved purely domestic, rather than a global, crisis. The impact of the global crisis, which started in developed economies, might therefore be quite different. Morgan and others (2004) and others propose a model where multinational banks extend capital to protect affiliates in countries facing serious shocks (support effect) but also shift capital away from countries facing serious shocks to other countries where they operate (substitution effect). The relative impact depends on whether supply or demand shocks are more important.

Although financial sector integration was high, Europe and Central Asia did not appear to suffer as significantly from the collapse in world trade as other regions. Although export growth slowed significantly in the region—from 7.3 percent in 2007 to -7.0 percent in 2009—the slowdown was more modest than in other regions (see Table 2). In comparison, export growth fell from 15.6 percent in 2007 to -9.9 percent in East Asia and the Pacific.

Table 2. Export growth during the crisis

	2007	2008	2009	2010	2011
World	**7.9**	**3.4**	**-10.7**	**14.1**	**6.0**
High Income					
European Union	5.5	1.6	-11.7	10.6	6.1
United States	9.3	6.1	-9.1	11.1	6.7
Low and Middle Income					
Europe & Central Asia	7.3	3.1	-7.0	7.4	4.3
Sub-Saharan Africa	6.1	4.0	-9.7		
Middle East & North Africa	8.0	12.0	-11.3		
Latin America & Caribbean	5.9	1.6	-9.7	12.6	6.1
East Asia & Pacific	15.6	7.1	-9.9	23.8	8.5
South Asia	6.1	11.7	-4.6	20.2	15.0

Source: World Bank (2012).

The financial crisis threatened firms in the region in three ways. First, it made it more difficult for firms to get access to credit. Using firm-level data from the beginning of the crisis, Clarke and others (2012) find that financial constraints had increased significantly for firms, and especially for large firms, between 2005 and the end of 2008. Second, the collapse in exports was a serious threat for firms that were integrated into the global marketplace. Finally, the collapse in domestic demand threated all firms. Previous studies from the early part of the crisis suggest that the drop in demand—both foreign and domestic—had the greatest impact on firms during the early months of the crisis (Correa & Iootty, 2010; Correa and others, 2010). [12]

The focus of this paper is how firms performed during the financial crisis and at the beginning of the recovery. To look at this, we use firm-level data from two sets of surveys conducted by the World Bank's Enterprise Survey group: [13] the Business Environment and Enterprise Performance Survey (BEEPS); and three follow-up surveys, the Financial Crisis Surveys (FCS), that were conducted in six countries in the region (Bulgaria, Latvia, Lithuania, Hungary, Romania, and Turkey). All of these countries suffered from significant drops in per capita GDP in 2009 and, to greater or lesser extent, recovered in 2010. Since the three rounds of the FCS were conducted in May/June 2009, February/March 2010, and May/June 2010 and the surveys compare firm performance at the time of the survey with performance from the previous period, we are able to look at firm performance at the beginning of the crisis and at the beginning of the recovery. These surveys help us to establish

[12] The question that they use refers to a "drop in demand for [the firm's] products or services" and does not distinguish between

[13] The data are available on the World Bank's Enterprise Survey website (http://www.enterprisesurveys.org)

a link between macroeconomic factors, firm characteristics and firm performance in the pre- and post- crisis period.

Given the impact that the crisis had on trade and access to credit, our study focuses on these two issues. We look at whether firms that had access to credit and firms that were exporters were more or less affected by the crisis than other firms. We look at both firm growth and managers' self-reported perceptions about how the crisis affected their firms.

Having access to credit before the crisis does not appear to have benefitted firms during the crisis. Firms that had access to credit grew at roughly the same rate during the crisis as other firms and managers of these firms did not report that they were affected differently than managers of similar firms without access to credit. Once the crisis was over, however, although firms with access to bank credit before the crisis did not report faster growth, they were more likely to report that their situation was improving. This provides further evidence that the main impact of the crisis was on sales rather than access to credit.

We also examine whether export-oriented firm were more or less affected by the crisis. Given the collapse in trade, it seems plausible that these firms might have been more vulnerable than other firms. Our econometric results do not generally support this idea. At the beginning of the crisis, export-oriented firms appear to have been affected to similar degrees as other firms. Managers of export-oriented firms did, however, report faster growth between March 2009 and March 2010 suggesting that they might have recovered more quickly than other firms.

The rest of the article is organized as follows. Section II discusses impact of the crisis in Eastern Europe. In section III, we describe the data. Section IV presents econometric models and discusses the results of the same. Section V concludes.

II. The Impact of the Crisis in Eastern Europe

Although the crisis is often seen primarily as a financial crisis, financial integration was not the only way that the crisis spread between countries. An additional important way that the financial crisis was propagated was through trade. As noted above, trade collapsed more significantly than GDP during the crisis (Amiti & Weinstein, 2011). [14]

The decline in trade was not limited to a few sectors or countries. Freund (2009) notes that "declines [in trade] have been widespread across countries and products, largely reflecting the sharp drop in global demand." Others, however, suggest that the collapse in trade was more important in some export sectors than others. Lane and Milesi-Ferretti (2010), in particular, note that the collapse in trade was specifically related to reduced demand for durable and investment goods, which was made worse by difficulties associated with access to credit. Consistent with this, Berkmen and others (2009) find that developing countries that export hi-tech manufacturing products were hit harder in terms of growth forecasts than similar countries exporting food.

[14] Consistent with this, Freund (2009) notes that trade volumes have become more sensitive to fluctuation in world GDP since the 1960s, especially during global downturns. Levchenko and others (2010) find the trading activities in the United States were reduced more than in earlier crises. Bems and others (2010) find that the trade collapse to the extent of 70 percent resulted from demand forces alone in the United States and the European Union. Using data on French firms, Bricongne (2012) demonstrate that the demand shock can be blamed on the collapse in trade.

International trade, however, was not the only way that the crisis spread throughout the world. As financial markets have become increasingly globalized, the risk that financial crises in one country or region could cause crises in other regions has grown. In the 2008-09 crisis, although the crisis started in the sub-prime market in the United States, it quickly spread into other markets in the United States and across the globe. [15] Although there are a number of ways that this can occur, cross-border banking can contribute to the propagation of financial shocks (Popov & Udell, 2012). Consistent with this, De Hass and Van Neeltje (2012) showed that cross-border lending by foreign banks fell by 58 percent after Lehman Brothers collapsed in Sept. 2008.

Several studies have found results consistent with the idea that the globalization of financial services affected the transmission of shocks. For example, De Haas and van Lelyveld (2011) find that subsidiaries of multinational banks reduced lending almost two times faster than that of domestic banks. They find that the slowdown was especially pronounced in large multinational banks that were dependent on wholesale funding. They concluded that the subsidiaries of large multinational banks act as a gateway to foreign financial shocks.

Even if foreign subsidiaries were affected more than domestic banks, this does not mean that purely domestic banks are unaffected by global financial crises. Cetorelli and Goldberg (2010) show that both domestic and foreign banks lent less after the start of the crisis. They noted that domestic banks reduced lending in part because cross-border lending between banks fell after the start of the crisis resulting in a shock to the domestic banks' balance sheets.

It is also important to note that how foreign banks responded to the crisis appears to depend on bank and country characteristics. De Haas and van Lelyveld (2010) conclude that foreign subsidiary banks that have a strong financial support of their parent banks are able to extend credit fast. Kamil and Rai (2010) find that Latin America and the Caribbean were not affected as much as other regions during the crisis because foreign banks lend money through local subsidiaries, which are financed with domestic deposits. Furthermore, De Haas and others (2012) found that banks that were members of Vienna Initiative and state-owned domestic banks were relatively stable lenders during the financial turmoil. Finally, De Haas and Van Horen (2011) show that the largest banks were more likely to continue providing financial support in countries that they were geographically closer to, where they had a relationship with domestic banks, and where they were regular borrowers. They also concluded that international banks were more stable sources of credit when they had a presence on the ground.

The globalization of financial markets might be especially important for the six emerging markets in Eastern Europe that we look at this study due to the high level of cross-border banking activity in these countries. [16] De Hass and Van Neeltje (2012) argue that firms in emerging markets in Eastern Europe are particularly at risk from the collapse in cross-border lending. They note (p.235) that their "results do not bode well for firms, such as in many

[15] Longstaff (2010) claims that the subprime crisis in the U.S. spilt over into other markets and was instrumental in the near collapse of global financial system. Altunbas *et al.,* (2012) claim relaxed regulations and innovation in financial markets resulted in the banking industry grown larger, developing a global presence, and is so doing, this increased interconnectivity.

[16] Berger and others (2000) show that after deregulating cross-border economic activity, there was substantial cross-border mergers and acquisition across most types of financial institutions in Europe. The impact of the crisis was more severe on emerging economies than on developed ones (Llaudes and others, 2010).

countries in emerging Europe, that depend on cross-border lending from Western European banking groups." European Bank of Reconstruction and Development (2012) makes a similar point, noting that cross-border banking activities, along with the large number of non-performing loans, meant that credit growth in the EU region was hit hard during the financial crisis. Berkmen and others (2009) argue that the effect on the financial sector was more important in terms of its immediate impact on growth expectations in emerging markets, in which they include all six countries covered in this study, than the effect of trade. [17]

Table 3. Sample distribution

Sector	
Manufacturing	
Textiles	7%
Garments	6%
Food and Beverage	10%
Chemicals	4%
Construction Materials	4%
Furniture	4%
Metal	6%
Paper and Publishing	2%
Plastics	3%
Machinery and Equipment	3%
Electronics	2%
Automobiles and parts	1%
Other manufacturing	1%
Services	
Retail and wholesale trade	32%
Hotels and Restaurants	3%
Other services	1%
Construction	6%
Transportation	5%

Table 4. Average firm-level sales growth, by country

	Jan 05-Dec 07	June 08-June 09	June 09-June 10
Average	**13.8**	**-24.2**	**-12.8**
Bulgaria	8.1	-21.2	-22.6
Hungary	4.0	-15.2	-11.5
Latvia	10.3	-41.1	-17.3
Lithuania	25.2	-40.8	-14.9
Romania	13.5	-25.4	-25.5
Turkey	15.6	-24.0	-5.3

Source: Authors' calculations based upon data from survey.

Note: Growth rates for the second FCS are excluded because the period overlaps with the first and third FCS. Country averages are weighted averages for survey firms.

[17] Berglöf and others (2009)show that when the crisis hit these countries during Oct 2008 to Mar. 2009, bank lending, foreign direct investment, and export volumes turned negative.

III. DATA

This paper uses firm-level data from four surveys conducted by the World Bank. [18] The initial survey, the 2008/09 Business Environment and Enterprise Performance Survey (BEEPS), was conducted in 27 countries in Eastern Europe and Central Asia in late 2008 or early 2009. It covered firms with more than 5 employees in the following industries (according to ISIC, revision 3.1): all manufacturing sectors (group D), construction (group F), retail and wholesale services (sub-groups 52 and 51 of group G), hotels and restaurants (group H), transport, storage, and communications (group I), and computer and related activities (sub-group 72 of group K). The surveys were delivered to the managing director or his or her direct representative. [19] Fully state- owned firms were excluded from the sample. [20] Table 3 shows the distribution of firms by sector. Relatively few firms are in those sectors (e.g., machinery and equipment and electronics) that were most affected by the collapse of world trade (see previous section).

The World Bank conducted follow-up surveys, the Financial Crisis Surveys (FCS), in six countries in the region: Bulgaria, Hungary, Latvia, Lithuania, Romania and Turkey. Three rounds of the financial crisis surveys were conducted in May/June 2009, February/March 2010 and May/June 2010. Firms that were part of the 2008-9 BEEPS were re-interviewed to see how they were affected by the financial crisis. Because firms were interviewed in BEEPS at the beginning of the crises (i.e., late 2008/early 2009) and then again in 2009 and 2010 in the FCS, we are able to follow the same firms through the global financial crisis. We focus on the six countries from the BEEPS survey where the follow-up FCS were conducted. Since FCS were not conducted in the other 21 countries, we are unable to include these countries in the analysis.

Table 5. Simple correlation between firm-level sales growth before and during the financial crisis

	Jun 09-Jun 10	Jun 08-Jun 09	Jan 05-Dec 07
Jun 09-Jun 10	1.00		
Jun 08-Jun 09	0.17***	1.00	
	(0.00)		
Jan 05-Dec 07	0.04	0.02	1.00
	(0.25)	(0.50)	

Source: Authors' calculations based upon data from survey.

***,**,* Statistically significant at 1,5, and 10 percent significance levels.

Note: Growth rates for the second survey are excluded because the period overlaps with the first and third FCS.

[18] This data is available at www.enterprisesurveys.org

[19] World Bank (2009) describes sampling methodology. In one country, Turkey, the financial crisis survey only resurveyed manufacturing firms (Ramalho and others, 2010).

[20] Moreover, less than 0.5 percent of the firms are majority state-owned in the surveys used in this paper.

Growth Rates over time

Table 4 shows average sales growth for firms in the three years before the crisis, the first year of the crisis (June 2008-June 2009) and the second year of the crisis (June 2009-June 2010). [21] Sales growth collapsed between June 2008 and June 2009. In the three years before the crisis, average sales growth in the six countries was between 4.0 percent in Hungary and 25 percent in Lithuania. [22] Sales growth collapsed most dramatically in Latvia and Lithuania, with the average firms reporting that sales fell by over 40 percent between June 2008 and June 2009. Although sales fell less in the other four countries, there was a large contraction in these countries as well. During the first year of the crisis, average sales growth in the other four countries was between -15 percent in Hungary and -25 percent in Romania.

Sales growth bounced back in most countries between June 2009 and June 2010. Although average sales growth remained negative over this period, sales grew faster between June 2009 and June 2010 than between June 2008 and June 2009 in four of the six countries (Hungary, Latvia, Lithuania, and Turkey). In the remaining two countries, Bulgaria and Romania, average sales growth was very close to the growth observed between June 2008 and June 2009.

Sales growth rates between June 2008 and 2009 and June 2009 and 2010 are positively and significantly correlated (see Table 5). That is, firms that grew slower between June 2008 and June 2009 also tended to grow slower between June 2009 and June 2010. Although statistically significant, the correlation is however fairly small (0.17). In contrast, pre-crisis growth rates are not highly correlated with post-crisis growth rates. Firms that were growing quickly before the crisis (i.e., between 2005 and 2007) did not appear to suffer smaller drops in sales than other firms after June 2008. Although the correlations between pre- and post-crisis sales growth are positive, they are very small (0.02 and 0.04) and are not statistically significant at conventional significance levels.

In the first round of the FCS, managers were asked about their expectations for growth between June 2009 and June 2010 (see Table 6). Managers were more optimistic about prospects for growth between June 2009 and June 2010 than their experience had been between June 2008 and June 2009. In three countries (Bulgaria, Romania and Turkey), the average manager expected their firms to grow after June 2009 rather than continuing to shrink. In the other three countries, managers expected sales to continue to contract, although at slower rate than in the earlier period.

In all six countries, managers were overly optimistic. Actual growth rates between June 2009 and June 2010 were slower than mangers had expected them to be in June 2009 in all six countries (see Table 6). Expectations and outcome were, however, generally positively correlated at the firm-level. That is, although growth was slower than expected over this period, managers that expected faster growth than other mangers did, on average, experienced

[21] We omit growth rates from the second FCS because the period overlaps with the periods from the first and third crisis.

[22] The averages are weighted averages at the country level. We do not use weights for the cross-country averages because it is not clear that the weights are comparable across countries. Different countries use different survey agencies and use different source of information for setting up their sample universes making pooling weights across countries difficult. Ayyagari and others (2011) discuss using sample weights in the Enterprise Surveys in more depth.

faster growth. Expectations were correlated with the firm's growth experience between June 2008 and June 2009 (0.18) but not with the firm's experience before the crisis (0.00).

Table 6. Expected and actual firm-level sales growth between June 2009 and June 2010

	Actual	Expected (in June 2009)	Firm level correlations
Bulgaria	-22.6	8.7	0.20*
Hungary	-11.5	-8.8	0.30***
Latvia	-17.3	-10.5	0.07
Lithuania	-14.9	-7.7	0.1
Romania	-25.5	0.4	0.16*
Turkey	-5.3	10.9	-0.03

Source: Authors' calculations based upon data from survey.

***,**,* Statistically significant at 1,5, and 10 percent significance levels.

Note: Expected growth rates are the manager's expectations about growth between June 2009 and June 2010 in June 2009. Correlations are firm-level correlations between expectation and actual experience.

Table 7. GDP Growth in the sample countries

	2006	2007	2008	2009	2010	2011	2012
Bulgaria	6.5	6.4	6.2	-5.5	0.4	1.8	0.8
Latvia	11.2	9.6	-3.3	-17.7	-0.9	5.5	5.6
Lithuania	7.8	9.8	2.9	-14.8	1.5	5.9	3.6
Hungary	3.9	0.1	0.9	-6.8	1.3	1.6	-1.7
Romania	7.9	6.3	7.3	-6.6	-1.1	2.2	0.3
Turkey	6.9	4.7	0.7	-4.8	9.0	8.5	3.0

Source: Eurostat.

IV. Econometric Analysis

This section presents results from the empirical analysis. We look at things that appear to affect how firms in the region were affected by the crisis while controlling for other things that might affect the depth of the crisis.

Econometric Models

The first question that we look at is whether firms reported lower sales than in the same month one year earlier. The first FCS was conducted in May/June 2009 and so compares June 2009, after the crisis had started, with June 2008, before the crisis. The second FCS was conducted in February/March 2010 and so compares this month with February 2009/March 2009. The final survey compares May/June 2010 with May/June 2009. Since GDP growth was slowest in all countries in 2009 (see Table 7), the first survey is close to the peak of the crisis, while the third survey is towards the end of the worst of the crisis in the region. The model that we estimate

$$Sales\ Growth_i = \alpha + \beta\ Firm\ Characteristics_i + \gamma\ country\ dummies + \varepsilon_i$$

The regression includes several variables representing characteristics of the firm. Given the focus on the collapse in trade and problems in the banking sector, the main variables of interest are variables representing firm's exposure to international markets and their use of credit. Exposure of trade is measured by percent of firm sales that are exported. Exports are measured in 2007, before the crisis started, to reduce the likelihood of reverse causation. Access to credit is measured with a variable indicating whether the firm had a loan or overdraft facility. Unlike the export variable, information on borrowing was not available for 2007. Instead, this variable is measured at the time of the BEEPS survey. Although conducted before the first round of the FCS survey (mid-2009), the BEEPS surveys were mostly conducted between September and December of 2008. As a result, they are measured at the very beginning of the crisis rather than in the year before the crisis. To the extent that banks either extended loans or overdrafts very early in the crisis to firms that they thought had long-term potential if they could survive temporary liquidity problems or ended lines of credit or loans for firms that they believed were the most likely to fail during the crisis, this could affect our estimates for this variable.

The regressions include several other controls. It is important to control for these because they might be related to both firm growth and both exposure to international markets and access to credit. The most important variable is a variable representing firm size before the crisis. The measure that we use is the natural log of the number of full-time workers that the firm had at the end of 2007. It is good that this measure of firm size predates the crises—concern about reverse causation mean that we would like to measure firm size before the crisis affected employment. The regression also includes a variable representing the firm's age. Finally, the regressions include an additional variable indicating that the firm was privatized (as opposed to being established as a private enterprise). Since the sample excludes fully state-owned enterprises, this variable represents whether the firm was established as a private enterprise or as a state-owned enterprise that was later privatized. [23]

The regressions include an additional variable that was measured at the time of the BEEPS survey—the percent of the firm that is foreign owned. As with access to credit, this means that this variable was measured at the beginning of the crisis rather than in the year before the crisis, and although, we would like to have earlier data from 2007, this is not available. In practice, this is probably not as great a concern for this variable as for our measure of access to credit. It is unlikely that there were significant ownership changes at the very beginning of the crisis.

As discussed above, macroeconomic conditions differed between the countries (see Table 7). Lithuania and Latvia in particular suffered from more severe contractions in 2009 than the other countries. Rather than trying to control for all aspects of the macro economy, we instead include a set of country dummies. This will more completely control for macroeconomic differences than including a few country level variables. Since we omit the dummy indicating

[23] As noted in footnote 8, there are very few majority state-owned firms in the 2008/09 BEEPS samples for these countries.

that the firm is in Latvia, the coefficients on the country dummies can be interpreted as the average difference in growth between each country and Latvia.

The second question that we look at is whether firms report that things have improved since the previous survey. So, for example, in June 2010, firms were asked whether the firm's overall situation had improved since the previous survey three months earlier. They were asked whether things had improved, remained the same or worsened. This is a useful robustness check for the previous results because it is broader than the previous questions. Even though sales might be recovering, it is possible that other things (e.g., debt levels or access to credit) remain bad. The model that we estimate regresses firm responses on firm characteristics to see whether there are systematic differences by firm type and the set of country dummies to control for macroeconomic differences between countries that might affect firm outcomes. As noted above, firm characteristics are characteristics of the firm from the original BEEPS survey and most are reported values for 2007 (i.e., before the start of the crisis). This reduces the likelihood of reverse causation.

$$Situation_i = \alpha + \beta\ Firm\ Characteristics_i + \gamma\ country\ dummies + \varepsilon_i$$

The dependent variable takes three possible values (1 to 3) corresponding to "improved", "remained the same", and "worsened". Because the dependent variable is ordered (i.e., improved is better than 'remained the same'; and 'remained the same' is better than 'worsened') and categorical, the model is estimated as an ordered Probit model.

The question in June 2009 was slightly different than the question in later surveys. Firms were only asked whether they had been affected by the crisis (a 'yes'/'no' answer). For the purpose of the analysis, we assume that most firms that were affected by the crisis were negatively affected by it (i.e., that all responses are either 'remained the same' or 'worsened'. Although it is possible that some firms might be have benefitted from the crisis, this does not appear to be a likely scenario .

First, sales dropped for most firms in the sample during the early part of the crisis. Second, when managers were asked how they were affected, over 90 percent responded with one of the given negative options (increased debt, increased costs, reduced access to credit, and drop in demand). Moreover, nearly all of the remaining managers gave an open response that suggests that the crisis had a negative effect on their firm (i.e., increased taxes, decreased profits, or increased debtors). [24]

A positive coefficient on a variable indicates that an increase in that variable will increase the likelihood that the manager will say that things have become worse since the previous survey. A negative coefficient indicates the reverse—that an increase in that variable means that the manager is more likely to say that things are better. So, for example, a negative coefficient on firm size would indicate that managers of large firms are less likely to say that things have become worse since the previous survey than managers of small firms.

24 Of the 96 'other' responses, 60 responses were coded in English. Only one of these 60 responses explicitly indicated that things had improved. A few additional managers reported things that could be negative or positive (competition, prices, government intervention, state policies, and exchange rates). The rest reported things that appear negative such as decreased profits or turnover, increased number of debtors, increased taxes, and government indecision.

Regression Results

Exporters

The coefficients on percent of sales that is exported are mostly statistically insignificant (see Table 8). In particular, they did not report faster growth between June 2008 and June 2009 than other firms. They also did not report fast growth between June 2009 and June 2010. Finally, managers of exporters were no more or less likely to report that they were unaffected by the crisis or that their situation improved between March 2010 and June 2010 (see Table 9).

Table 8. Firm-level sales growth during financial crisis

Dependent Variable	Sales Growth		
Period	(Jun 08-Jun 09)	(Mar 09-Mar 10)	(Jun 09-Jun10)
Observations	1,416	1,403	1,172
Sector Dummies	Yes	Yes	yes
Firm Characteristics			
Number of workers (2007)	2.304***	3.642***	2.636***
[natural log]	(4.19)	(5.88)	(3.78)
Age (2008)	0.577	1.723	1.645
[natural log]	(0.45)	(1.15)	(1.01)
Firm has bank credit (2008)	0.794	0.725	2.019
[dummy]	(0.47)	(0.36)	(1.04)
Percent foreign owned (2008)	0.012	0.089**	0.074**
[percent]	(0.42)	(2.19)	(2.36)
Firm was privatized	1.378	-6.315*	2.396
[dummy]	(0.60)	(-1.82)	(0.82)
Exports as percent of sales (2007)	-0.035	0.080**	0.029
[percent]	(-1.21)	(2.11)	(0.71)
Country Dummies[a]			
Turkey	14.395***	18.113***	13.744***
[dummy]	(5.12)	(5.43)	(3.89)
Romania	7.753***	6.551**	-6.766**
[dummy]	(3.10)	(2.09)	(-2.24)
Hungary	18.148***	15.175***	2.464
[dummy]	(7.65)	(4.84)	(0.83)
Lithuania	0.219	5.382	0.412
[dummy]	(0.08)	(1.38)	(0.12)
Bulgaria	13.596***	4.831	-3.355
[dummy]	(4.62)	(1.11)	(-1.00)
Constant	-49.868***	-47.912***	-23.707**
	(-7.04)	(-4.58)	(-2.33)
R-Squared	0.136	0.133	0.122

Source: Authors' calculations based upon data from survey.

Note: t-statistics are in parentheses. ***,**,* Statistically significant at 1,5, and 10 percent significance levels. All regression include sector dummies.

[a] The omitted country in Latvia.

Table 9. Impact of firm characteristics on manager's perceptions about the crisis

Dependent Variable	Has establishment's situation changed?		
Period	Start of Crisis-June 2009	Sept 2009-Mar 2010	Mar 2010-June 2010
Observations	1,228	1,460	1,220
Firm Characteristics			
Number of workers (2007)	-0.012	-0.135***	-0.085***
[natural log]	(-0.34)	(-5.86)	(-3.40)
Age (2008)	0.080	0.087*	0.014
[natural log]	(1.03)	(1.73)	(0.25)
Firm has bank credit (2008)	0.205*	-0.087	-0.190***
[dummy]	(1.84)	(-1.21)	(-2.62)
Percent foreign owned (2008)	-0.001	-0.002**	-0.001
[percent]	(-0.33)	(-1.99)	(-0.64)
Firm was privatized	0.010	0.205*	0.172
[dummy]	(0.05)	(1.91)	(1.48)
Exports as percent of sales (2007)	-0.001	-0.005***	-0.002
[percent]	(-0.78)	(-3.84)	(-1.32)
Country Dummies			
Turkey	-0.340*	-0.765***	0.010
[dummy]	(-1.87)	(-6.80)	(0.08)
Romania	-0.607***	-0.092	0.699***
[dummy]	(-3.68)	(-0.81)	(6.08)
Hungary		-0.046	0.644***
[dummy]		(-0.43)	(6.19)
Lithuania	0.107	0.160	0.421***
[dummy]	(0.52)	(1.32)	(3.48)
Bulgaria	-0.428**	0.030	0.426***
[dummy]	(-2.18)	(0.25)	(3.44)
Pseudo R-Squared	0.0627	0.101	0.0640

Source: Authors' calculations based upon data from survey.

Note: t-statistics are in parentheses. ***, **,* Statistically significant at 1, 5, and 10 percent significance levels. All regressions include sector dummies. Since the dependent variable is ordered, an ordered Probit model is estimated

[a] The omitted country in Latvia.

They did however report faster growth between March 2009 and March 2010 and were more likely to report that their situation improved between September 2009 and March 2010 than other managers. This improvement does not, however, appear to be sustained. In particular, they did not experience faster growth between June 2009 and June 2010 and were no more likely to report that their situation improved between March 2010 and June 2010.

Overall, these results do not provide strong support for the idea that the collapse in trade during the crisis was particularly problematic for firms. Firms that were exporting before the crisis do not appear to have been particularly negatively impacted by the crisis.

Table 10. Firm-level sales growth during financial crisis including pre-crisis sales

Dependent Variable	Sales Growth		
Period	(Jun 08-Jun 09)	(Mar 09-Mar 10)	(Jun 09-Jun10)
Observations	931	908	783
Sector Dummies	Yes	Yes	Yes
Firm Characteristics			
Sales growth between 2005 and 2007	0.051*	0.052	0.049
[percent]	(1.88)	(1.64)	(1.40)
Number of workers (2007)	2.667***	3.336***	2.553***
[natural log]	(4.13)	(4.08)	(2.86)
Age (2008)	4.451**	3.750*	-0.034
[natural log]	(2.38)	(1.66)	(-0.02)
Firm has bank credit (2008)	-1.914	1.839	2.295
[dummy]	(-0.94)	(0.72)	(0.98)
Percent foreign owned (2008)	0.025	0.129**	0.091**
[percent]	(0.75)	(2.29)	(2.52)
Firm was privatized	0.655	-9.027**	2.112
[dummy]	(0.23)	(-1.98)	(0.61)
Exports as percent of sales (2007)	-0.038	0.104**	0.003
[percent]	(-1.06)	(1.97)	(0.07)
Country Dummies [a]			
Turkey	11.695***	14.031***	13.528***
[dummy]	(3.40)	(3.53)	(3.33)
Romania	10.468***	8.925**	-9.470***
[dummy]	(3.41)	(2.32)	(-2.59)
Hungary	20.277***	16.374***	2.483
[dummy]	(7.62)	(4.48)	(0.73)
Lithuania	3.758	5.939	1.394
[dummy]	(1.26)	(1.21)	(0.36)
Bulgaria	15.186***	7.128	-2.553
[dummy]	(4.67)	(1.26)	(-0.62)
Constant	-55.931***	-19.235*	-19.992*
	(-4.43)	(-1.81)	(-1.71)
R-Squared	0.158	0.138	0.136

Source: Authors' calculations based upon data from survey.

Note: t-statistics are in parentheses. ***, **,* Statistically significant at 1, 5, and 10 percent significance levels. All regression include sector dummies

[a] The omitted country in Latvia.

Bank Credit

The coefficient on the variable indicating that firms had bank credit is statistically insignificant in all three growth regressions (see Table 8). This indicates that firms with bank credit do not appear to have grown faster than other firms in any of the periods studied.

Previous studies have found that having access to credit was associated with greater likelihood of survival during the crisis (Clarke and others, 2012). Given that these firms did not appear to fare better during the crisis, this suggests that although having access to credit helped firms cope with the drop in demand, firms with access did not face smaller drops in demand than other firms.

Interestingly, managers of the firms with bank credit were more likely to say that they were affected by the crisis by June 2009 than other firms. This provides further evidence that firms with access to credit did not fare better in the early part of the crisis than other firms. There is, however, some evidence that even after controlling for other factors, firms that had access to credit before the crisis managed to recover more quickly after the crisis. The coefficient on having access to credit is statistically significant and negative in the regression for whether the firm's situation improved between March and June 2010.

Firm Size

Consistent with previous studies (Correa and others, 2010; Ramalho and others, 2010), large firms appear to have been less affected by the financial crisis between June 2008 and 2009 (see Table 8). The coefficient on the natural log of the number of workers is positive and statistically significant in the regression using the data from the first round of the FCS. The coefficient suggests that sales at a firm with about 30 workers (the weighted 75th percentile) grew about 3.2 percentage points faster than sales at a firm with 7.5 workers (the weighted 25th percentile).

The results in this paper show that large firms also appear to have recovered more quickly after the crisis (see Table 8). The coefficients on firm size are statistically significant and positive in the regressions using the second and third rounds of the FCS. The coefficients indicate that sales at firms with 30 workers grew about 5.0 percentage points faster between March 2009 and March 2010 and about 3.6 percentage points faster between June 2009 and June 2010 than at firms with 7.5 workers. Overall, these results suggest that large firms did better during the crisis and recovered faster after the crisis.

The results from second set of regressions are basically consistent with the growth regressions (see Table 9). Larger firms were more likely to say their establishment's situation had improved between September 2009 and March 2010 and between March 2010 and June 2010. The coefficient in the final regression is negative but statistically insignificant. It is possible that since about 90 percent of firms said that they were affected by the crisis by June 2009, that there are too few firms that did not respond that they were to find significant results.

Foreign Ownership

Foreign-owned firms appear to have been affected similarly to other firms at the beginning of the crisis. The coefficient on foreign ownership is statistically insignificant in the regressions for both sales growth between June 2008 and June 2009 and in the regression for whether the firm had been affected by the crisis by June 2010.

There is, however, some evidence that foreign-owned firms situations improved faster than other firms in 2010. Fully foreign owned reported that sales growth was about 8.9 percentage points faster than fully domestic firms between March 2009 and March 2010 and that it was about 7.4 percentage points faster between Jun 2009 and June 2010. Managers of these firms were also more likely to say that their situation improved between September

2009 and March 2010 and between March 2010 and June 2010 than managers of fully domestic firms.

Country Dummies

The omitted country dummy is for Latvia – the country that experiences the slowest growth (see Table 7) in 2009. The coefficient can, therefore, be interpreted as the difference between that country and Latvia. The coefficients suggest that firms in Latvia and Lithuania were more affected by the crisis in the first half of 2009 than firms in other countries. The coefficients on the other country dummies are statistically significant and positive in the regressions for growth between June 2008 and June 2009. This is consistent with the macroeconomic growth data that suggests that Latvia and Lithuania suffered the largest drops in output over this period.

By June 2010, these differences have dissipated. Although firms in Turkey reported faster growth over this period than firms in other countries and firms in Romania reported slower growth, the other coefficients are statistically insignificant at conventional significance levels. This is also consistent with the macroeconomic data. Although Turkey recovered quickly after the crisis—with growth reaching 9.0 percent in 2010—the other countries continued to have slow growth. Similarly, growth in Romania remained slower than in the other countries (-1.1 percent in 2010).

Growth before the Crisis

As a robustness check, we include pre-crisis sales growth between 2005 and 2007 in the base regression (see Table 10). Because this variable substantially reduces sample size, we omit it from the base regressions. Pre-crisis sales growth is positively, but weakly, correlated with post-crisis sales growth. The coefficient is statistically significant in the regression for growth between June 2008 and 2009 at only a 10 percent significance level and is marginally insignificant at conventional significance levels in the other two regressions. Moreover the coefficients are small. Firms that grew one percentage point faster in the pre-crisis period, grew only 0.05 percentage points faster in the later periods.

For the most part, including this variable does not affect the earlier results. The main exception is that the coefficient on firm age becomes statistically significant and positive in two of the three regressions suggesting that older firms grew faster after the crisis. This could be because older firms tend to grow slower than young firms in most countries. [25] When previous growth is included in the regression, this might correct for this omission.

CONCLUSION

In this study, we investigate how the impact of the crisis varied for different types of firms. Although the primary focus is on whether the firm had access to credit before the crisis and whether the firm exported, we also look at firm size, ownership and age.

Because of the integrated financial systems around the globe, the crisis resulted in a near global financial meltdown. Whether firms had access to finance their activities was therefore

[25] Haltiwanger and others (2008, 2010) find young firms tend to grow faster than older firms in the United States. Growth also appears is faster for small and young firms in developing countries (Dinh and others, 2012).

a vexing question during the crisis. Our regression results show that firms with bank credit did not shrink less than other firms during the crisis or recover more quickly in the immediate aftermath of the crisis. Given that manager said that their biggest problem was a decrease in demand, this suggests that having access to credit did not save firms from economic woes.

The econometric results also indicate that large firms appear to be less affected by the crisis. They appear to have suffered less during the early part of the crisis and recovered more quickly in the aftermath of the crisis. This suggets that large firms find it easier to weather severe economic downturns. At the onset of the crisis, foreign-owned firms appeared to have been impacted in a magnitude similar to that of the other domestic firms. There is some evidence that foreign-owned firms' performance improved faster than that of the other firms in 2010.

Finally, we perform a robustness check by incorporating pre-crisis sales growth between 2005 and 2007 in the base regression. The correlation of sales growth between pre- and post-crisis is positive, but weak. Thus, firms that were growing quincly before the crisis did not grow faster during the crisis or in the immediate recovery from the crisis.

The work presented in this paper can be expanded in various directions. One interesting question is whether the results would hold in other regions. Although Eastern Europe suffered from a particular severe economic contraction, exports fell by less than in other regions. Looking at the impact of the crisis in other developing regions such as East Asia, where growth remained strong even as exports collapsed, or Latin America would be an interesting extension.

REFERENCES

Amiti, M., & Weinstein, D. E. (2011). Exports and financial shocks. *The Quarterly Journal of Economics, 126*, 1841-1877.

Ayyagari, M., Demirguc-Kunt, A., & Maksimovic, V. (2011). *Small vs. Young firms across the world: Contribution to employment, job creation and growth.* Policy Research Working Paper No. 5631.Washington DC: World Bank.

Bems, R., Johnson, R. C., & Yi, K.-M. (2010). Demand spillovers and the collapse of trade in the global recession. *IMF Economic Review, 58*, 295-326.

Berger, A. N., DeYoung, R., Genay, H., & Udell, G. F. (2000). Globalization of financial institutions: Evidence from cross-border banking performance. *Brookings-Wharton papers on financial services, 2000*, 23-120.

Berglöf, E., Korniyenko, Y., Plekhanov, A., & Zettelmeyer, J. (2009). *Understanding the crisis in emerging Europe*. Working Paper No. 109.London UK: European Bank for Reconstruction and Development.

Berkmen, P., Gelos, R. G., Rennhack, R., & Walsh, J. (2009). *The global financial crisis: Explaining cross-country differences in the output impact.* IMF Working Papers No. 09/280.Washington DC: International Monetary Fund.

Bricongne, J.-C., Fontagné, L., Gaulier, G., Taglioni, D., & Vicard, V. (2012). Firms and the global crisis: French exports in the turmoil. *Journal of International Economics, 87*, 134-146.

Cetorelli, N., & Goldberg, L. S. (2010). Global banks and international shock transmission: Evidence from the crisis. *IMF Economic Review, 59*, 41-76.

Claessens, S., & Van Horen, N. (2012). *Foreign bank: Trends, impact and financial stability*. No. 12/10.Washington DC: International Monetary Fund.

Clarke, G. R. G., Cull, R., & Kisunko, G. (2012). External finance and firm survival in the aftermath of the crisis: Evidence from Eastern Europe and Central Asia. *Journal of Comparative Economics, 40*, 372-392.

Clarke, G. R. G., Cull, R., Martinez Peria, M. S., & S nchez, S. (2003). Foreign bank entry: Experience, implications for developing countries, and agenda for further research. *World Bank Research Observer, 18*, 25-40.

Correa, P., & Iootty, M. (2010). *The impact of the global economic crisis on the corporate sector in Europe and Central Asia: Evidence from a firm-level survey*. Enterprise Note No. 9.World Bank.

Correa, P., Iootty, M., Ramalho, R., Rodriguez-Meza, J., & Yang, J. (2010). *How firms in Eastern and Central Europe are performing in the post-financial crisis world*. Enterprise Note No. 18.Washington DC: World Bank.

De Haas, R., Korniyenko, Y., Loukoianova, E., & Pivovarsky, A. (2012). Foreign banks and the Vienna initiative: Turning sinners into saints?

De Haas, R., & Van Horen, N. (2011). *Running for the exit: International banks and crisis transmission*: European Bank for Reconstruction and Development.

De Haas, R., & Van Horen, N. (2012). International shock transmission after the Lehman Brothers collapse: Evidence from syndicated lending. *American Economic Review Papers & Proceedings, 102*, 231-237.

De Haas, R., & Van Lelyveld, I. (2010). Internal capital markets and lending by multinational bank subsidiaries. *Journal of Financial Intermediation, 19*, 1-25.

De Haas, R., & Van Lelyveld, I. (2011). *Multinational banks and the global financial crisis: Weathering the perfect storm?* Working Paper No. 135.London UK: European Bank for Reconstruction and Development.

Dinh, H. T., Mauvridis, D. A., & Nguyen, H. B. (2012). The binding constraint on firms' growth in developing countries. In H. T. Dinh & G. R. G. Clarke (Eds.), *Performance of manufacturing firms in africa: An empirical analysis* (Vol. 5485, pp. 87-137). Washington DC: World Bank.

European Bank for Reconstruction and Development. (2012). *Transition report 2012: Integration across borders*. London UK: European Bank for Reconstruction and Development.

Freund, C. (2009). *The trade response to global downturns: Historical evidence*. World Bank Policy Research Working Paper No. 5015.Washington DC: World Bank.

Gorton, G., & Metrick, A. (2012). Getting up to speed on the financial crisis: A one-weekend reader's guide. *Journal of Economic Literature, 50*, 128-150.

Haltiwanger, J., Jarmin, R. S., & Miranda, J. (2008). Business formation and dynamics by business age: Results from the new business demography statistics. College Park, MD: University of Maryland.

Haltiwanger, J., Jarmin, R. S., & Miranda, J. (2010). *Who create's jobs? Small vs. Large vs. Young*. Center for Economic Studies Research Paper No. 10-17.Washington DC: U.S Census Bureau.

Kamil, H., & Rai, K. (2010). *The global credit crunch and foreign banks' lending to emerging markets: Why did Latin America fare better?* : International Monetary Fund.

Lane, P., & Milesi-Ferretti, G. M. (2010). The cross-country incidence of the global crisis. *IMF Economic Review, 59*, 77-110.

Levchenko, A. A., Lewis, L. T., & Tesar, L. L. (2010). The collapse of international trade during the 2008–09 crisis: In search of the smoking gun. *IMF Economic Review, 58*, 214-253.

Llaudes, R., Salman, F., & Chivakul, M. (2010). The impact of the great recession on emerging markets. *IMF Working Papers*, 1-34.

Lo, A. W. (2012). Reading about the financial crisis: A twenty-one book review. *Journal of Economic Literature, 50*, 151-178.

Longstaff, F. A. (2010). The subprime credit crisis and contagion in financial markets. *Journal of Financial Economics, 97*, 436-450.

Mishkin, F. S. (2011). Over the cliff: From the subprime to the global financial crisis. *Journal of Economic Perspectives, 25*, 49-70.

Morgan, D. P., Rime, B., & Strahan, P. E. (2004). Bank integration and state business cycles. *Quarterly Journal of Economics, 119*, 1555-1584.

Popov, A., & Udell, G. F. (2012). Cross-border banking, credit access, and the financial crisis. *Journal of International Economics, 87*, 147-161.

Ramalho, R., Rodriguez-Meza, J., & Yang, J. (2010). *How are firms in Eastern and Central Europe reacting to the financial crisis?* Enterprise Note No. 8.Washington DC: World Bank.

World Bank. (2009). *Enterprise survey and indicator surveys: Sampling methodology.* Washington DC: World Bank.

World Bank. (2012). *World development indicators*. Washington, D.C.: World Bank.

In: Financial Crises
Editor: Cooper A. Hawthorne
ISBN: 978-1-62808-293-7

Chapter 5

A SURVEY OF COUNTRY VERSUS INDUSTRY EFFECTS IN INTERNATIONAL EQUITY RETURNS

Ye Bai*

Bai: Business School, University of Nottingham, UK

ABSTRACT

Numerous studies have sought to determine whether investors should diversify across countries and/or industries to improve their risk-return tradeoffs. The common methodological framework is to identify the country effects and industry effects embedded in cross-sectional variations in international stock returns. In general, empirical findings in the literature suggest that country effects are more important overall especially in emerging stock markets, but that the importance of industry effects has increased in the recent years and may have overtaken the dominant position of country effects in OECD countries especially in euro zone countries. It is still an open question whether geographical importance has permanently diminished on a global basis or that industry importance has increased globally. This survey aims to summarise and evaluate key studies on the relative importance of the country and industry effects in determining the cross-sectional variations in stock returns according to some key issues involved that may have contributed to the inconclusive results and also point to several directions that derived from this topic for future research.

Keywords: portfolio diversification; cross-sectional variation; country effects; industry effects; Heston and Rouwenhorst dummy variable model; emerging stock markets

* Corresponding author: Business School, Jubilee Campus, University of Nottingham, Nottingham, NG8 1BB, United Kingdom, Tel: +44(0) 115 846 8487; fax: +44(0) 115 846 6667, E-mail addresses: ye.bai@nottingham.ac.uk.

1. INTRODUCTION

In the standard mean-variance model of portfolio selection, international diversification increases welfare by improving the risk-return trade-off available to investors in comparison with that trade-off available using only domestic country securities as documented in Levy and Sarnat (1970) and Solnik (1974). Gains from international diversification are generated from the imperfect correlation between national stock market returns (Goetzmann, Li and Rouwenhorst, 2005). Some literature show that despite the increasing trend of globalisation and liberalisation of capital markets recently, there is only weak evidence supporting increasing cross-country co-variance in returns especially for small-cap stocks (Longin and Solnik, 1995; Huang, 2007).

A large volume of research has focused particularly on the effects that have impeded perfect integration among national equity markets. Following Lessard (1974), the common methodological framework is to identify the country effects and industry effects as the main driving forces of international stock return variations. The more important are the country effects the more should investors diversify across countries; similarly for the industry effects. This procedure mimics to some extent the portfolio selection 'top-down' approach of international portfolio managers. Sparked by the conflicting conclusions of the seminal studies by Roll (1992) and Heston and Rouwenhorst (1994), the study of the relative importance of global, country and industry effects blossomed in 1990s. In stead of fading away after the millennium, studies in this area are thriving mainly due to new data becoming available, the progress of economic and financial integration (such as the introduction of euro) and impacts of various financial crises. Although recent findings suggest that industry effects have increased in importance and may even have overtaken country effects in some OECD countries (Cavaglia, Brightman and Aked, 2000; L'Her, Sy and Tnani, 2002; Baele and Inghelbrecht, 2006; Campa and Fernandes, 2006; Philaktis and Xia, 2006; Baele and Inghelbrecht, 2009), the ongoing debate on the relative importance of industry and country effects is far from drawing a definite conclusion.

This survey aims to summarise and evaluate key studies in this rapidly growing field according to some key issues involved that may have contributed to the inconclusive results and need further attention in the future research. First, we briefly summarise the key literature and their key findings so far. Second, early studies suggest that the increasing importance of industry effects is due to the permanent impact of liberalisation or integration measures in these countries. However, more recent work suggests that such increase may be short-lived, either due to long swings in the correlations or to contagion from a financial crisis. If true this would imply that there may still exist substantial unexploited diversification gains in these market equities. Since comovement varies over time in response to different kinds of shock, we summarise and discuss how different kinds of shock and their combinations may lead to the time-varying pattern in the relative importance of country and industry effects. Third, a popular methodological framework for evaluating the relative importance of country versus industry effects is the orthogonal decomposition into country, industry and global effects introduced by Heston and Rouwenhorst (1994). However, this method also has its critics. Alternative methods have been developed in more recent literature in response to these criticisms. Fourth, we discuss different data specifications and their implications to empirical findings. Finally, this paper also points to some directions that derived from this topic for future research.

Section 2 presents an overview of studies on the country and industry effects debate. Section 3 discusses the dynamic pattern in the relative importance of industry and country effects in response to different kinds of shock. Then it is followed by a review of the basic methodological framework and the alternatives. Section 5 covers data specification issues, and then followed by a brief discussion of future research directions. Finally section 7 concludes.

2. A Brief History of the Debate of Industry *vs.* Country Effects

Since four decades ago, following early work by Lessard (1974) and Solnik (1974) a large number of studies have focused particularly on the relative importance of country and industry effects in driving the cross-sectional variation in national equity returns. The debate comes into full force with conflicting conclusions drawn by Roll (1992) and Heston and Rouwenhorst (1994). Roll (1992) decomposes daily dollar-denominated national index return data for 24 countries and seven industries into weighted average of global industry index returns plus a country-specific disturbance. Roll by using a cross-country Fama/MacBeth-type (Fama and MacBeth, 1973) regression, from 1988 to 1991 finds that the low correlation of returns between countries arises from diversity of industrial structure across countries, mirrored by national stock market indices that have a different industrial composition. On the other hand, Heston and Rouwenhorst (1994) (Hence force: H-R) among others[26] by decomposing returns of 829 European stocks into seven industry components and 12 country components from 1978 to 1992 show that only a small amount of the cross-country variation in stock returns can be attributed to the industrial composition of the national indices (so called industry effects). Country effects seem to be the dominant force in international stock returns according to their results. H-R propose that local monetary and fiscal policies, domestic economic shocks and differences in institutional and legal regimes lead to the relatively large country-specific variation in stock returns. H-R argue that their conclusions differ from Roll (1992) because Roll's regressors include the average return across all the sampled markets, whereas they measure industry effects as deviations from the average return across the sampled markets.[27] Beckers, Connor and Curds (1996) apply H-R method to a similar dataset used by Roll (1992) but still fail to find dominant industry effects.

In the last decade there has been an increasing liberalisation of financial markets (Bekaert and Harvey, 2000) and associated globalisation of the world's economies. We would expect that the progress of integration should lead to the increased correlations among international financial markets.

[26] Grinold, Rudd, Stefel, 1989; Heston and Rouwenhorst, 1995; Beckers, Connor and Curds, 1996; Griffin and Karolyi, 1998; Rouwenhorst, 1999.

[27] An alternative explanation is that Roll's dataset covers just too short a period to draw robust conclusions.

Country specific effects should become less important in the pricing of investments and global industry effects should become more important. Studies[28] carried out after the millennium[29] with the extended dataset have generally shown that country effects still play an important role but the importance of industry effects relative to country effects has increased and even overtaken country effects in importance in some OECD countries between late 1990s and early 2000. Grisolia and Navone (2007) obtain a similar result and suggest that the country effects are dominated by regional effects (Asia-Pacific, North America, European Monetary Union (EMU) and non-EMU Europe), suggesting a two-step approach to asset allocation: first diversify across regions, and then across countries or companies within a region. Some even suggest that the persistence of country effects in liberalised countries (for example, OECD) may be attributable partially to a small firm effect (Steliaros and Thomas, 2006; Eun, Hung and Lai, 2008 and Bekaert, Hodrick and Zhang, 2009). So far, the debate on the relative importance of country and industry effects is far from conclusive.

3. The Dynamic Pattern in the Relative Importance of Industry *vs.* Country Effects: In Response to Different Kinds of Shock

Although the consensus of studies in the last decade is that the relative importance of industry effects is growing since mid-1990s even in some emerging markets, a more complicated time-varying pattern has been constantly appearing in various studies employing different samples.

Table 1 presents a comparison between some of these studies. A difficulty in interpreting these findings is that comovement may increase over time in response to different kinds of shock, including: permanent shocks such as increasing international integration, as in the euro-zone (Eiling, Gerard and de Roon, 2012); temporary global shocks, such as the boom in technology stocks at the turn of the century (Brooks and Del Negro, 2004); or temporary local shocks that spread across international markets by a process of contagion, especially during the financial crisis (Fedorova, 2011).

If a local shock spreads to other markets, diversification across these markets is evidently less useful in reducing risk than is diversifying more widely.

As the comparison in Table 1 shows that in general, between around mid-1996 to 1999, there is an increase in the magnitude of industry effects. Then after a small drop between 1999 and 2000, a sharp increase in the magnitude of industry effects is the most noticeable change, which lasts until around 2001. What has not been paid much attention in most of the literature is that after the sharp increase at the turn of the century, industry effects exhibit a downward trend until the end of sample periods of these studies. The latest one is 2007 in Baele and Inghelbrecht (2009).

[28] Given the large number of published and ongoing studies in this area, the author is not trying to exhaust the list of studies here.

[29] Baca, Garbe and Weiss, 2000; Cavaglia, Brightman and Aked, 2000; Serra, 2000;L'Her, Sy and Tnani, 2002; Brooks and Del Negro, 2004; Flavin, 2004; Ferreira and Gama, 2005; Campa and Fernandes, 2006; Chen, Bennett and Zheng, 2006; Phylaktis and Xia, 2006; Ferreira and Ferreira, 2006; Baele and Inghelbrecht, 2009; Bekaert, Hodrick and Zhang, 2009; Ferreira and Gama, 2010; Bai, Green and Leger, 2012;

Table 1. Comparisons of studies showing time-varying pattern of industry effects magnitude

Reference	Method	Sample countries	Increase in industry effects period	Decrease in industry effects period
Brooks and Del Negro (2004)	H-R + MAD	25 IND, 17 ESM	General increase: Early 1997 – end of 1999 Sharp increase: end of 1999 – mid 2000	Mid 2000 - 2002
Ferreira and Gama (2005)	Volatility decomposition	21 IND	General increase 1997 - 1999 Sharp increase: 2000 - mid 2001	Small drop: 1999-2000; late 2001- the end of 2002
Chen, Bennett and Zheng (2006)	H-R + MAD	23 IND, 26 ESM	General increase mid 1997- late 1999 Sharp increase: 2000-2001	Mid 1999 - 2000; the end of 2001 - 2005
Campa and Fernandes (2006)	H-R + MAD	27 IND, 19 ESM	General increase late 1996 – late 1999 Sharp increase: 2000 – early 2001	late 1999 - 2000; 2000 - 2005
Phylaktis and Xia (2006)	H-R + MAD	23 IND, 11 ESM	General increase early 1997 - early 1999 Sharp increase: mid 1999 - mid 2000	late 2000 - the end of 2001
Baele and Inghelbrecht (2009)	Structural regime-switching spillover model	21 IND	Sharp increase: mid 1996 – 2002 (with TMT) Sharp increase: mid 1997 – 2002 (without TMT)	2002 -2007
Bai, Green and Leger (2012)	H-R+*F*-test + MAD	13 ESM	General increase: mid-1997 – 09.2003 Sharp increase: early 1999 – early 2000	07.2003-07.2004

Note: 1. H-R: Heston and Rouwenhorst (1994) model; MAD: Mean Absolute Deviation; IND: Industrial countries; ESM: emerging stock markets; NAFTA: North American Free Trade Agreement

2. Except Ferreira and Gama (2005), Baele and Inghelbrecht (2009) and Bai, Green and Leger (2012), all the other relative importance of industry effects is only based on MAD plots.

3. Ferreira and Gama (2005) measure the global industry volatility as annualized global industry standard deviation. Baele and Inghelbrecht (2009) measure change in industry effects by idiosyncratic volatility aggregated over industry. Bai, Green and Leger (2012) also measure the importance of industry effects by inspecting the significance of the industry dummies over time.

Explanations to the observed dynamic pattern in industry effect relative importance are quite diverse. Some studies argue that the sharply increasing importance from 1998 to 2002 is only limited to the Technology, Media and Telecommunication (TMT) industries attributed to IT bubble and is temporary. It is a reflection of the 'new economy' power being more 'internationalised' than the 'old economy' one (Brooks and Del Negro, 2004; Chen, Bennett and Zheng, 2006; Ciner, 2006; Grisolia and Navone; 2007). Therefore in the post-bubble period, country effects are still the dominant force explaining stock return variations so that it is still more effective to diversify across countries. On the other hand, robustness test in various studies excluding the TMT industries from the sample shows that IT bubble cannot explain the decline, instead that the general upward trend up to the 21st century is a worldwide phenomenon cross different industry sectors beyond TMT industries.[30]

Some incline to explain the upward trend as a reflection of permanent shocks such as worldwide economic and financial integration. As countries become more integrated in regional and world financial markets, country specific effects become smaller at the same time national equity returns are more sensitive to global industry effects. For example, economically and financially harmonised areas such as European Monetary Union (EMU) provide near to a natural experiment as we are likely to find in financial economics. Studies on this issue come to no consensus either. Rouwenhorst (1999) extends H-R data over the post-Maastricht Treaty time period up to August 1998, and finds that despite increased monetary and fiscal policy coordination among EMU member states, country effects still dominate industry effects. Empirical results in Heston and Rouwenhorst (1995) and Griffin and Karolyi (1998) provide support to this conclusion. Flavin (2004) does find an increase in industry effect importance following the introduction of the euro, which is, however, not exclusive to the euro zone. Bekaert, Hodrick and Zhang (2009) find the increasing importance of industry effects is a short-lived phenomenon. However, another group of studies notes that since the adoption of the single currency euro, euro zone countries are more integrated with low correlations because fiscal and monetary policy differences are no longer applicable to these national equity markets (Adjaouté and Danthine, 2005; Bekaert, Harvey and Ng; 2005 and Baele and Inghelbrecht, 2006). With more detailed analyses, some studies suggest that the risk premia differences in the euro equity markets depend on the extent of the integration of the euro markets. Balli and Balli (2011) argue that existing literature has produced different results depending merely on the time interval of the dataset. In the very first years of the euro, the potential gains of sectoral diversification across all sector equity indices are measured as being relatively higher (see Baca *et al.*, 2000, Cavaglia *et al.*, 2000 and Moerman, 2008). Balli and Balli suggest that the potential gains of the industrial diversification within the region depend on different industry reactions to the aggregate euro return fluctuations. For example, the euro regional shock impacts on basic industry sectors diminish considerably after the start of the EMU but are still very significant on the financial sectors.

Some see such upward trend due to a combination of some of these shocks. First, studies suggest that both IT bubble and integration effects enhance each other. Therefore there are two stages of increasing trend observed in the results. The more permanent and fundamental-based increase has been amplified for a short time period over the IT bubble period especially in highly technology-concentrated countries. However, IT bubble effect soon lost its dominance after the burst of the bubble (Chen, Bennett and Zheng, 2006; Phylaktis and Xia, 2006). Second, the alternative explanation combines IT bubble effect with the contagion theory. The least discussed but similarly interesting part of the time-varying pattern is the decreasing trend of industry effects from 2001 onwards. If the general upward trend is indeed due to more permanent and fundamental changes in real economy, then without any noticeable reversion of these liberalising and integration trend, one does not expect that the previous changes will reverse. One cannot help but doubts that integration may not be as widely spread as expected. Stulz (2003) shows that despite the significant decline in those explicit international investment barriers over the last 60 years, the impact of financial

[30] Ferreira and Gama, 2005; Chen, Bennett and Zheng, 2006; Phylaktis and Xia, 2006; Campa and Fernandes, 2006; Baele and Inghelbrecht, 2009.

globalisation has been surprisingly limited. Such upward trend may be explained by temporary local shocks that spread across international markets by a process of contagion, especially during the financial crisis. During 1997 Asian financial crisis, there was an increase in residual correlation among the affected countries. The increase (decrease) in global industry effects (country specific effects) after 1997 due to contagion may have been amplified during the IT bubble period (Bekaert, Harvey and Ng, 2005; Bai *et al.*, 2012). Therefore, when both temporary shocks die down, the general trend driven by more fundamental reasons emerges again after 2001.

It is not yet totally clear that geographical importance has permanently diminished on a global basis or that industry importance has increased globally.

4. THE BASIC METHODOLOGICAL FRAMEWORK AND THE ALTERNATIVES

4.1. H-R Dummy Variable Model: Specification and Testing

Following H-R, the dummy variable (fixed-effect) model has been employed by most studies (e.g. refer to Table 1) in this area as standard practice to separate country and industry effects. The decomposition of returns in any time period is given by:

$$R_i^{\$} = \alpha + \sum_{j=1}^{J} \beta_j D_{i,j} + \sum_{k=1}^{K} \gamma_k C_{i,k} + e_i \tag{1}$$

$R_i^{\$}$ = The return on security i in industry j (j = 1,...,J) and country k (k = 1,...,K), denominated in US dollars

α = A base level of return

β_j = The industry j factor

γ_k = The country k factor

e_i = Idiosyncratic disturbance for firm i, where:

$E(e_i) = 0$, $Var(e_i) = \sigma^2$ and $\text{Cov}(e_i, e_g) = E(e_i\, e_g) = 0, \forall i \neq g$

$D_{i,j}$ and $C_{i,k}$ are industry and country dummy variables where

$$C_{i,k} = \begin{cases} 1 & \text{if security } i \text{ belongs to country } k \\ 0 & \text{otherwise} \end{cases} \qquad D_{i,j} = \begin{cases} 1 & \text{if security } i \text{ belongs to industry } j \\ 0 & \text{otherwise} \end{cases}$$

Eq. (1) states that each return observation is explained as the sum of a constant, an industry component, a country component, and an error term. It is not possible to estimate the equation due to the perfect collinearity in the dummy variables $C_{i,k}$ and $D_{i,j}$ since each firm belongs to one industry and one country. This is solved by measuring industry and country effects relative to the average firm in the sample. Define w_j and v_k as the shares of industry j and country k respectively in total sample capitalisation.

$$\sum_{k=1}^{K} v_k \gamma_k = 0 \text{ and } \sum_{j=1}^{J} w_j \beta_j = 0, \text{ where } \sum_j w_j = \sum_k v_k = 1 \qquad (2)$$

Under these restrictions, the Ordinary Least Squares estimators (OLS) of γ and β are fully identified, and the estimated disturbances are by construction orthogonal to all the industry and country dummies so that the average residual is zero in every country and industry. Applying the constraints (2) to eq. (1) gives

$$R_i^{\$} = \alpha + \sum_{j=1}^{J-1} \beta_j d_{i,j} + \sum_{k=1}^{K-1} \gamma_k c_{i,k} + e_i \qquad (3)$$

where $d_{i,j} = (D_{i,j} - (w_j / w_J) D_{i,J})$ and $c_{i,k} = (C_{i,k} - (v_k / v_K) C_{i,K})$. The application of OLS to eq. (3) is equivalent to Weighted Least Squares (WLS) estimation of eq. (1) with weights $p_{i,k}$ equal to the share of firm i in the total sample market value of country k, and $p_{i,j}$, the share of firm i in industry j, where $\sum_{i \in k} p_{i,k} = 1$, and $\sum_{i \in j} p_{i,j} = 1$.

On top of the basic methodological framework, Bai and Green (2010) and Bai, Green and Leger (2012) also perform F-tests separately on the industry and country dummies in eq. (3) for each month of the returns series. They suggest that comparing the F-statistics gives a precise picture of the significance of the country and industry effects and their variation over time, which provides a foundation for more detailed decomposition of returns. Furthermore, based on the inspection of the F-statistics time series, they are also able to identify the time-varying pattern in the importance of country and industry effects, which provides supplementary information to the decomposition and Mean Absolute Deviation analysis at the following stages.

4.2. Decomposition of Returns

Multiplying eq. (3) by $p_{i,j}$, and summing over all firms in industry j leads to the following decomposition of the value-weighted industry index return in any time period:

$$R_j^{\$} = \hat{\alpha} + \sum_{k=1}^{K-1} p_{j,k} \hat{\gamma}_k c_{i,k} + \hat{\beta}_j \qquad (4)$$

where $p_{j,k}$ is the share of the total market value of industry j included in country k, and $\sum_{j=1}^{J-1} p_{i,j} e_j = 0$. Thus, $R_j^{\$}$ is decomposed into a component common to all industries, $\hat{\alpha}$, a weighted average of k country components, $\sum_{k=1}^{K-1} p_{j,k} \hat{\gamma}_k c_{i,k}$, and an industry-specific component, $\hat{\beta}_j$. Eq. (4) states that the return in industry j (e.g. Utility) may differ from the sample average return for two reasons: i) the geographical distribution of Utility industry is different from that of sample as a whole; ii) the return of Utility stocks may differ from that of stocks in the same country but in a different industry.

Similarly, each value-weighted country index return $R_k^{\$}$ can be decomposed into:

$$R_k^{\$} = \hat{\alpha} + \sum_{j=1}^{J-1} p_{k,j} \hat{\beta}_j d_{i,j} + \hat{\gamma}_k \tag{5}$$

Here $p_{k,j}$ is the share of the total market value of country k included in industry j.

Repetition of the cross-section estimation of Eqs. (4) and (5) over all months yields a time series of a geographically-diversified portfolio of firms in the jth industry, $\hat{\alpha} + \hat{\beta}_j$ (the "pure industry" effect) and a time series of an industrially-diversified portfolio of firms in country k, $\hat{\alpha} + \hat{\gamma}_k$ (the "pure country" effect). Calculating the standard deviation/variance of these effects measures the relative importance of country and industry effects in explaining the cross-sectional return variations.

Furthermore, studies also apply Mean Absolute Deviations (MADs) to measure the magnitudes of the industry and country effects (for example, Rouwenhorst, 1999; Cavaglia, Cho and Singer, 2001; Bai and Green, 2010; Bai *et al.*, 2012).

$$MAD_{jt} = \sum_{j=1}^{11} w_{jt} \mid \beta_{jt} \mid \tag{6a}$$

$$MAD_{kt} = \sum_{k=1}^{13} v_{kt} \mid \gamma_{kt} \mid \tag{6b}$$

These are defined as the absolute values of the estimated pure industry or country effects at time t, multiplied by the corresponding share of industry j or country k in total sample capitalization. A higher $MAD_{j,t}$ ($MAD_{k,t}$) means that pure industry (country) effects have greater magnitudes on average and are more dispersed around the sample average in that month.

4.3. Some Alternative Methods and Criticisms on H-R Model

Although H-R model has been widely adopted by studies in this area as a standard method, it has its critics. Eq. (1) can be interpreted as a factor model in which the factor sensitivities, $C_{i,k}$ and $D_{i,j}$ are set to unity by the 0-1 dummy restriction, implying that all firms in the same country are exposed to same country risk and that all firms in the same industry are exposed to the same industry risk (Brooks and Del Negro, 2004; Phylaktis and Xia, 2006). However De Moor and Sercu (2011) argue that H-R is not modelling a return generating process, but providing an algorithm to combine pre-defined country and industry portfolio returns so that different industry effects in country indices (and vice versa) can be modelled. De Moor and Sercu find that a Fama-MacBeth variant of H-R, which allows non-unit sensitivities, produces almost the same effects as H-R. However, Moerman (2008) argues that a mean-variance approach produces results more favourable to the industry effects. Some criticise that since the relative importance of industry and country effects are based on the variance of these dummy coefficients in each cross section calculated over arbitrarily specified time windows, there is an implicit assumption in the H-R model that the factors driving country and industry effects either remain constant or, at the most, change very gradually (Catao and Timmerman, 2003).

With the criticisms on H-R model on mind, some recent studies in this area start focusing on the application of different methods. Baele and Inghelbrecht (2009) relax the common assumption of unit or constant factor exposures explicitly allowing both country and industry exposures and asset-specific volatilities to vary over time in a structural regime-switching volatility spillover model. Their results largely support the common findings in other studies but they also find that when they allow betas to change over time, the relative importance of country effects over industry effects is substantially lower than those based on H-R model.

Up to a decade ago, most of the existing studies of industry and country effects have concentrated exclusively on decompositions of the stock returns. However, as argued in Bai and Green (2010), since risk reduction is one of the main benefits expected from portfolio diversification, stock return variations should reflect to some extent the outcome of portfolio shifts in response to perceived changes in stock risks. Theory suggests that market risk is the most important factor driving stock returns in a fully integrated world market since individual risk can be diversified away. However, in practice, it is still useful to look directly at the cross-section of individual stock risks. For example, sufficient evidence in the literature suggests that international stock markets are not yet fully integrated, especially emerging stock markets(ESMs) (Bekaert, Harvey, Lundblad and Siegel, 2008). Furthermore, different groups of investors (e.g. Pension funds) are restricted in their portfolio selection due perhaps to asymmetric information, corporate policies and domestic law and regulations (Kalev, Nguyen and Oh, 2008; Silva and Chavez, 2008). Both individual and market risks are unavoidably important to these constrained investors. Finally, empirical results in Bai and Green (2010) suggest that the determinants of stock risks in ESMs follow a generally similar pattern over time to those of ESM stock returns. However, since the decomposed risk in their study is total risk,[31] such correspondence between returns and total risk is less expected. It implies that investors who base their cross-border diversification strategies solely on the return decomposition results may move towards assets with greater total risk which in turn could diminish the expected covariance risk reduction.

Ferreira and Gama (2005) also decompose the total volatility of individual assets into specific sources of risk by extending the Campbell, Lettau, Malkiel, and Xu (2001) volatility decomposition method to an international setting. Ferreira and Gama take the variance of the local industry return in excess of its country of origin return as a measure of local industry risk, which relaxes H-R model assumption of the unit asset exposures across countries to global industry shocks. In general, their results are in line with the common findings of studies using H-R method.

5. DATA

Although studies in this area have adopted relatively standard methodological framework, in terms of data employed, there are a number of discrepancies that may have

[31] Bai and Green estimate monthly conditional total risk for a group of individual stocks, using stock-specific models of the conditional mean return, with (G)ARCH-type errors to model the time-varying risks. Then they apply the standard H-R model to the estimated monthly risk series.

implications to their diverse findings. In this section, we compare different studies on several related data specification issues.

5.1. Emerging Stock Markets

It is well established that ESM equities have different characteristics from equities in developed capital markets – in particular, higher average returns, higher volatility, greater predictability and low correlations with developed market returns (Bekaert and Harvey, 1997). Studies suggest that some investment barriers in ESMs have impeded effective global equity-market integration, such as poor credit ratings; high and variable inflation; controlled exchange rate; absence of a high-quality regulatory system and limited size of some stock markets. Although studies[32] on integration suggest that the correlations may have increased in ESMs over time with the increasing degree of economic integration and financial liberalisation, ESMs are still not as effectively integrated as developed markets (Bekaert, 1995; Bekaert, Harvey, Lundblad and Siegel, 2008). It implies that there are still unexploited portfolio diversification opportunities in ESMs. We would expect to observe investor portfolio holdings gradually shifting away from domestic assets in the major industrial countries and towards ESMs. Theoretically, during this process, risk sharing among international investors should increase, and therefore ESMs become less sensitive to domestic economic shocks and more integrated with the rest of the world. The change may have a significant impact on the relative importance of country and industry effects on ESM returns and therefore on the portfolio diversification strategies. However, most of the studies on this issue focus on OECD countries. Studies[33] in the last decade turned their attentions to ESMs. In general, they suggest that the dominant country effects have remained relatively stable while industry effects have significantly increased in importance at the beginning of the 21st century. Since ESM firms are mostly smaller on average than those in the OECD, it may be argued that any "ESMs effect" in stock returns, particularly the dominant country effects, could in reality be due to the predominance of small firms rather than any intrinsic differences between ESMs and the industrial countries. However, according to De Moor and Sercu (2010), the role of ESMs cannot be reduced to just a small-firm phenomenon. Studies using ESMs data have more or less all experienced the limited data and short sample period issue. Especially, as discussed in section 3, these short sample periods also include various financial crises and market events. Limited number of studies on ESMs with these data complications make the composition of ESM stock returns therefore still a matter of debate.

5.2. Data Specifications

The first data specification issue concerns the datasets used in the decomposition literature. The majority of the studies in this area base their results on industry components of national stock market indices rather than on individual companies. Bai *et al.* (2012) argue that

---

[32] Scheicher (2001) finds regional integration among three Eastern Europe emerging markets: Hungary, Poland and the Czech Republic. Phylaktis and Ravazzolo (2002) show that the substantial trade between a group of Pacific-Basin emerging stock markets and Japan and US plays an important role in economic integration.

[33] Examples can refer to Table 1.

the use of industry indices has several limitations. First, active portfolio managers construct their own portfolios and do not necessarily use ready-made industrial indices, either due to the flexibility of their fund's mandate or due to fiduciary limitations.[34] Second, decomposition results based on indices will depend in part on the rules that are applied to determine the definition and composition of the indices. Both are typically reviewed and can be revised at least quarterly. Third, Marsh and Pfleiderer (1997) argue that studies using indices have to ask: how much of the variation in (say) the Taiwan index is explained by the industry composition of the Taiwan market, and how much is attributable to a country effect that affects all Taiwan stocks? However if the results are based on decomposing individual firm data, the question is changed to: how much of the variation in (say) Acer stocks is because of the fact that Acer is in the Technology industry and how much is because of the fact that Acer is a Taiwan company? Being in the Technology industry may be important even if the industry composition of the Taiwan market explains very little of Taiwan stock returns. Fourth, many country indices include cross-listed companies. Therefore studies use these indices effectively double-count the domicile and industry of such firms. Although according to Griffin and Karolyi (1998), the H-R method produces numerically identical results irrespective of whether stock indices or individual stocks in the indices are used in the analysis, this applies only to indices using an identical weighting procedure and to a sample of firms with an identically-changing composition of companies. Also, it does not mitigate the issue of double-counting cross-listed firms. See Marsh and Pfleiderer (1997) for a detailed discussion.

The other data specification issue concerns the industry classification level. Marsh and Pfleiderer (1997) test different industry classifications with the same dataset and find that industry classification does not have a critical impact on the final results. Griffin and Karolyi (1998) argue that the seven-industry grouping in Roll (1990) and Heston and Rouwenhorst (1994) fails to provide adequate cross-sectional variation in industry returns in order to allow country- and industry-specific influences to be disentangled. Griffin and Karolyi (1998) and Phylaktis and Xia (2006) used 66 and 51 industry groups respectively. Bai *et al.* (2012) argue that classifying a firm's industry is somewhat subjective: an excessively coarse classification will bundle together firms engaged in different activities, on the other hand, an overly fine classification will include arbitrary allocations of multi-activity firms to specific industries. In particular, ESMs tend to have more conglomerates than the main OECD stock markets while at the same time having, in general, a narrower industrial base and a narrower range of industries. Hence it is more reasonable to use a more aggregated industry classification in ESMs return decomposition. Bai *et al.* (2012) use 11 industry sectors classified according to the level three Dow Jones/FTSE Industry Classification Benchmark (ICB). Hence their sample includes 11 industry groups in 13 ESMs, which is arguably a more balanced sample in industry and country dimensions than many other studies. In general the above studies find similar results. However, the classification level does matter in some cases. Some studies following Griffin and Karolyi (1998) report the decomposition results grouped by traded and non-traded goods industries. It is expected that a larger proportion of return variation would be explained by pure industry effects in traded goods industries than in non-traded goods industries since we would expect traded goods industries to be more directly influenced by international competition for inputs and sales. On the other hand, variation in non-traded

[34] Exchange traded funds could track industry indices, but in practice they mostly track major market indices.

goods industries should be more exposed to the country effects as such industries are more shielded from the direct impacts of international competition. Bai *et al.* (2012) argue that one of the reasons behind their different results to Griffin and Karolyi (1998) is due to the use of different industry classification levels. Griffin and Karolyi identify traded and non-traded goods industries on the basis of their 66-industry classification. The level 3 ICB classification used in Bai *et al.* (2012) is coarser and may lead to a different grouping as between traded and non-traded goods industries.

6. Future Research

From the above discussions, it seems that with the development of globalisation and the occurrence of different market events, the debate on the relative importance of industry and country effects in determining the cross-sectional variation in stock returns is still very active if not more so than three decades ago. The inconclusive debate is calling for researchers to pay attentions to the following. First, with the new development in the world economy especially more data becoming available in ESMs, it is more likely to conduct research with longer sample period which covers various important shocks such as financial crises; capital market liberalisation; the adoption of new technology; the establishment of new trade and economic unions and economic cycles. With controlling different shocks in the same methodological framework, researcher may find evidence regarding to whether the decreasing importance in country effects and increasing importance in industry effects are short-lived or based on more fundamental changes across the markets.

Second, as argued in Heston and Rouwenhorst (1994), the standard decomposition of country and industry effects is purely descriptive without giving direct insight into the underlying sources of the country and industry effects, or why one or other effect should be more important at any point in time. Very few studies including Campa and Fernandes (2006) investigate the determinants of industry and country effects and conclude that country effects are smaller for countries integrated in world financial markets. In addition, greater integration within an industry increases the importance of industry effects in explaining returns, but countries with a more specialised production structure have higher country shocks. However, Bai and Green (2011) argue that these results are limited due first to their focus on index instead of individual firm returns, then due to a limited range of determinants of country and industry effects analysed and finally, due to their focus on the magnitudes of the country and industry effects only without considering the directions of the stock return cross-sectional variations. Bai and Green (2011) investigate whether country effects will gradually disappear with the progress of liberalisation; or whether there are other fundamental reasons which underlie the importance of country effects, and which may be more slow-moving or ambiguous in direction than the impact of liberalisation. Their results show that some traditionally recognised macroeconomic variables such as the change in exchange rate and risk free interest rate together can contribute to about 73% cross-sectional variation of pure country effects. Financial sector development and the legal environment also have significant influences on cross-section variation in stock returns. Their estimations also find evidence to support the argument that the legal origin of the market does matter to stock returns, which suggests that no amount of liberalisation is likely to lead to a complete dissipation of country effects as a driving force in the cross-sectional distribution of returns. With limited research in this area, it is still important to conduct further research from different aspects on the underlying reasons of the country and industry effects in the future.

Third, regarding to the limitations of the standard H-R model, it is useful to develop more flexible models but still retain the simplicity of H-R model as far as possible in future research in this area.

CONCLUSION

The principal aim of this chapter is to summarise and evaluate key studies on the relative importance of the country and industry effects in determining the cross-sectional variations in stock returns according to some key issues involved that may have contributed to the inconclusive results and need further attention in the future research. A brief summary of the key studies shows that in general, country effects are still important but the importance of industry effects has increased in the last decade and may have overtaken the dominant position of country effects in some OECD countries especially in highly integrated euro zone countries. This survey then discusses how different kinds of shock and their combinations with each other may lead to the dynamic patterns found in the relative importance of these two effects. In particular, the time-varying pattern may be due to permanent shocks like international integration, temporary global shocks such as IT bubble or temporary local shocks that spread across international markets by a process of contagion, especially during the financial crisis or in some markets, due to the combination of these shocks happening around the same time period. Therefore it is still an open question whether the decreasing importance in country effects and the increasing importance in industry effects is a permanent phenomenon happening cross the world. After reviewing the standard H-R fixed effect dummy variable model along with various criticisms on it, we summarise some alternative methods adopted in response to those criticisms. Then, this survey summarises some key data issues including the importance of ESMs in the decomposition literature, the advantage of using individual firm returns instead of index returns and the implication of industry classification level to the empirical findings. This survey shows that the on-going debate is calling for further studies hence finally we briefly discuss some potential directions in future research.

REFERENCES

Adjaouté, K. & Danthine, J. (2005). Equity returns and integration: Is Europe changing?. *Oxford Review of Economic Policy*, *20*, 555-570.

Bai, Y. & Green, C. J. (2010). International diversification strategies: Revisited from the risk perspective. *Journal of Banking & Finance*, *34*, 236–245.

Bai, Y. & Green, C. J. (2011). Determinants of cross-sectional stock return variation in emerging markets. *Empirical Economics*, *41*, 81-102.

Bai, Y., Green, C. J. & Leger, L. (2012). Industry and country factors in emerging market returns: Did the Asian crisis make a difference?. *Emerging Markets Review*, *13*, 559-580.

Baca, S., Garbe, B. & Weiss, R. (2000). The rises of sector effects in major equity markets, *Financial Analysts Journal*, *56*, 34-40.

Baele, L. & Inghelbrecht, K. (2006). Structural versus temporary drivers of country and industry Risk, Tilburg University Working Paper, 2006/413.

Baele, L. & Inghelbrecht, K. (2009). Time-varying integration and international diversifying strategies, *Journal of Empirical Finance*, 16, 368-387.

Balli, F. & Balli, H. (2011). Sectoral equity returns in the Euro region: Is there any room for reducing portfolio risk? *Journal of Economics and Business*, *63*, 89-106.

Beckers, S., Connor, G. & Curds, R. (1996), National versus global influences on equity returns. *Financial Analysts Journal*, 31 - 38.

Bekaert, G. (1995). Market integration and investment barriers in emerging equity markets. *The World Bank Economic Review*, *9*, 75-105.

Bekaert, G. & Harvey, C. R. (1997). Emerging equity market volatility. *Journal of Financial Economics 43*, 29–77.

Bekaert, G. & Harvey, C. R. (2000). Foreign speculators and emerging equity markets, *Journal of Finance*, *55*, 565-613.

Bekaert, G., Harvey, C. R., Lundblad, C. T. & Siegel, S. (2008). What segments equity markets? University of North Carolina Working Paper.

Bekaert, G., Harvey, C. R. & Ng, A. (2005). Market integration and contagion. *Journal of Business* ,*78*, 39-69.

Bekaert, G., Hodrick, R. J. & Zhang, X. Y. (2009). International Stock Return Comovements. *The Journal of Finance*, *LXIV*, 2591-2626.

Brooks, R. J. & Del Negro, M. (2004). The rise in comovement across national stock Markets: Market integration or global bubble?. *Journal of Empirical Finance*, *11*, 659–680.

Campbell, J., Lettau, M., Malkiel, B. & Xu, Y. (2001). Have Individual Stocks Become More Volatile? An Empirical Exploration of Idiosyncratic Risk. *Journal of Finance*, *56*, 1–43.

Campa, J. & Fernandes, N. (2006). Sources of gains from international portfolio diversification. *Journal of Empirical Finance*, *13*, 417-443.

Catao, L. & Timmerman, A. (2003). Country and industry dynamics in stock returns. IMF working paper WP/03/52, Washington D.C., International Monetary Fund.

Cavaglia, S., Brightman C. & Aked, M. (2000). The increasing importance of industry factors. *Financial Analysts Journal*, *56*, 41-54.

Cavaglia, S., Cho, D. & Singer, B. (2001). Risks of sector rotation strategies. *Journal of Portfolio Management*, *27*, 35-44.

Chen, J., Bennett, A. & Zheng, T. (2006). Sector Effects in Developed *vs*. Emerging Markets. *Financial Analysts Journal*, *62*, 40-51.

Ciner C. (2006). A further look at linkages between NAFTA equity markets. *The Quarterly Review of Economics and Finance*, *46*, 338–352.

De Moor, L. & Sercu, P. (2010). Country v sector effects in equity returns and the roles of geographical and firm-size coverage. *Small Business Economics*, *35*, 433–448.

De Moor, L. & Sercu, P. (2011). Country v industry factors in equity returns: The roles of non-unit exposures. *Journal of Empirical Finance*, *18*, 64–77.

Eiling, E., Gerard, B. & de Roon, F. A. (2012). Euro-Zone equity returns: country versus industry effects. *Review of Finance*, *16*, 755-798.

Eun, C. S., Huang W. & Lai, S. (2008). International diversification with large and small-cap stocks. *Journal of Financial and Quantitative Analysis*, *43*, 489–524.

Fama, E. & MacBeth, J. D. (1973). Risk, return, and equilibrium: Empirical tests. *Journal of Political Economy*, *38*, 607-636.

Ferreira, M. A. & Ferreira, M. A. (2006). The importance of industry and country effects in the EMU equity markets. *European Financial Management*, *12*, 341–373.

Ferreira, M. A. & Gama, P. M. (2005). Have world, country, and industry risks changed over time? An investigation of the volatility of developed stock markets. *Journal of Financial and Quantitative Analysis*, *40*, 195-222.

Fedorova, E. (2011). Transfer of financial risk in emerging eastern European stock markets: A sectoral perspective. Bank of Finland, BOFIT Discussion Papers 24/2011.

Flavin, T. J. (2004). The effect of the Euro on country versus industry portfolio diversification. *Journal of International Money and Finance*, *23*, 1137–1158.

Goetzmann, W. N., Li, L. & Rouwenhorst, K. G. (2005). Long-term global market correlations. *Journal of Business*, *78*, 1-38.

Griffin, J. M. & Karolyi, G. A. (1998). Another look at the role of the industrial structure of markets for international diversification strategies, *Journal of financial Economics*, *50*, 351-373.

Grinold, R., Rudd, A. & Stefel, D. (1989). Global effects: fact or fiction? *Journal of Portfolio*, *16*, 79-88.

Grisolia, E. & Navone, M. (2007). Cross-industry diversification: Integration or bubble? Bocconi University Working Paper, September.

Heston, S. L. & Rouwenhorst, G. K. (1994). Does industrial structure explain the benefits of international diversification? *Journal of Financial Economics*, *36*, 3-27.

Heston, S. L. & Rouwenhorst, G. K. (1995). Industry and country effects in international stock returns. *Journal of Portfolio Management*, *21*, 53 - 58.

Huang, W. (2007). Financial integration and the price of world covariance risk: Large- vs. small-cap stocks. *Journal of International Money and Finance*, *26*, 1311-1337.

Kalev, P. S., Nguyen, A. H. & Oh, N. Y. (2008). Foreign versus local investors: Who knows more? Who makes more?. *Journal of Banking and Finance*, *32*, 2376- 2389.

Lessard, D. R. (1974). World, national and industry factors in equity returns. *Journal of Finance*, *29*, 379-391.

Levy, H. & Sarnat, M. (1970). International diversification of investment portfolios. *American Economic Review*, *60*, 668-675.

L'Her, J., Sy O. & Tnani, M. Y. (2002). Country, industry, and risk factor loadings in portfolio management. *Journal of Portfolio Management*, *28*, 70-80.

Longin, F. & Solnik, B. (2001). Extreme correlation of international equity markets. *Journal of Finance*, *LVI*, 649-676.

Marsh, T. & Pfleiderer, P. (1997). The role of country and industry effects in explaining global stock returns. Mimeo. U.C. Berkeley and Stanford University.

Moerman, G. A. (2008). Diversification in euro area stock markets: Country versus industry. *Journal of International Money and Finance*, *27*, 1122–1134.

Phylaktis, K. & Ravazzolo, F. (2002). Measuring financial and economic integration with equity prices in emerging markets. *Journal of International Money and Finance*, *21*, 879-903.

Phylaktis, K. & Xia, L. (2006). The changing role of industry and country effects in the global equity markets. *European Journal of Finance*, *12*, 627 – 648.

Roll, R. (1992). Industrial structure and comparative behaviour of international stock market indices. *Journal of Finance*, *47*, 3-42.

Rouwenhorst, G. K. (1999). European equity markets and the EMU. *Financial Analysts Journal*, *55*, 57-64.

Serra, A. P. (2000). Country and industry factors in returns: evidence from emerging markets' stocks. *Emerging Markets Review*, *1*, 127-151.

Scheicher, M. (2001). The comovements of stock markets in Hungary, Poland and the Czech Republic. *International Journal of Finance and Economics*, *6*, 27-39.

Silva, A. C. S. & Chavez, G. A. (2008). Cross-listing and liquidity in emerging market stocks. *Journal of Banking and Finance*, *32*, 420- 433.

Solnik, B. (1974). Why not diversify internationally rather than domestically? *Financial Analyst Journal*, *30*, 48-54.

Steliaros, M. E. & Thomas, D. C. (2006). The cross-sectional variability of stock-price returns: Country and sector effects revisited. *Journal of Asset Management*, *7*, 273-290.

Stulz, R. M. & Williamson, R. (2003). Culture, openness, and finance. *Journal of Financial Economics*, *70*, 313–349.

In: Financial Crises
Editor: Cooper A. Hawthorne

ISBN: 978-1-62808-293-7

Chapter 6

CHINESE ECONOMY ON TRANSITION

Liang-Xin Li*
Business School, Hunan International Economics University
Hunan, Changsha, China

ABSTRACT

This paper will demonstrate what China was doing, is doing and will do for its economic expansion during and after global crisis. Many thoughts and theories about Chinese economic reforms are analyzed. The road map and goal of Chinese economic growth are examined and outlined in this paper. How to keep Chinese economy fast growth is this paper's key issue which is thoroughly discussed.

Keywords: Chinese economy, high growth, economic reform, competitive, global crisis

JEL code: C1

INTRODUCTION

Since 2008, the global economy has been experiencing the deepest downturn in the post–World War II period, as the financial crisis rapidly spreads around the world. A large number of advanced economies have fallen into recession, and economies in the rest of the world have slowed abruptly. Global trade and financial flows are dramatically shrinking, while output and employment losses huge. Credit markets remain frozen as borrowers are engaged in a drawn-out deleveraging process and banks struggle to improve their financial health.

The recovery is being led by strong growth in emerging Asian powerhouses such as China and India, real GDP growth is forecast to reach almost 5 percent in 2010, up from 1.75 percent in 2009, while the US, Europe and Japan are just beginning to emerge from

* Email: apolo1@sina.com. Mailing address: Business school, Hunan International Economics University, Changsha 410205, Hunan, China

devastating recessions. Advanced economies are projected to expand sluggishly through much of 2010, with annual growth in 2010 projected to be about 1.25 percent, following a contraction of 3.50 percent in 2009, and with unemployment continuing to rise until later in the year. Europe could face unemployment of nearly 12 percent by the end of 2011, while the US jobless rate will peak at 10 percent in 2010, the IMF said.

As the world economy comes out of a deep global recession, global activity is forecast to expand by about 3 percent in 2010 after contracting by about 1 percent in 2009, according to the International Monetary Fund (IMF) projections.

With the slowdown of the economy, Chinese jobs are suffering. Global downturn means falling demand for Chinese exports, resulting in factory closures and layoffs on a daily basis in many parts of China, especially in the Southeast. Domestically, overcapacity has long resulted in over production which translates as over-employment. Now the global recession exacerbates the situation by throwing out more workers due to decelerating industrial output and reduced foreign investment, hence unemployment is climbing in China. In addition, there are annual additions to the army of job seekers including more than 6 million university graduates and at least 10 million immigrant farmers looking for a job in the city. Estimates of the number of jobs which have already been lost vary, but most put it at around 20 million (Economist, 19 March 2009). To make things worse, the Chinese economy is decelerating. According to the World Bank, the forecast growth for China is 6.5% in 2009, which tends to further reduce job opportunities. By any standards, it is no small task for China to copy with the growing pressure of unemployment.

Over the past several years, China has enjoyed one of the world's fastest growing economies (Table 1 and Figure 1) and has been a major engine to world economic growth. However, the current global financial crisis threatens to significantly slow down China's economy growth. Several Chinese industries, particularly the export sector, have been hit hard by crisis, and millions of workers have reportedly been laid off. This situation is of great concern to the Chinese government, which views rapid economic growth as critical to maintaining social stability. China is a major economic power and holds huge amounts of foreign exchange reserves, and thus its policies could have a major impact on the global economy.

What China as an important economy entity had done, is doing and will do will have a significant influence to the global economy. Much is therefore hinged on how well China is coping with the devastating effect of the current crisis (Prasad, 2009). If China can successfully muddle through, the world will see a more confident China that opens her arms wider for globalization. However, if fails, the rising tide of nationalism within the nation may drag China into a state in which wheels of reforms are reversed. The world then will have to face a China that is resistant to globalization with mighty forces. The implications of this are huge and the world will be affected in many ways by its adverse consequences (Yep, 2009). This paper will provide all around insights on the following aspects on Chinese economy: global crisis influence; China's response to global crisis; Chinese economy in a long run; Chinese economy's fast growth; Chinese economic reforming; China as global economic growth engine. It is my goal to provide broad views on Chinese economy and some thoughts on global economy after global crisis. For the rest of the paper, we will first introduce Chinese economic effects on the global financial crisis in Section I, which sets the background for understanding China's responses for crisis management in Section II. Section

III will be devoted to China's long term economic policy and its role in Chinese economy expansion in a long run.

Table 1. The growth rate for each year of 1978 - 2008

1978	11.7%
1979	7.6%
1980	7.8%
1981	5.2%
1982	9.1%
1983	10.9%
1984	15.2%
1985	13.5%
1986	8.8%
1987	11.6%
1988	11.3%
1989	4.1%
1990	3.8%
1991	9.2%
1992	14.2%
1993	13.5%
1994	12.6%
1995	10.5%
1996	9.6%
1997	8.8%
1998	7.8%
1999	7.1%
2000	8.0%
2001	7.5%
2002	8.3%
2003	9.5%
2004	10.1%
2005	10.4%
2006	11.6%
2007	13%
2008	9%
2009	9.1%
2010	10.3%
2011	9.2%
2012	7.8%
Average	9.66%

In Section IV, I will discuss China's strategy which sustains a fast growth of Chinese economy. Section V presents the Chinese economic reforming before, during and after the crisis. Chinese way as a leading growth engine of world economy is presented in Section VI. The summary remarks are in Conclusions section.

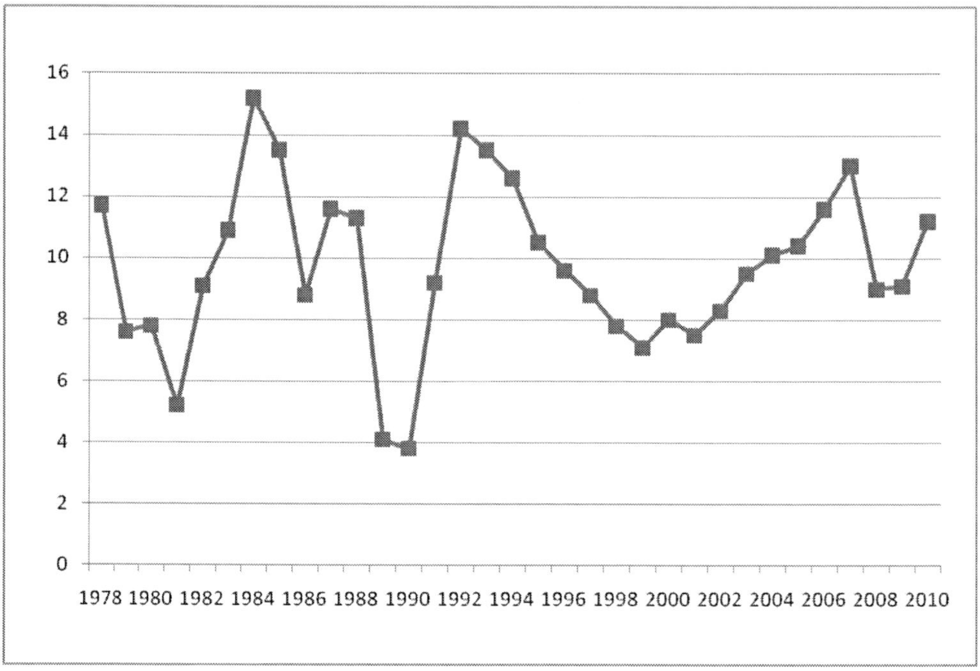

Figure 1. Chinese GDP growth rate [in %, 2010 projected] during 1978-2010.

Section 1. The Impact of the Global Crisis on Chinese Economy

Chinese economy growth rate reached the peak in 2007, it starts to slow down since the third quarter of 2007, but keeps a growth rate above 10%. The global crisis's effect emerges since the third quarter of 2008: the fourth quarter's growth rate was just 6.8%, and decreased to 6.1% in the first quarter of 2009. Some analysts contend annual economic growth of less than 8% could lead to social unrest in China, given that an estimated 20 million people seek jobs every year (including migrant workers that move to urban centers and high school and college graduates). According to the International Monetary Fund (IMF), China was the single most important contributor to world economic growth in 2007.3 Thus, a Chinese economic slowdown (or recovery) could also have significant global implications.

As for the real economy, the real estate market in several Chinese cities has exhibited signs of a bubble that is bursting, including a slowdown in construction, falling prices and growing levels of unoccupied buildings. This has increased pressure on the banks to lower interest rates further to stabilize the market. For the first four months of 2009, industrial output rose by 5.5% year-on-year, well below 12.9% growth rate in 2008.

The global crisis effect to Chinese financial market is small due to the fact that Chinese capital market is not completely open to international funds, foreign capital can't flow into Chinese capital market freely; Chinese banks didn't purchase much subprime debts; foreign reserve mostly is in dollar-valued US government debts; therefore, the direct influence of the global crisis to Chinese bank sector is light and most Chinese banks are doing very well. The value of China's main stock market index, the Shanghai Stock Exchange Composite Index, lost nearly two-thirds of its value from December 31, 2007, to December 31, 2008.

The influence of global crisis to Chinese export industry is very heavy. Since October 2008, Chinese export has started to decrease. Chinese exported $1.43 trillion goods and growth rate slowed by 8.6%; in the first season of 2009, china exported $245.5 billion goods; it slowed 19.7% compared with the same season of last year. At the same time, the import is $183.2 billion; it lowered 30.9% than last year.

As a result of the global financial crisis a large number of export-led private enterprises in China's coastal provinces have gone bankrupt, with around 20 million unskilled workers losing their jobs. Furthermore, the slowdown in China's exports, along with the decline in real estate investments, has led to a decrease in GDP growth from 13% in 2007 to 9% in 2008.

China's economy is heavily dependent on exports and investment flow-ins. In 2007, China overtook the United States to become the world's second largest merchandise exporter after the European Union (EU). China's net exports (exports minus imports) contributed to one-third of its GDP growth in 2007. China's exports of goods and services as a share of GDP rose from 9.1% in 1985 to 37.8% in 2008.

The Chinese government estimates that the foreign trade sector employs over 80 million people, of which 28 million work in foreign-invested enterprises. Foreign direct investment (FDI) flows to China have been a major factor behind its productivity gains and rapid economic growth. FDI flows to China in 2007 totaled $75 billion, making it the largest FDI recipient among developing countries and the third largest overall, after the EU and the United States. The current global economic slowdown (especially among its major export markets—the United States, the EU, and Japan) is having a significant negative impact on China's export sector and industries that depend on FDI flows.

The misalignment of the RMB exchange rate has been one of the major factors to have caused the Chinese economy's external and internal imbalances. To solve this problem, Chinese government started to reform the RMB's exchange rate mechanism in July 2005. Its sticking to the US dollar was replaced by managed floating with reference to a basket of currencies, and the pace of the RMB's appreciation against the dollar accelerated from July 2005 to the first half of 2008. However, after the aggravation and spreading of the global financial crisis, China's exports declined significantly.

To sustain the relative competitiveness of China's export goods, the PBC (People's Bank of China) increased its intervention in the foreign exchange market to prevent the further appreciation of the RMB from the third quarter of 2008. In an environment of declining external demand and increasing protectionism, it is doubtful that managing the RMB's exchange rate will help stimulate China's exports. To make things worse, the bank's heavy intervention in the foreign exchange market will sustain or even aggravate the country's external and internal imbalances.

Obviously, China is not crisis proof. As an open economy, China is striving to handle the crisis damages without losing the benefit from the openness and going backward to closeness.

SECTION 2. CHINA'S RESPONSES TO THE GLOBAL CRISIS

To reduce the effects of global crisis and recover quickly, Chinese government takes many decisive and high efficient procedures to tackle the financial turmoil which include:

A) Implement expansionary monetary policy

These measures include:

1) Lower the deposit reserve rate

In order to stimulate banks to release loans, the government lowered the deposit reserve rate four times consecutively since September, 2008.

2) Cut the interest rate of deposits and loans

The 3-year loan rate lowered from 7.56 in December of 2007 to 5.4% of present, it was lowered by 2.16%.

3) Encourage loans

In the first quarter of 2009, total loan increased by 4.58 trillion RMB; total loan grew 4.91 trillion RMB in the whole year of 2008, part as shown in Table 2.

Table 2. Projected GDP for China [growth rate 10%] and USA[growth rate 3%]

year	China GDP[$ trillion]	USA GDP[$ trillion]
2008	4.222	14.333
2009	4.642	14.76
2010	5.106	15.203
2011	5.617	15.659
2012	6.179	16.129
2013	6.796	16.612
2014	7.476	17.111
2015	8.224	17.624
2016	9.046	18.153
2017	9.951	18.697
2018	10.95	19.258
2019	12.04	19.836
2020	13.24	20.431
2021	14.57	21.044
2022	16.03	21.675
2023	17.63	22.326
2024	19.39	22.995
2025	21.33	23.685
2026	23.46	24.396
year	China GDP[$ trillion]	USA GDP[$ trillion]
*2027	25.81	25.128
2028	28.39	25.882
2029	31.23	26.658
2030	34.35	27.458

As a matter of fact, the growth rate of national loan keeps at a rate above 27% /month, mostly financed by commercial papers.

B) Increase Government Spending Heavily

The central government made a two year plan to invest 4 trillion RMB. It is equivalent to 16% of Chinese 2007 GDP. The plan includes central government investment of 1.18 trillion RMB, and the rest are from the local government. The major goal is pushing for a better housing、peasants' living in rural area; an modernized railway transportation ; more environmental protection projects and recovery of earth quake of Sichuan province. The plan is developing very well now.

The package (as shown in Figure 2) would finance public transport infrastructure (including railways, highways, airports, and ports) affordable housing, rural infrastructure (including irrigation, drinking water, electricity, and transport), environmental protection projects, technological innovation, health and education, and rebuilding areas hit by disasters (such as areas that were hit by the May 12, 2008 earthquake, primarily in Sichuan province). Shortly after the central government announced its stimulus package, many local governments announced their own stimulus package. Thus, the total level of China's economic stimulus could be much higher than the official 4 trillion yuan ($586 billion) figure.

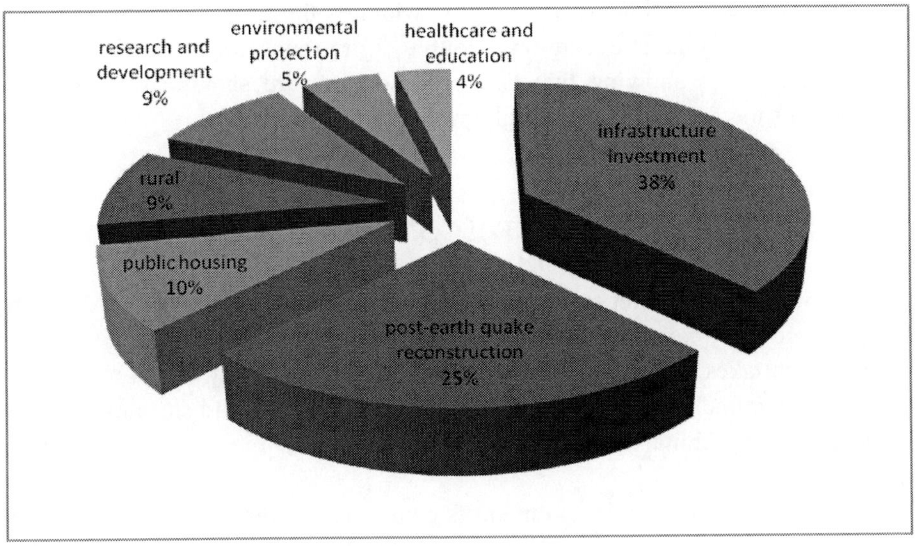

Figure 2. The breakdown of the stimulus package.

On April 7, 2009, Chinese government announced plans to spend $124 billion over the next three years to create a universal health care system. The plan would attempt to extend basic coverage to most of the population by 2011, and would invest in public hospitals and training for village and community doctors. A number of efforts have been made to boost rural incomes and spending levels and to narrow the gap in living standards between rural and urban citizens (as well as between coastal and western regions of the country). For example, since February 2009, an estimated 900 million Chinese rural residents have been eligible to receive a 13% rebate for purchase of home appliances. Public housing projects, education, and infrastructure projects are largely targeted to rural area low income peasants. The government has also announced plans to boost agricultural subsidies to farmers.

C. Take Structural Reduce of Taxes

This procedure includes medium to small size enterprises and housing industry favorable tax reform; eliminating and stopping 100 administration Services fee. Together, the policy will reduce corporates' and individuals' cost by 500 billion RMB each year.

D. Undertake Reform and Promotion of Industry

The central government outlined reform and promotion plan for steel, auto, equipments, electronics and information, textile, chemical, oil, color-metal, ship, light-industry, logistics industry. The major goals are taking decisive steps to regroup industry, to get rid of production of low-tech, to develop advanced productivity, to concentrate enterprises and to raise the resource allocation efficiency.

Despite some concerns on China's response package, as results of these procedures, Chinese economy made a 9.1% growth in 2009 which is the fastest growing economy in the world after recession. China is eyeing on a double digit growth for 2010. Now all the macro-economic indicators are showing that Chinese economy are shaking off the global crisis influence and runs toward a full swing high growth development.

SECTION 3. CHINESE ECONOMY IN A LONG RUN

Since 1978, the free market reform has been the major task of Chinese economy. Since then, Chinese economy keeps growing at a rate around 9.6% each year for more than 30 years. Now China takes over Japan as the second largest economy in the world which is an obvious economic miracle of the world. In order to secure a fast and sustainable development of Chinese economy, China now is taking many important measures to facilitate Chinese economy's growth.

The strategy of sustainable development is considered as the center piece of guidelines of Chinese future development. In China, any level enterprise and public must make a plan for its own sustainable fast growth. The center government and local government are working jointly to make sure the sustainable development is the major policy making strategy. According to the strategy, all level government must outline an operational plan、stimulate creativity and eagerness of enterprises and individual、efficiently allocate resources、push free market reform、enhance intension management、encourage participation of enterprises and individuals.

1. *Enhance the ability to lead the sustainable growth.* China now is training its governing body and advertising the ideology of the sustainable development to build it into its political system、market mechanism、public and enterprises decision procedures. The goal is obviously to enhance the decision making ability of all aspects of the nation's economy to secure the high efficient realization of the sustainable development strategy.
2. *Environmental protection and management are reformed to facilitate the free market requirements.* The procedures include: a) setting up and complete the environmental legal system and laws; b) using market procedure to protect environment, such as pollution fee、environmental tax, etc. c) enhancing the public service in the environmental protection sector, such as, protecting clean drinking water, clean air, clean living conditions.
3. *Turn the traditional industry society toward a knowledge-based economy informational society.* Technology and knowledge take over natural resources as the major factor of the economic growth. In informational age, sustainable development goes with a new development direction: a) global net of information leads to a complete open sustainable development system which leads to a global resource efficient allocation. b) high technology industry is the leading growth point of the economy. c) knowledge-based economy growth leads the production factor change from natural resources consumption to the knowledge production.
4. *The international corporation entities and channels are becoming more diversified.* China as a WTO member will enjoy as a equal trade partner to corporate with any other members. This will widen china's corporation channels and strongly enhance china's development opportunities.
5. Enhancing the competitiveness of Chinese industries. China is urging its all level industries to form its own research and development centers, utilizing new technology, participating international competition, educating high quality workers in order to sustain Chinese industries high growth.
6. Raising people's knowledge and quality. Through educating Chinese people with scientific knowledge and law-governing ideology, China is trying to form a supportive culture base for the long run into its modernization era.

For the effective long term growth, China will attach greater importance to long-term optimization of the economic structure. For this, workable measures have to be adopted to expedite the country's social construction in an all-round way in order to clear the path for sustained and healthy economic development.

A number of emerging Asian economies had to face the so-called "middle-income trap" during their economic development because of their sluggish social construction process. Some countries such as Brazil, Argentina, Mexico, Chile and Malaysia have suffered even a long economic slowdown or stagnation because of their failure to resolve economic contradictions, or owing to their ill-conceived development strategies or outside impacts.

One of the main reasons why such a situation arose in those countries was because they attached too much importance to economic growth but failed to pay enough attention to social construction. As a result, the rich-poor income gap widened further, leading to slackened domestic demand. The formation of a new dual social structure during their accelerated urbanization process and the absence of a social security net aggravated the existing severe social contradictions. Besides, inadequate expenditure on education and human capital aggravated the imbalance in their industrial structure and fuelled an extensive economy.

Entering this economic stage (Figure 3), a related problem is the widening gap between rural and urban income. At the beginning of the 1980s, the rural–urban income gap in fact narrowed, since agricultural income was boosted by the implementation of the household responsibility system in the countryside while urban reforms were slow to gather momentum. Over time, however, the gap has widened sharply. In 1981, urban income was on average about two times that of rural income. In 2005, this ratio rose to 3.2. It is probably the result of institutional restrictions on migration and faster productivity growth in the urban economy.

China will expedite its social construction and overcome the "middle-income trap" as an important part task of the scientific development outlook. China is striving to complete its building for harmonic society, from employment generation and social security to housing and healthcare to improve people's livelihood, though its expenditure on public services and other social areas is still far from enough now. Another important measure to sustain its high growth is that China will put more emphasis on raising people’s quality by educating them scientific knowledge and strengthening the ideology governing the country by law.

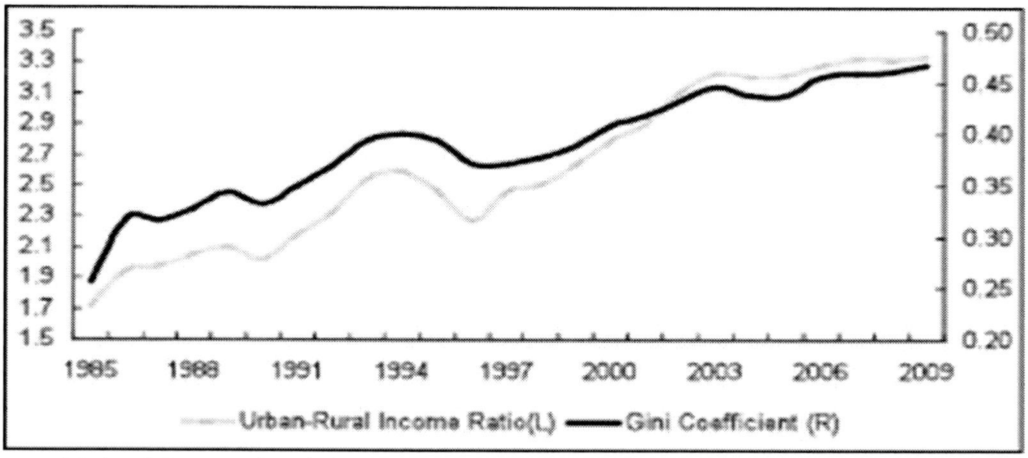

Source: National Bureau of Statistics (NBS) various years, *China Statistical Yearbook*, China Statistics Press, Beijing.

Figure 3. Gini coefficient among households and the urban–rural income gap.

Greater efforts will be made to reduce the country's excessive dependence on investments (Figure 4) for economic growth. The government adopted an unprecedented expansionary fiscal policy in the first quarter of this year to stop the economic slide, with investments into fixed assets reaching 2.8129 billion yuan ($412.33 million)), a 28.8 percent increase year-on-year. In fact, investments have been used as a forcible tool to sustain the country's high economic growth over the past three decades. It is true, large investments have bolstered the country's decades-long rapid growth. But it is also true that they have consumed huge amounts of natural resources and energy. To reverse the trend, the governments has to take some concrete and effective measures for boosting technological innovation and accelerating the cultivating of a more efficient human capital market and improving its investment performance. This will help prevent building up of surplus production capability under the investment-pushing growth pattern.

Besides, the existing national income distribution pattern should be modified to raise the ratio of people's consumption to the GDP. The fast economic growth of the past three decades has boosted China's wealth accumulation. But the growth in people's wealth has been far behind the nation's level. An imbalance in wealth distribution has been a key cause for the rising economic structural imbalance and soft demand. Statistics show people's consumption level has fallen on a yearly basis during the past three decades, with its ratio to the country's GPD being less than 60 percent. From 1998 to 2005, the average income of labors grew by an average of 9.9 percent per year, less than one-third than the 30.5 percent annual growth in the country's industrial profits. Between 1995 and 2007, the shares of the corporate sector and the government in total national income increased steadily. As a result, the income share of households decreased from 68 per cent to 50 per cent. This trend could be important for explaining the declining share of consumption in GDP.

China's strategy is endeavoring to reform all those sectors that hurdle its sustainable growth without sacrificing its high growth rate with controllable、well-regulated reforming approaches.

SECTION 4. FAST GROW TOWARD THE TOP OF GLOBAL ECONOMY

Chinese economy has grown at an average rate above 9.6% since 1978 when the free economy reform started. How to keep the high growth rate for next 20-30 years is the key issue of any policy making in China. But the fact to improve the quality of Chinese people living standard is the only fundamental driving force for Chinese economy to grow. To satisfy this goal, China will take the following steps to realize the modernization of Chinese people's life, include: industrialization, urbanization, informationalization, technology-driving economy toward all around modernized and homogenous economy for a new China.

1. Industrialization Process Will Be a Leading Driving Force for Chinese Economic Growth

A. Regional Cooperation As a Driving Force

Due the fact that Chinese is a huge territory which leads to a non-homogeneous economy development for the present, China will push for the regional - corporation to utilize compensate advantages to speed up the growth of the industries. The regional corporation will take advantages of resources reallocation, production redistribution, position advantage, infrastructure development, raw materials supplies, labor movement in a large scale fashion to stimulate the demands, raise the industrial structure, drive economy fast growth.

B. Industrial Structure Reshaping As a Driving Force

China will push for its service industry growth and modernization. At the same time, the high technology manufacture industry is also a direction for Chinese further industrialization. Chinese manufacture industry will put its development strategic emphasis at those advanced and high-tech ends such as equipment making、 airspace and aerospace equipment making . This kind of industry restructuring will stimulate new growth rounds of Chinese industrialization and economy. Specifically, China will do the following two things to secure its high growth in industrialization:

1. Strategic Industries Integration And Strengthen

China will push for the strategic industries fast growth, such as advanced equipment making, aerospace equipment manufacturing, information industry, resource industry, logistic industry, nano-structure industry, etc.

2. Resource Industries Development

China is full of all kinds of nature resources, such as, minerals、 forestry and agriculture, sea, ecological resources. China will develop large scale resource-based industries, the goal is to further develop and utilize Chinese natural resources, extend the production-chain, enhance the added value and change the resource advantage to industries and economic fast growth.

C. Financial System Modernization As a Driving Force

China will complete its financial system modernization process, which include: completing the laws for financial system; developing more instruments for the financial market; reducing the government control of the investment and financing; pushing for a global free conversion RMB; participating the international capital flow; building a more efficient and high informational financial system, etc. The modernization of Chinese financial industry will be a supporting factor of china economic growth.

1. Urbanization Will Be a Key Push for China Economic Growth

By 2009, China urbanization rate is just 46.6%. To 2030. China will try to reach a goal to put this rate at 65%, which is a completion of Chinese basic urbanization process. In order to realize this goal, China will raise 1% population each year into the urban living standard. Due to this process, China will keep a high growth rate for its economy. The reasons are:

a) Urbanization will enlarge the scale of cities and its population. This process will build more infrastructures, houses, high ways, which eventually expand the demands and drive the economy grow.
b) Newly urbanized people will produce new demands for those durable consumption products. Such as houses, cars, TVs, computers, schools, etc. The new demands will stimulate the growth of economy.
c) Urbanization will produce more service industries. In 2009, Chinese service industry is just 43.3% Chinese GDP, which is lower than world average 68% much. Urbanization will produce more demand for service industry and stimulate its fast grow.
d) Urbanization will leave smaller population of farmers which will raise the production efficiency and income of individual farmer. Eventually It will enhance the productivity and technology of agriculture industry.

2. Informationalization Will Be an Important Way to Speed Up Chinese Economy

Information technology is the key modernization criteria for every country. How to obtain and use the information is a key issue for all modern life.

a) Information will enhance the efficiency of modern decision making, management, living. So to push for the informationalization, i.e. to use information to decide what to do will basically change people's management precision and significantly reduce the cost of all production、consumption and living processes. Information is a productivity, which leads to high quality growth of economy.
b) To build up Chinese information system will stimulate the demands、speed up Chinese modernization and support china economy growth.

3. Technology Is the Key Factor for Chinese Economic Growth

By using high technology, China can reduce the cost for its products, produce new products which lead to new broad consumption market, raise the efficiency of its production, enhance its competitiveness of its goods. The discovery and innovation will take place each every day, which will change our life in daily basis. China can keep a sustainable and efficient growth road in a long run through technology innovation. China is pushing its industry to build up research and development sectors, and will invest more money into those strategic high tech industries, such as nano-structure、aerospace、gene engineering、 new energy、 new materials, etc. China will produce more scientists and engineers by invest more to its education system and pushing for research-oriented universities. In order to lead the world in technology innovation in the long run, China will raise its huge population resources into a innovation resources. Technology-driving economy will be a key for China to succeed.

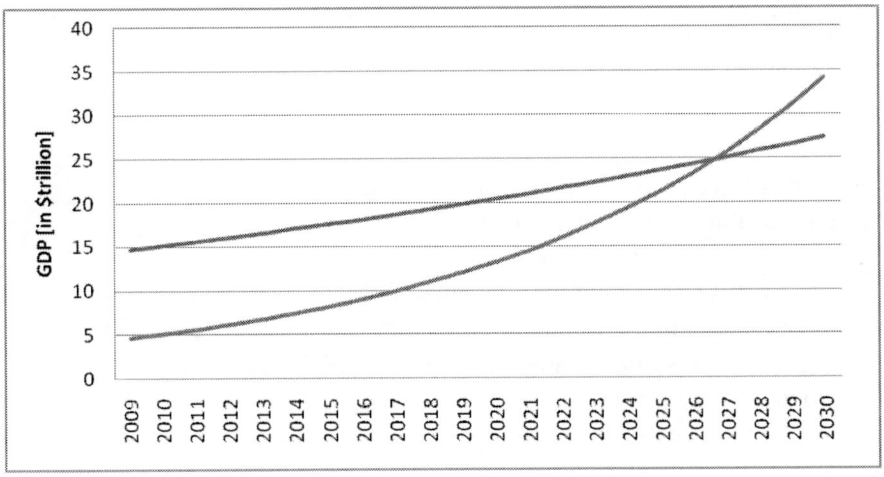

Figure 4. Projected Chinese and USA GDP in the near future. Red line: USA GDP; Blue line: Chinese GDP. The cross point is at the year 2026.

These driving forces will support china economy high growth rate which basically is the fact that Chinese people will complete a modernization process which delay too much. China will take many rational policies to use all these driving forces to keep its growth rate above 8% for next few decades. By 2030, China will be No.1 economy in the world. China already passed Japan as the world No.2 economy earlier this year. The road toward the top is bright (Table 2, Figure 4) and fast though China will have to face many challenges, such as, energy shortage, political reforming, international competitiveness, etc.

As projected, China will pass USA as No.1 economy in the year 2026.

SECTION 5. CHINESE ECONOMIC REFORMS

Since 1978, China has undertaken many decisive reforms of its old style political and government - controlled economy. From economic point, It can be viewed as four stages by now: 1) The starting stage: 1978-1984, it is the period of free marketing idea emerging and breaking through from the government-planned economy. 2) All around reforming stage: 1984-1992. China takes steps to reform its state-owned enterprises toward private enterprises. 3) System innovation: 1992-2003. It is a stage to find new and suitable economic system to release Chinese economic productivity. 4) Perfection of reforms:2003-now. It is a stage to improve and perfect the free marketing reforms.

To guide this historical reform of huge-population long history country, China used many useful and effective theories, such as the theory to build a Chinese characteristic society; the theory to develop a Chinese style free market; the theory to proceed stage by stage reform of Chinese economy; the theory to form a harmonic society. Specifically, China put its reform emphasis on the following fields:

1. Reform the agriculture economy and rural peasants management;
2. Open economy and set up many special economic regions for free market;
3. Privatize enterprises and develop other economic systems from free economy;
4. Reform public finance and modernize financial system;
5. Reform price forming mechanism and market system;
6. Reform employment and income distribution and build up an efficient social security system;
7. Restructure education, science and technology, culture system
8. Reform health and human services sector.

For the past five years, China has recognized the need to rebalance the economy. China will place less emphasis on investment and exports and more on consumption, services and innovation. Now that transition can no longer be delayed. There already is a long list of policy proposals to boost consumption. The top priority for many economists is healthcare reform. Shifting the balance of the economy will demand more than well-executed policies, it will oblige shifts in political culture and in the institutions that govern the economy. In much of the service sector, from finance to telecoms, the state still dominates. Even creative industries are trapped in its shadow. The privatization process is a long lasting reform.

The key approaches for Chinese reform are lying in three aspects:

1. Reform from the local to central government: this kind of reforms include rural peasants, non-state-owned economy.

2. Reform from the central to local government: such as public finance, financial system, foreign currency system, administrative examination and approval system reform.
3. Reform by the cooperation of central and local government: such as, state-owned enterprises, price reform, market system building, open economy.

Since 2003, China uses a new theory named scientific development outlook to guide nowadays economic reform. The central pieces of this theory are human oriented ideology and sustainable development. That is to say Chinese economy reform are based on improving peoples 'life and will take a road to develop Chinese economy in a sustainable fashion. Through more than 30 year's reform, Chinese economic reform is going further into a new stage, which characterizes as the following changes:

1. from government control to market-oriented economy;
2. from large amount of public enterprises to small number of quality public corporations;
3. from efficiency and fair to free market;
4. from managing the state-owned economy well to develop all economy in the country effectively;
5. from state-owned economy reform to public administration reform.

So far, Chinese reform is a success and a miracle of economy in Chinese and world history. With the guidance of the new theory, China is endeavoring to become a stable, progressive, harmonic nation. It is china's ambitious goal to make its people living in a prosperous and peaceful environment and in the world No.1 economy and innovation center in about 20 years.

Section 6. Leading the World Economy as a Major Economic Growth Engine

After recession, China quickly and strongly restored its high economic growth. China achieved a 9.1% growth in the year 2009, which is the fastest recovery of the world. In 2010, China reached a 11.9% growth rate in the first quarter. As expected China will obtain a 11% growth in the year 2010.

With the huge potential of Chinese market, Chinese economy shall be able to expand in a fast fashion for next few decades. Eventually, not in a long time, China will overtake USA as the world No.1 economy. And naturally China will become the major growth engine of the world economy.

According to IMF's calculation, China count a 25% share of world economic growth last year, already No.1 driving force in the world. At the same time, in 2009, USA is a decline in its economy which is the largest growth driving force for last few decades.

In order to lead the world in economy effectively, China will enhance its GDP scale and the competitiveness. In 2008, USA GDP is around $14.3 trillion; China GDP is about $4.2 trillion. USA GDP is about 4 times bigger than Chinese GDP. China just passed Japan as the

No.2 in the world economy. It will take another 10-20 years to take over USA if China takes an average 10%-8% growth rate. Even China reach the No.1, but in GDP per capital, China is still far below USA. This means as the world No.1 Economy, China's potential to develop is still huge.

The advantages for Chinese economy to compete and grow fast are:

1. The low cost of fundamental production factors

The cost for workers' is just 1/30 of Japan, 1/40 of USA. China has educated around 40 million college level work forces, with 3 million college graduates each year. Chinese workers are diligent and hard-working, which is attractive for many big international companies.

2. Huge potential and volume of Chinese market

China is now growing rapidly, its demand for product and services is strong. This fact will make many products huge in amount and scale even if with low ratio of share in Chinese market, for example, The number of Chinese mobile phones already passed USA but the mobile owners account still a lower portion of its population than US. The huge growth potential attracts many famous companies and big investments to Chinese market, which speed up high technology and capital transferring to China.

3. Jump start of many products by using advanced skills of the world

By using advanced and already existing skills and management experiences, China will take a more straight way toward the efficient production of many high tech goods and services. It will reduce large amount of cost and time for china to catch up. In the catch up process, China grow rapidly to lead the economy grow. But eventually, with Chinese own innovation power, China will lead the technology innovation.

To strengthen China's competitiveness, China will take the following steps:

1. Raise productivity and lower the unemployment rate.
2. Improve state-owned enterprises' efficiency and scale up private enterprises.
3. Push for products and enterprises upgrade.
4. Modernize education and scientific research system.
5. Protect environment and peaceful utilize world energy resources.
6. Form a stable financial and political circumstance.
7. Strengthen defense power to secure Chinese national interests.
8. Push for multi-polarized world for a peaceful growth environment.
9. Build up a rational social security system to narrow the poor-rich differences.
10. Develop a homogeneous economy for the whole nation.

China's influence becomes more and more important: China owns the biggest foreign reserve; China is the largest consumer of energy; China produces and consumes largest amount of cars, computers, TVs and mobile phones; China generates more electricity power than any other countries in the world, etc. With all rightful and rational efforts, China will be the leading driving force in economy for next 100 years after USA. When China's modernization level finally passes USA in about 100 years, Chinese economy will be four times bigger than that of USA, which is a huge goal to achieve for Chinese people and for any nation in the world by all measures.

CONCLUSION

China takes expansionary fiscal and monetary policies to deal with the global crisis, by investing huge capital to the infrastructures, reducing taxes for individuals and small businesses, cutting bank loan interest rates, lowering deposit reserve rates, etc. China achieved a 9.1% growth in 2009 for its GDP, which is a demonstration of its effective policies against global recession. This year, China will harvest an 11% growth as it is right in the track now. The global crisis forced China to reform its economic structure to put more emphasis on domestic consumption instead of export, which will significantly reduce the Chinese economic reliance on foreign economies and secure Chinese economy against future international crisis. China's position on international reserves is to use them as self insurance rather than an avenue for international leverage. Within this framework and if safety of its foreign assets can be assured, China can be cooperative with needy countries by providing financial support to them through international financial organizations. China made efforts to achieve substantial progress in the reform of international financial institutions. China wants the reform to increase the representation of developing countries. China *economy* wants an international financial governance system that allows China to play an bigger and rational role to form a financial atmosphere for smoother Chinese economy expansion globally. China will actively seek international opportunities to enhance its economy, such as Asian-pacific rim free economic zone, China-Africa regional cooperation, etc. All these policies will not only keep Chinese economy expansion as fast as usual and also will have a long term effect for Chinese economy to grow effectively.

By obeying the following two principles, China is going to handle all kinds of obstacles that hurdle china's economic growth and modernization development.

Principle 1: in all circumstances, there will be at least one field as a growth point whose growth and development will lead and drive the whole economy to grow.

Principle 2: to a developing economy, its growth will generally classified as two phases: quantitative growth and qualitative growth.

By using the first principle, China will adopt different growth points to drive its economy toward a fast and strong development, such as information industry as a growth point now, with environmental industry, energy industry, life industry, space industry following on. This principle means to any economy, at any situation, there is always one or few key growth fields that will break throw and grow fast to lead the whole economy to expand, either for the driving of raising people's living standard or by technology innovation. The more growth points, the larger the potential the economy grow, and the faster the economy will grow. For Chinese economy, right now, the growth points are lying for the enhancement and modernization of people's living conditions. For example, the information industry, auto industry, and materials industry, infrastructure industry, environmental industry, energy industry, transportation industry, etc. There are so many growth points which means Chinese economy can be stimulate to grow easily and will sustain for a long period fast expansion.

For the second principle, in the long run, China's economic development can be classified as two stages: first, China will try to get all its people a modernized living standard as fast as possible, that is to say, China will be a manufacture center of modern products. Chinese economy will expand real fast at this stage due to its huge population and its large demand for good living. I will call this stage the quantitative expansion period. In the second stage, China will expand its market and economy by technology innovation mainly, which I will call it a qualitative expansion stage. At this stage, China will use new technology products to create consumption and keep its people already-modernized living standard abreast with the brand new technology frontier. In the second stage, Chinese economic growth rate will significantly rely on scientific and technologic breakthroughs and shall be slower than the first stage. But with its largest human resources, China will be able to create more new products if Chinese education、scientific and research systems are effective.

In the long run, China's economic development can be classified as two stages: first, China will try to get all its people a modernized living standard as fast as possible, that is to say, China will be a manufacture center of modern products. Chinese economy will expand real fast at this stage due to its huge population and its large demand for good living. I will call this stage the quantitative expansion period. In the second stage, China will expand its market and economy by technology innovation mainly, which I will call it a qualitative expansion stage. At this stage, China will use new technology products to create consumption and keep its people already-modernized living standard abreast with the brand new technology frontier. In the second stage, Chinese economic growth rate will significantly rely on scientific and technologic breakthroughs and shall be slower than the first stage. But with its largest human resources, China will be able to create more new products if Chinese education、scientific and research systems are effective.

In about 20 years, China will reach the top of the world economy by overtaking USA. But Chinese average individual people's living standard is still 1/4 of USA. Urbanization has been one of the main driving forces and by some calculations the process is only half-complete. Despite all the progress since 1978, China is still a much poorer country than most people realize – it is not even in the top 100 in the International Monetary Fund's ranking of gross domestic product per capita. That means plenty of room to keep fast expanding. The 11 per cent growth in the third quarter of 2010 is still exceptional by historical standards, higher than Japan or South Korea's growth during their boom years. The last time the US grew that quickly was more than half a century ago.

China will keep its fast growth for another 20 years and will be the top driving force for world economy. China's modernization is a long and fast process. By finishing this process, China will contribute the world a 1.3 billion good living people and stronger economic growth engine than ever before and any other country in the world history. It is a beautiful thing to see China's run toward its modernization era.

REFERENCES

All data are from Chinese National Bureau of Statistics.

Liang-Xin Li, Research on the Quantitative Dynamic Structure of Shocks in Macroeconomics.

Business Cycle, *International Journal of Business and Management* Vol 5, No.6, 2010.

Chinese 30 years' reform, published by People's press, first edition, 2008.

Global Financial Stability Report: *Financial Stress and Deleveraging — Macro - Financial Implications and Policy* (Washington, October) International Monetary Fund (IMF), 2008.

World Development Report. Tsinghua University Press, 2006.

World Economic Outlook 2010, IMF.

In: Financial Crises
Editor: Cooper A. Hawthorne

ISBN: 978-1-62808-293-7

Chapter 7

LESSONS NOT LEARNED - ICELAND'S FINANCIAL CRISIS COMPARED TO THE NORDIC COUNTRIES

***Mar Wolfgang Mixa*[*,1] *and Throstur Olaf Sigurjonsson*[1,2]**
[1] Reykjavik University, Reykjavik, Iceland
[2] Copenhagen Business School, Frederiksberg Palace, Denmark

ABSTRACT

The financial crisis of 2008 had different effects on countries within the same regions of the world. The Nordic countries mostly sailed through the crisis smoothly, comparatively at least compared to the rest of Europe, with Iceland being the major exception. Finland, Sweden and Norway went through a financial crisis during the late 1980s and beginning of the 1990s, with Finland and Sweden experiencing an especially severe meltdown in their financial systems. These three countries seem to have learned from that experience some twenty years ago. Iceland, still in the early 1990s bound to political and economic restrictions, entered the recent financial crisis especially vulnerable. This research shows that warnings signs leading up to crises were very similar. All of the Nordic countries were caught in an overconfident mood and structural deficiencies.

Keywords: Financial crisis, Liberalization, Scandinavian crisis, Iceland

INTRODUCTION

Although the implications of the financial crisis that erupted during the fall of 2008 will take years to unfold in large parts of the world, Iceland´s crash during that period are becoming clear. The crash is in many ways historically unprecedented. The stock market lost within a few days about 90% of its market value (Halldorsson & Zoega, 2010), with all of its three major banks set into a liquidation process, having lost approximately half of their

[*] E-mail address: marmixa@ru.is

combined balance sheets. The losses of foreign creditors are enormous, currently estimated being in the area of $60 to $70 billion. That is the equivalent of almost twice the market value of all of Iceland´s property value, including land, hotels, offices, halls, summer cottages etc. (Mixa, 2010). It is generally accepted today that all possible factors in preventing such a collapse broke down, both within themselves and also interactively.

This happened within 20 years from Iceland´s last banking crisis in the early 1990s; one that became within a very short time span all but forgotten. Gylfason (2010) argues that the magnitude of the crisis in Iceland was similar to the severe and better documented crisis in the other Nordic countries[35] during the same period, with the Icelandic government allocating about 4-5% of the country´s GDP to prop up the banking system, a similar level as in the Nordic countries. Gylfason (2010) maintains that the government hid the losses by exerting very high spread in interest rates[36] and the absence of a stock market concealed the extent of the crises. Nordic countries have also felt the extent of the current global financial crisis, but to a much smaller degree than Iceland did. The Nordic societies resemble in many ways, often considered bearing similar value systems according to cross-cultural studies (Adalsteinsson, G. D., Gudmundsdóttir, S. and Gudlaugsson, 2011; Eyjolfsdottir & Smith, 1997; Olafsson, 2003), indicating that these nations would behave in a similar manner. The distinct difference of the magnitude of the recent crisis raises the question what main points differed in the creation of the recent financial bubble between those nations, which relates to how they possibly learned lessons from the 1990s crisis and to what degree those lessons were applied within the separate Nordic countries.

This paper compares the differences between the Nordic countries during the build-up of the financial crisis, focusing on the similarity and possible contrasts, illuminating the magnitude of the asset bubble in Iceland. The comparison explores differences between the countries′ public policy area, social trends and possible explanations of why such similar countries from standard cultural standpoints differ as much in their financial behavior. However, an underlying question throughout this discussion is what went wrong within the banking institutions and how the changes within the public policy arena (itself being influenced by general social trends) may have contributed to the crisis.

Firstly, this paper will examine the main reasons for the sudden and extraordinary growth of the Icelandic banks. We review and compare trends in part two concerning the increased vulnerability of the banks and the following collapse in Iceland set in contrast to other Nordic banks. This involves an examination of similarities between the two subjects, and the identification of factors that are unique between Iceland and the rest of the Nordic nations. Lastly, is a short summary regarding what lessons may be learned from the recent crisis and what policy recommendations can be derived from this experience. Of special interest is the fact that the crisis occurred within a banking environment where the separation of investment and commercial was no longer intact in the U.S., following the abolishment of the Glass-Steagall Act of 1999, which resulted in the banking landscape changing worldwide: meaning that banks' risk appetite increased. We maintain that such complacency spread to the general

[35] Reinhart and Rogoff define the Nordic countries' crisis as being among the five ,"big ones" in their historical overview of banking crises since WWII.

[36] The high interest rate spread gave banks, that were almost exclusively state owned, the opportunity to make massive profits on the interest rate differential, which was much higher than is normal within banking industries. It can thus be argued that the costs were to a large extent born by all who were either lenders or borrowers, lenders receiving much lower interest for their money and borrowers paying much higher interest cost, around 7-8% real interest rates, than under normal conditions.

public as well. After the abolishment of the act, it took less than a decade for the international banking system to collapse, the meltdown being worst in Iceland. Our starting point is thus 1999 in our comparisons in this paper, along with some historical overview.

Iceland's Short Banking History

Iceland became in 1994 one of the founding members of the European Economic Area (EEA) agreement which granted Icelandic banks the right to operate within the border of the EU countries. At the same time, Iceland instituted the EU regulatory framework for financial institutions and markets. Still, it was not until 2003 with the privatization of the Icelandic public banks that they multiplied their size by capitalized money market funding, opened branches abroad and acquired foreign financial institutions in large numbers (Sigurjonsson, 2010a). Only five years later Iceland experienced the worst financial collapse of any western country when its banking system collapsed in fall 2008. The bankruptcy of the three largest banks (with $182 billion in assets) combined created the second largest credit default collapse after Lehman Brothers (Bibler, 2010).

The combined Icelandic banking industry had total assets of approximately the same amount as Iceland's GDP during the beginning of the century (Halldorsson & Zoega, 2010), swelled to approximately 7 to 8 times its country's GDP in less than ten years. The drivers for this growth were favorable international conditions, a mature domestic market and an investment banking style established partnership with major clients in their fast growing international M&A deal making. The partnership did not only consist of lending but became, in many instances, joint ventures in which banks invested their own equity in projects in which their clients were involved. That gave later rise to speculation regarding conflict of interests and dependence on a few large customers, some of whom were the largest owners of the banks and were not necessarily geographically diversified nor diversified by industry (Portes and Baldursson, 2007).

The governance style that characterized the Icelandic banks had its source in the ownership structure. That structure had its origin in the privatization of the public banks, a process conducted somewhat differently from privatization in many other countries. Many countries privatized their banks with at least some foreign ownership whereas the Icelandic government initially decided to encourage foreign ownership, but then backed away from that decision. Instead, individual domestic entities gained controlling interests in the banks, being investors with no prior experience in banking but with considerable ownership in other industries (Sigurjonsson, 2010b). This resulted couple of years later in criticism coming from abroad on potential cross ownership and lack of transparency (Central Bank of Iceland, 2006a: Valgreen, 2006). When cross-ownership in Iceland was scrutinized, the lack of transparency was evident and corporate governance within the banks became a real issue. A leak of one of the bank's loan book unveils unusual lending practices[37] generally identified as being crony lending. The highest loans (5.5 billion Euros) were given to companies that were related to six clients, four of them were major shareholders in the bank. Collateral was none or only partial (Morgunbladid, 2009). The Icelandic banks, over a period of a few years, had leveraged their capital base to buy up banking assets worth several times Iceland's GDP and

[37] See wikileaks: http://wikileaks.org/leak/kaupthing-bank-before-crash-2008.pdf.

the potential depreciation of assets made the leveraged banking sector highly vulnerable. Furthermore, little leeway was left for declining assets values, which had been mostly purchased during the years of the banking and credit boom period of 2003-2007, which caused the banks' equity to dry up. Neither the National Treasury nor the Central Bank of Iceland had the necessary foreign reserves to support any of the larger banks. A lender of last resort in foreign currency, therefore, did not exist in Iceland's post-privatization era.

In 2007, liquidity difficulties were beginning to accumulate when severe flaws in the US housing credit market were revealed. Trust within financial markets was diminished and the trouble only accelerated in 2008. Financing through bond markets became difficult and at the same time, assets became less liquid. The Icelandic banks became a gauge of the negative effects to come. Their assets became extremely vulnerable and when creditors began believing that other creditors would refuse to roll over present loans and extend new credit the banks lost all remaining credibility. This is a classic situation that leads to the failure of banks.

A point of no return for the Icelandic banks was reached. After the fall of Lehman Brothers in September 2008, a bank run began, not on a single Icelandic bank, but the complete Icelandic financial system. Interestingly, all of the Icelandic banks had passed stress tests only a few weeks earlier (FSA, 2008), but these stress tests did not account for vulnerability to a liquidity nor currency crisis.

COMPARISON OF CRISES

A study by Reinhart and Rogoff (2008) has identified 18 financial crises from WWII until 2007 when the subprime crash unfolded. Among the five "Big Ones" are the crises in Norway, Sweden and Finland at the beginning of the 1990s.[38] They conclude that the crises followed a similar pattern although tipping point in each case seems to differ. The crisis' usually follow a pattern which is a change in regulations that leads to some sort of increase in lending (Easy Money) that develops into an asset bubble. When such bubbles burst, especially related to real estate, asset prices tumble with the consequence of mass bankruptcies. Losses related to write-offs and asset depreciation causes a banking crisis that, along with a currency crisis, exacerbates losses especially in circumstances where financing during the bubble has been performed via loans denominated in foreign currencies. The consequence is a contraction in loans to companies that are still in business, adding further pressure on a systematic collapse and necessary governmental interference to assist the financial system (Englund, 1999).

This chapter focuses on the crises in the Nordic countries with a main emphasis of comparing Iceland to other Nordic countries. This involves concrete financial data, corporate governance, legislation issues and differences between cultures affecting financial behavior. Although all countries had endured a major financial crisis prior to the one occurring 2008, the lessons those neighboring countries seem to have differed greatly.

---

[38] The crash in Norway actually occurred in 1987-1989 but is generally scaled towards 1990 in comparison studies. External factors, with the aid of 20/20 hindsight vision, merely hastened an inevitable process of a trend that occurred there in a similar fashion as in the comparison countries.

All countries had similar banking systems before the seeds of destruction were sown, with highly restrictive banking systems. That ensured that banking crisis were unlikely but with the costs of highly inefficient systems where political purposes dominated often lending decisions. There was hence a need of added efficiency with increased liberalization within the banking industry. The processes of added liberalization differed somewhat between countries, but the start and ending points were similar in nature (Englund, Vihriala, 2003). The main characteristics were the liberation of interest rates and the free flow of capital in international markets, importantly including financing (Jonung, Kiander, Vartia, 2008).

The new financial landscape escaped regulators in Sweden where the laws remained largely unchanged following the rapid development and in addition, changes to the tax system resulted in incentives for households and corporations to increase lending (Honkapohja, 2009). Whilst the liberalization process took less than a decade in Scandinavia from start to finish, with the indirect effects in increased lending taking three to four years to materialize, the period in Iceland was much longer.

The main years of liberalization were 1982 to 1986 for Scandinavia but for Iceland it was 1984 to 2003. However, the lending growth period was immediate in Scandinavia from 1986 to 1990; while in Iceland such growth started during the latter part of the 1990s but the explosive growth, leading to the bust, began after 2003. Nevertheless, the seeds of growth were planted once the interbank lending started in 1998, which quickly spread to add fluidity in currency market dealings.

The starting point for the comparison period may appear subjective. When comparing lending growth to assess how the banking systems expanded, we look at the start of the liberalization process as a starting point in Scandinavia, i.e. in 1982. In Iceland, the liberalization process began during a similar period, but took longer and the effects were for a long time barely visible. We, therefore, use 1999 as the starting point in Iceland, which is four years prior to the lending boom really taking hold (which is the same as the Scandinavians starting point), but also an approximation of when the liberalization process began in reality to change the Icelandic financial landscape. At that time, the privatization processes in two of the three Icelandic state owned banks had just begun coinciding with the implementation of rapid changes.

Using the above assumptions, we use the year 1982 as the starting point for Scandinavia in this paper and 17 years later for Iceland. Thus, we define year 1999 as Period 0 or T for Iceland and 1982 or T minus 17 for Scandinavia. The length of periods differs somewhat, mainly because some data is no longer available after the Icelandic banks went into default[39].

Expansion of the Banks' Balance Sheets Prior to Banking Crises

Following the liberalization process, the banks in Scandinavia decreased their emphasis on services and cost structure, and instead began to concentrate on pricing and added market

[39] We do not use Denmark in the first comparison because despite a banking crisis occurring there during the early 1990s, it was considerably less severe. This is in line with most research on the banking crisis from that period focusing usually on Finland, Sweden and to a lesser extent Norway. Denmark is however, used in later sections when comparing economic behavior between Nordic countries.

share. This resulted in additional risk taking (Honkapohja, 2009) and loans to new markets followed. However, financial institutions were working in a new environment where their ability to measure risk adequately became more difficult (Berg, 1998).

Initially the lending increase caused no alarm. After a long period of lending restriction, in which real rates were negative and thus there was some sort of privilege associated with receiving loans, a higher lending equilibrium was to be expected. Added demand for money caused interest rates to rise, leading to an increased rate difference between domestic rates and international rates. This made borrowing in foreign denominated currency even more tempting within the environment of free capital flow, making interest rate policies in Scandinavia increasingly toothless (Honkapohja, 2009). Due to the pegging of domestic currencies to the German Mark, domestic loan takers perceived the likelihood of currency losses to be minimal. Berg (1998) maintains that without the foreign capital inflow the increased lending growth would have been impossible.

The bank privatization process began in Iceland 1997 with the aim of establishing a widely distributed ownership structure. The policy change in 2003, amid the controlling interest in two of the three main banks falling into the hands of investor groups with little banking experience, set the stage for the banks' transformation in which lending growth exploded in Iceland. As in Scandinavia a few years earlier, the Icelandic banks (with savings banks following suit) began to concentrate on market share and pricing with added risk associated to their business model. The true explosive lending growth period thus began in 2003 in Iceland, 17 years after the same development in Scandinavia.

We compare two different periods yet side by side, the starting point defined for Iceland is 1999 and 1982 for other Nordic nations, in line with assumptions previously explained.

Comparison of the Creation of Bubbles

A major difference between the underlying growth between Iceland and its Nordic counterparts was the type of lending. Icelandic bankers did not restrict their increased lending to households and companies that caused this increase. Icelandic banks evolved quickly from being traditional commercial banks into becoming investment banks who took positions in their commercial customers' projects. Jannari (2009) explains this by stating that the majority holders who gained control in 2002-2003 had a mindset more like investment bankers rather than commercial bankers. Incentive systems were enacted in line with common features abroad where short term profits were paramount. This created an atmosphere in which the main objective was getting a deal done, as percentages of loans provided could be around 0.3% to 0.4% in the form of bonuses. As one banker we interviewed explained; if you did the numbers diligently before agreeing to the deal, another one across the street skipped the hard work, got the deal and gained the bonuses. The system was basically set that way up since those bonuses were given regardless of long-term consequences and inherent risks associated with the deals. In fact, as McLean and Elkind (2003) described the situation with Enron a few years earlier, an incentive scheme evolved in which it became advantageous to minimize the potential risk associated with deals taking place in order to make sure that they were completed and thus commissions paid.

Recent information (for example, the leaked loan book of Kaupthing Bank) indicates that the loans were not merely ill considered but were even questionable from legal and ethical standpoints. The collateral for loans was in an abnormally low percentage range or even simply only the equity being used to buy by use of the loans. In some instances, such loans were used to finance purchases of the bank's own shares, so in effect banks were lending money to buy shares in themselves, with those shares being the only collateral (Special Investigation Commission, 2010).

As with Japan in the late 1980s, where loans were increasingly made to holding companies with the main purpose of investing in other companies (Chancellor, 1999), loans by Icelandic banks were often related to cross-ownership or other relations between parties in which dubious collateral was placed (Jannari, 2009). This was not a concern in Scandinavia (Jonung, 2008). Figure 1 shows the increase in total lending Icelandic holding companies scaled to April 2005, compared to the growth in lending to domestic households, many of whose sole purpose was investing in equities of other companies (Jannari, 2009).

Despite the frenzied increase in lending to households, it pales compared to the increase in lending to holding companies. Often with little (if any) collateral on the table, the owners of the holding companies stood a chance of striking it rich if they were successful in their investments, while the end result is that bondholders and taxpayers have picked up the entire amount of the tab associated with such loans.

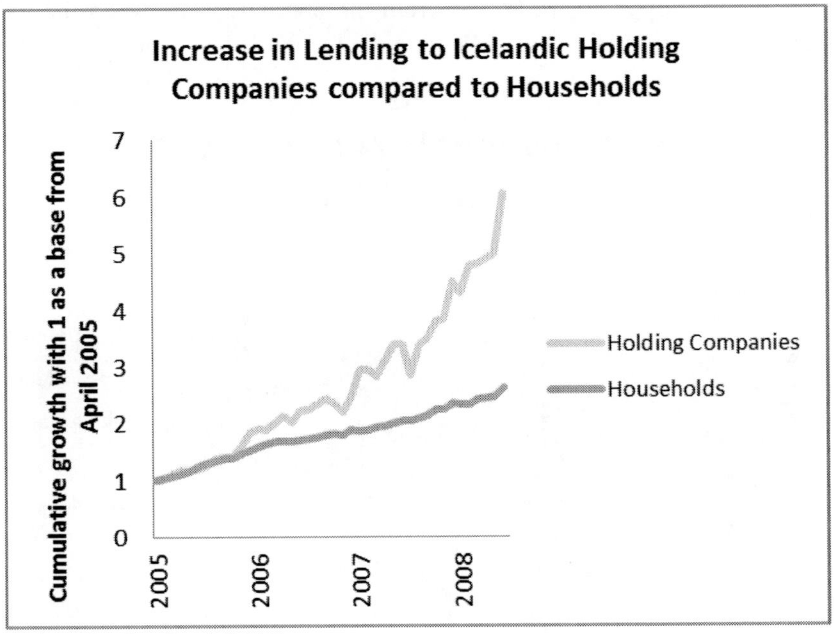

Source: Central Bank of Iceland (2009).

Figure 1. Lending Growth to Icelandic Holding Companies and Households.

With increased lending within the Icelandic system aimed more at holding companies rather than households and traditional business lending, with additional investments within banks as an increasing part of the picture with added ways to increase leverage, it should come as no surprise that the balance sheet growth was immense. Compared to Nordic nations prior to their banking crisis in the early 1990s, the cumulative growth rate of the size of

Icelandic banks' balance sheets was approximately 3 times as much during the 9 years prior to the crash in 2008.

One explanation of why the negative effects of liberalization filtered down so late into the Icelandic financial system is that the government retained its controlling stake in the banking system whilst the changes were taking effect. Thus, despite the free flow of capital, there were implicit restrictions on lending growth. That is not to say that lending growth was non-existent during those years; but during that period it was understandable due to the easing of lending restrictions leading to a natural higher lending equilibrium.

UNEMPLOYMENT, GDP AND (ASSET) INFLATION DURING THE 2000S

This section compares economic behavior during a same comparable period, which is 1999-2000 in order to see difference in economic behavior before the crash in fall 2008. The balance sheet growth comparison shows how much banks expanded before historical crises. This section compares the same period side by side in order to gain an insight of how much the countries learned from the crisis all nations faced in the early 1990s. Although the starting point for most countries shows unemployment within what is generally considered as being a normal range, it had dropped considerably from the previous years when the rate had in all countries gone up, especially Finland, following the banking bust during the early 1990s.

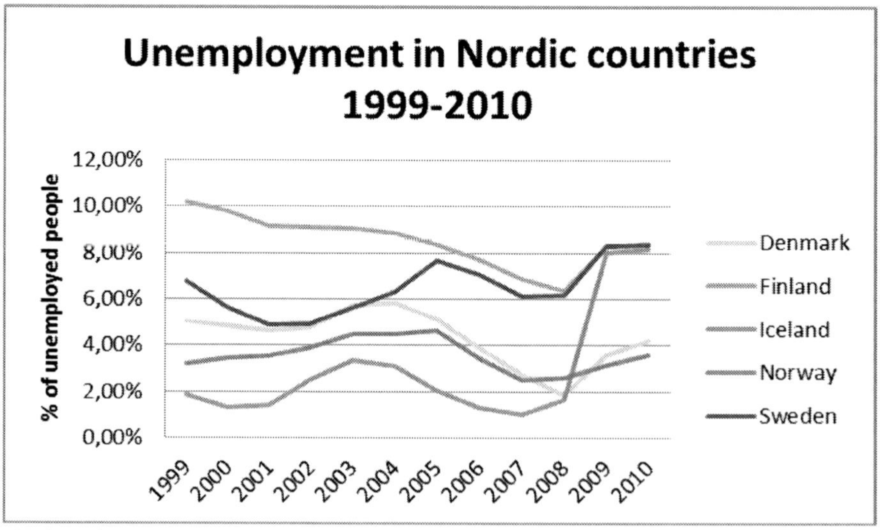

Source: IMF (2011).

Figure 2. Unemployment % Comparison – Iceland vs. Scandinavia.

As Figure 2 demonstrates, Iceland experienced almost non-unemployment during the euphoric part of the 2000s. It was to some degree explained by major construction projects that amounted to 11%-12% of GDP, with migrant workers flocking to Iceland during this period, with the number of foreign nationals residing in Iceland rising fivefold 1995 to 2007 (Loftsdottir, 2010). Other Nordic unemployment numbers were closer to the norm in western societies. Finland gradually saw its number decrease while Sweden and Norway hovered around 6% and 4% respectively. Denmark remarkably saw its unemployment numbers hit a record low only a few months before the 2008 financial crisis initially hit full force.

It is interesting that Denmark and Norway saw unemployment numbers only rise moderately since the crash but Iceland experienced unemployment that has not been experienced for decades (IMF, 2012) despite substantial emigration in 2009 and 2010 with a bit over 1% of the nation moving abroad in seeking work (Olafsson, 2011).

All the Nordic countries saw their GDP levels contract and even become negative during banking busts that developed during the early 1990s. GDP levels in all Nordic countries, however, reached the norm of 2-4% annual GDP growth in prior decades by the end of the 1990s. As Figure 3 demonstrates, GDP growth contracted 2001-2003 in tandem with international developments but returned back to normalcy a few years later.

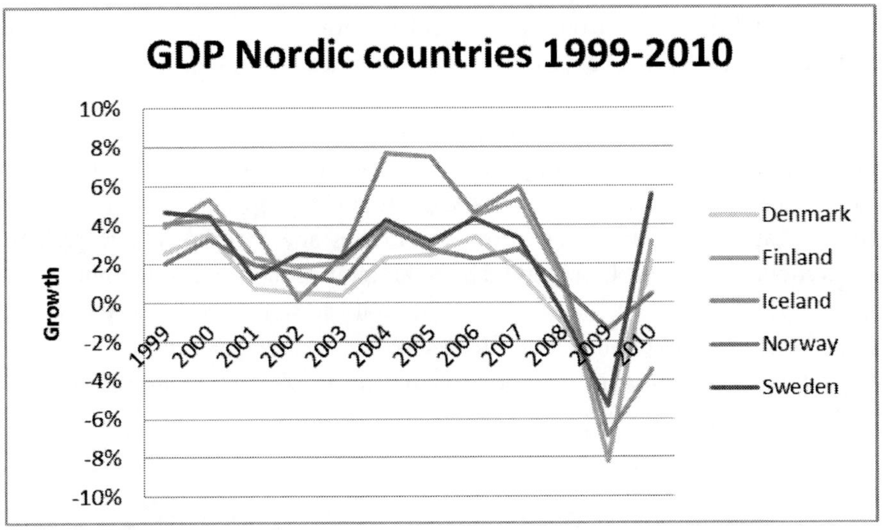

Source: IMF (2011).

Figure 3. Real GDP Growth Comparison – Iceland vs. Scandinavia.

The exception was Iceland once the boom period took hold, where annual GDP growth 2003-2007 was on average well over 6%, it hovered in Finland and Sweden around 4% and Denmark and Norway slightly below 3%. Municipalities engaged during the same period in various projects keeping demand for labor high, whilst adding their debt level to finance for example the construction of new buildings, many of which have since been written off by foreign creditors. Increased activity in the building industry most likely resulted in a great amount of Iceland's GDP growth. Such activities were caused by the massive expansion in consumer loans related to housing, which had poor foundations and was thus at least partly illusory. In his recent book, The Great Depression of Debt, Warren Brussee estimates that such an increase due to increased debt amounted to 70% of an illusory rise in the US GDP during the boom years of the 2000s (Brussee, 2009), which simply must be "paid" in some form later. The unemployment level in Iceland was thus in a way unsustainable since it was built upon a foundation in which the future was mortgaged for current GDP growth during those years.

The comparison of inflation is somewhat problematic. Iceland´s average annual inflation rate since 1940 is 16% (geometrical average is little below 15%) with inflation during 1980s only once creeping below 20% on an annual basis (Statistics Iceland, 2013). Despite leveling off a great deal during the 1990s it shot up again during the following decade, with average inflation in Iceland just above 5%, usually about twice the inflation in the other Nordic countries (Mixa, 2010). With this historic trend in mind, one could say that inflation in Iceland was relatively mild during the boom years as seen in Figure 4, It hardly ever still got down to the Central Bank's inflation goal of 2.5%. More worrisome was the fact that underlying inflation was in a sense camouflaged through the strength of the Icelandic Krona (ISK), making imports cheaper than otherwise. Domestic factors were thus the main causation of added inflation.

The inflation spike witnessed 2008 and 2009 was thus partially a due to a reversal of a currency high yield trend that was so severe that currency restrictions were set up under an emergency law, one step away from in effect seizing foreign creditors money. What had kept inflation back for a few years came in a sudden full force as imports spiked up in Icelandic krona prices.

Adding insult to injury, many Icelandic companies had seemingly been operating in a stable and profitable manner. No study has been done yet in this particular field, as far as the authors are aware, but many annual reports show that by comparing EBITDA numbers to net loans and fixed assets, under normal currency circumstances companies were losing money on their operations. However, by having a huge amount of their loans denominated in foreign currencies, interest costs were little[40], with artificially low interest rates and an increasingly strong ISK. Once the ISK depreciated, the strengthening reversed and exposed the 'hidden' risk via currency fluctuations in financing, leading to many companies' equity disappearing almost overnight.

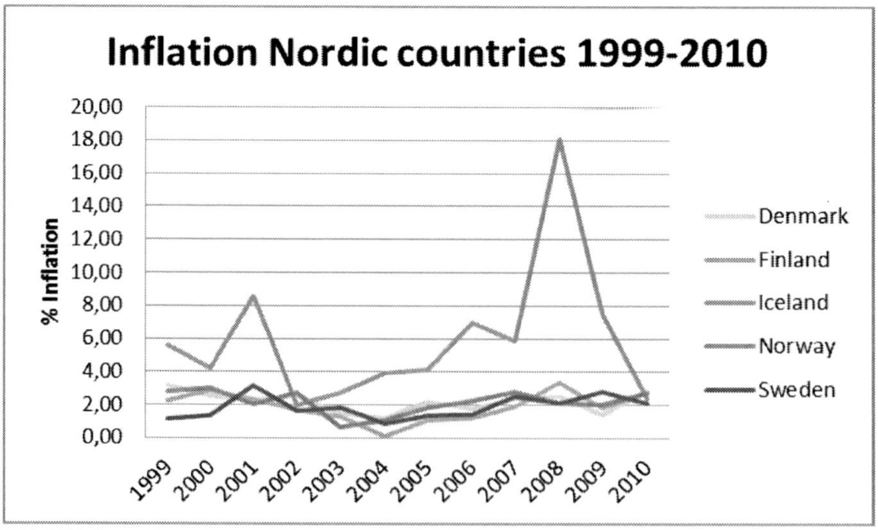

Source: IMF (2011).

Figure 4. Inflation % (end of period) Nordic Countries.

[40] Currency costs were even shown in many cases as profits since the debt measured in Icelandic currency was shrinking.

Therefore, measuring asset inflation during this period is difficult. The underlying factors that were taking place did not necessary show up in normal studies. A simple approach is looking at the nominal inflation price of real estate, which takes inflation, underlying inflation to some extent, and the level of risk appetite into account. It also measures the consequences of access to money, or M1. This development was extreme in Iceland. The government decided to raise the Loan-to-Value (LTV) ratio in a few steps during 2001 until 2004 from 65% to 90%. People began to take advantage of this by taking mortgage loans that were partially government sponsored in an indirect way and using the money, not only for household purposes, but also to increase spending and paying down overdraft loans. The banks responded in 2004 by lowering interest rates even more and in the spirit of gaining market share one bank began offering 100% LTV loans[41]. The fierce competition led to a negative interest rate spread. One of the major savings banks, for example, financed itself via long-term bonds paying 4.90% to 5.20% interest but lent its customers at the same time money to finance real estate at 4.15% (NASDAQ OMX Nordic (2009).

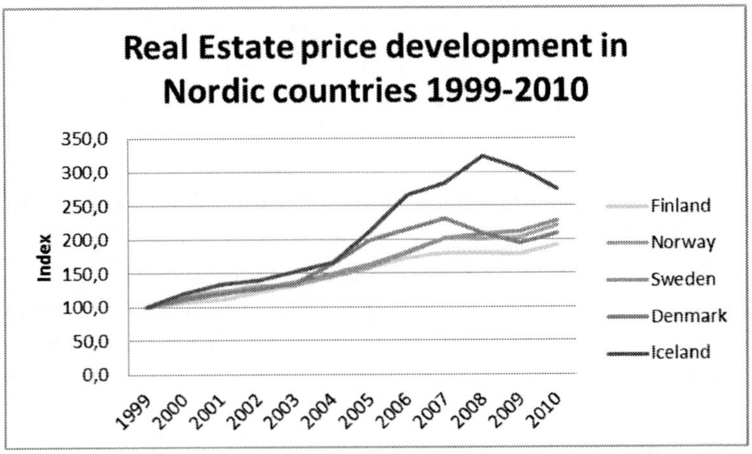

Sources: Statistics Finland, Statistics Norway, Statistics Sweden, Statistics Denmark and the Icelandic Property Registry (2011).

Figure 5. Real Estate Nominal Price Inflation Comparison (index set at 100 as starting point).

Figure 5 shows that the paths of Iceland and the other Nordic countries during the first comparative years in this study were similar. As the LTV ceiling was raised in Iceland, banks entered the market with lower interest rates and higher ceilings of lending amounts. This combination of increased lending, often termed "easy money," and increased wealth via stock ownership manifested itself in higher real estate prices.

Stock Market and Saving Comparisons during the 2000s

Another way to measure asset inflation is looking at the stock market. That can be tricky for a period stretching over a decade. During recent decades, GDP growth has been stable in

[41] http://www.sa.is/files/Sp%E11%-EDkan%20um%20%EDb%FA%F0afj%E1rfestingar_1723061657.pdf

most western countries, with price fluctuations often related to the swings in interest rates (Ilmanen, 2010). Despite interest rates fluctuations being rather mild in Iceland, and if anything, interest rates generally rising from 2003 (has in general a negative effect on stock prices), stocks in Iceland rose with a vengeance that is historically almost unknown in historical terms, worldwide.

Stocks in Nordic countries followed the general worldwide trend of rising a great deal in 1999 and showing gains for at least the most part of 2000. This took a quick turnaround when the tech bubble burst in 2001 with most major stock indices falling. The Swedish and Finnish stock market indices plummeted because of the heavy market weighting of Ericsson and Nokia respectively, both companies becoming major victims in the meltdown of companies in the tech industry. Their stock market, however, recovered with the banking sector being among the highest risers. Stocks in Denmark did not rose and fell less during the early stages but their ascent compared to Swedish and Finnish stock markets was slightly higher 2002-2008. Norway, however, saw only moderate gains and losses during the early stage of the comparison period, but enjoyed a phenomenal rise in stock returns after the surge of oil prices began and a rise in prices of banking stocks, with the major stock index's value rising more than 4x in value in 5 years from fall 2002 to fall 2007. Not only were those banks increasing profits but Icelandic banks began pursuing takeovers of such companies as the Finnish insurance company Sampo and the Norwegian life insurance company, driving their stock prices even higher up.

The rise in value of Icelandic stocks, however, dwarfed the other Nordic returns. The main stock exchange returned higher or the same returns each year in 2003, 2004 and 2005 than the best calendar year in the US during the previous century, 54% in 1933 (Fridson, 1998), with returns of 54%, 57% and 60% respectively. The stock index rose almost 7x from fall 2002 to fall 2007. This happened despite the fact that the weighted stock index of Iceland compromised mainly of banks, a sector not historically known for wild appreciation in stock prices.

This meant that not only had Icelanders easy access to money but their wealth kept on increasing with an increasingly higher worth of real estate and stocks. The above factors demonstrate not only an overheating of the economy, but also how the general population perceived the economy, i.e. added optimism leads to added consumerism. Therefore a vicious cycle forms, in which the main driver of economic growth is consumption (of various forms) financed by loans. In a sense, the current lifestyle is, in a similar manner as low unemployment and high GDP growth, funded by sacrificing the future, although that is usually not the general perception at such a given point. Carey (2009) points out that the savings ratio of Iceland was negative during the boom years, 2003 to 2007.

Households felt the wealth effect resulting in a lesser need to continue being financially thrift and even begin spending beyond what they produced within the nation, with the savings ratio in Iceland hitting negative territories in 2008.

Norway saved a remarkable percentage of their GDP, ranging from the high 30s during the early part of the period to the low 40s during the later part, when oil prices had gone from a historical low in 1999 up to a historical high only a decade later. This is partially due to their policy of setting the state's profits from the oil industry in a special fund[42]. The other Nordic countries savings ratio hovered between 20-30%.

[42] Commonly known as the Oil Fund.

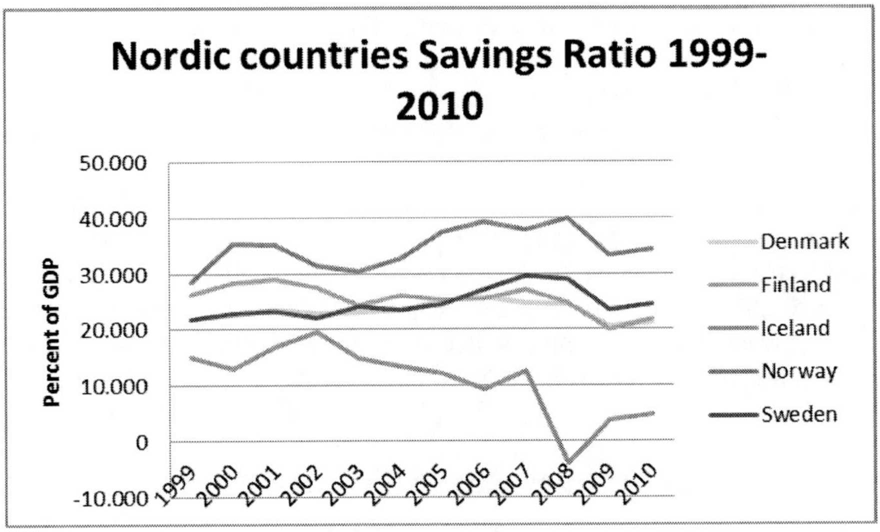

Source: IMF (2011).

Figure 6. Saving ratios in Nordic Countries.

As previously mentioned, the high interest rate policy of the Central Bank may have increased underlying inflation, being expansionary in a sense. However, the monetary policy regarding Easy Money was clearly accommodating; broad based monetary aggregates such as M1 grew above 20% or more every year from 2002 until the crash (Bagus & Howden, 2009).

Berg (1998) asserts that the Scandinavian banks would have not been able to increase their lending growth without access to foreign capital. This was the case in Iceland also, where people with loans in foreign currencies had enjoyed favorable interest rates for years and even had their underlying debts decrease in value due to the strength of the ISK. This was further amplified when people see others making money by speculative trading (not limited to the stock market but even to a larger degree housing loans in foreign denominated currencies), adding a tendency to follow the crowd. Kindleberger described this as "Monkey see, monkey do" (Kindleberger, 1996). Thus, by adding insult to injury, in the expansionary climate Icelanders began increasing their appetite for foreign loans considerably as the boom period continued.

The ever-increasing appetite for increased debts, and thus less inclination to save, made Iceland look less like other Nordic countries and more like countries that have dominated international financial news for all the wrong reasons in the aftermath of the banking crash in 2008.

CONCLUSION

Despite the Scandinavian crisis being defined as one of the five "Big Ones" by Rogoff and Reinhart, Iceland shows, by a wide margin, more significant signs of over-expansion in practically all aspects. An obvious question is how Iceland came to be a victim of such (a similar) euphoria so shortly after a similar crisis by their neighbours. Monetary issues are not the sole explanation. Galbraith (1997) maintains that credit has on numerous occasions (for instance both before and after the "Roaring Twenties") been easy without causing speculation. As with added liberalization, easy money by itself does not cause unsound speculation leading to disaster. Galbraith states that the mood is far more important than the rate of interest, some sort of conviction that ordinary people should be rich. The answer is in short provided by Reinhart and Rogoff (2009). Icelanders, in line with a common syndrome associated with financial crises, thought that they were smarter and had learned from past mistakes; such crises only happened to other people during other times. The reality was that not only had Icelanders not learned from past mistakes, but there are vast indications that past mistakes were visible both qualitatively and quantitatively. Striking similarities are also to be found in recent examples in Argentina a decade ago, Asia during the 1990s, and even the "Roaring Twenties" in the US (Mixa, 2009).

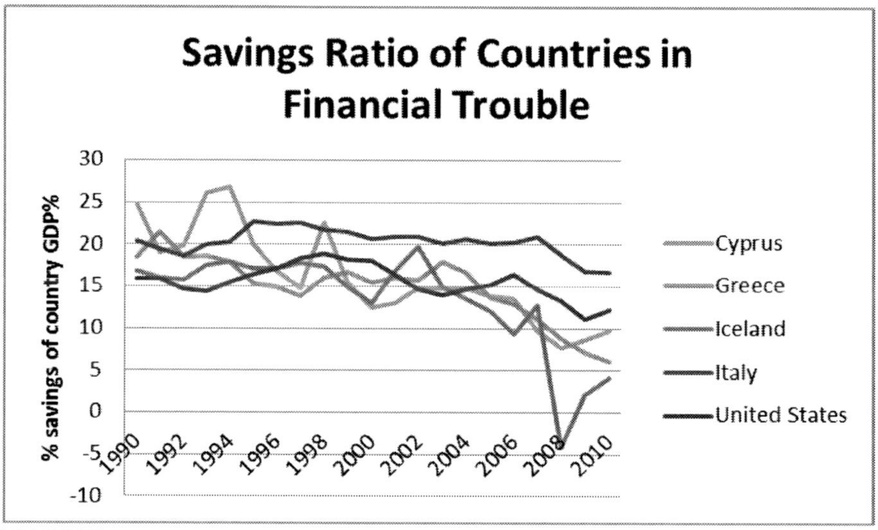

Source: IMF (2012).

Figure 8. Saving ratios in Countries in Financial Trouble.

Iceland imitated all the main features of Scandinavia such as increased liberalization, a real estate boom, huge lending increase and an increased amount of foreign capital flow. As the increase of lending to holding companies shows, lending growth was not only more prevalent in Iceland but had an added category where risk taking among insiders took constantly a bigger share of the lending pie. Such added risk appetite was also prevalent in banks' increased exposure in direct ownership of companies.

Business practices in Iceland became questionable and of such a scale that they ultimately facilitated the collapse of the Icelandic economy. The close-knit society, partially created by managerial relationships, cross-ownership and cross lending, established imbalances in favor of business over regulatory authority. This consequence was an extensive collapse; if one link in the chain was to fail a domino effect throughout the entire economy was certain to follow. As pointed out in this paper, this was not a problem in the other Nordic countries (Jonung, 2008). The foreign criticism from financial institutions, rating agencies and foreign media in 2006 did not manage to influence the general discussion in the Icelandic media in such a way that the international expansion of the Icelandic banks was scaled down. On the contrary, the growth only escalated.

One possible reason why things got so out of control in Iceland is that the Icelandic banks operated as if they were investment banks. In the shadow of the Great Depression, the Glass-Steagall Act was enacted in 1933, separating commercial banking and investment banking. During the Scandinavian crisis, those walls still held. They were, however, abolished 1999 and it was within that landscape that the Icelandic banks grew so quickly. It took the international banking system less than a decade to collapse after investment banking again became part of commercial banking. Icelandic banks, expanding partially because they had some sort of governmental guarantee, were the worst culprits and, as such, suffered the worst consequences. This questions how systematic the crash was in reality, whether the similarity of the buildup created the circumstance in which all of the banks stood a chance of failing within parameters of certain negative events, with or without domino effects.

The recent experience in Iceland and the one in Scandinavia two decades ago suggest that fiscal and monetary policies must involve consistent goals. Interest rate tools within an environment of free flow of capital were used in both instances, in Iceland with the aim of keeping inflation at bay with a floating currency whilst the Scandinavian countries aimed at stabilizing the economy by pegging their currencies. History shows that both these courses become toothless once speculation within an environment of rising asset inflation. The real rate of interest was disguised with foreign denominated loans freely available. During the prelude to the crash of 1929, the rate of interest of some margin loans for stock purchases went to 40-50% with added collateral required (Rappoport & White, 1994) without dampening the amount of speculation since the stock market had become a cornerstone in a sociological sense (Galbraith, 1997).

Much discussion has revolved around the effects of added liberalization in Scandinavia. Englund (1999) maintains that such a view simplifies reality. Demirgüç-Kunt and Detragiache (1998) find that a financial crisis occurs more likely in an unregulated environment, especially where a lack of respect is for the rule of law and corruption is widely spread. They find, however, no correlation between financial crises and changes from a tightly controlled banking system to a liberated one. Englund (1999) concludes that what counts is a balanced macro environment in keeping the financial system stable within a deregulated environment. While the costs of inefficiency were high in a tightly regulated market, recent experience shows that not do markets require some sort of regulations, but as Jonung has pointed out in 2012[43], their interrelatedness with each other and society demonstrates the importance of viewing and regulating them a part of a holistic system, both economically and social wise.

REFERENCES

[1] Adalsteinsson, G.D., Gudmundsdottir, S. & Gudlaugsson, T.O. (2011). Islensk thjodmenning i ljosi menningarvidda Hofstede [Icelandic Cultural Nationality within Hofstede's Culture Dimensions]. http://skemman.is/handle/1946/10399

[2] Bagus, P. & Howden, J. D. (2009). Iceland's banking crisis: The meltdown of an interventionist financial system. http://www.hayek.sk/wp-content/uploads/2012/12/deep_freeze.pdf.

[43] A lecture Lars Jonung gave at the Central Bank of Iceland in 2012.

[3] Berg, S. (1998). Bank failures in Scandinavia. In J. E. Hughes & S. B. MacDonald (Eds.), *International banking: Text and cases*, (pp. 198-207). Hong Kong: Pearson Education Asia Limited and Tsinghua University Press.
[4] Bibler, J. (2010). Hversu mikið var fall íslensku bankanna á heimsmælikvarða? [How extensive was the fall of the Icelandic banks internationally?]. http://fme.is/?PageID=14&NewsID=521.
[5] Brussee, W. (2009). *The great depression of debt: Survival techniques for every investor*. Hoboken: John Wiley & Sons, Inc.
[6] Carey, D. (2009). Iceland: The financial and economic crisis. http://www.olis.oecd.org/olis/2009doc.nsf/LinkTo/NT000069D2/$FILE/JT03271463.PDF
[7] Central Bank of Iceland. (2009). Advantages and disadvantages of changing Iceland's monetary policy framework. http://www.sedlabanki.is/lisalib/getfile.aspx?itemid=7219
[8] Central Bank of Iceland. (2006a). Fitch Ratings revises Iceland's outlook to negative. http://www.sedlabanki.is/?PageID=287 &NewsID=1124
[9] Central Bank of Iceland. (2006b). The Economy of Iceland. http://www.sedlabanki.is/lisalib/getfile.aspx?itemid=4689
[10] Chancellor, E. (2000). *Devil take the hindmost: A history of financial speculation*. New York: Plume.
[11] Demirgüç-Kunt, A. & Detragiache, E. (1998). Financial liberation and financial fragility. http://siteresources.worldbank.org/DEC/Resources /84797-1251813753820/6415739-1251813951236/demirguc.pdf
[12] Englund, P. (1999). The Swedish banking crisis: Roots and consequences. *Oxford Review of Economic Policy, 15*(3), 80-97.
[13] Englund P. & Vihrala V. (2003). *Financial crises in developed economies: The cases of Sweden and Finland*. Stockholm: Handelshogskolan.
[14] Eyjolfsdottir, H.M. & Smith, P.B. (1997). Icelandic business and management culture. *Int. Studies of Mgt. & Org., 26*, No 3, 66. 61-72.
[15] Fridson, Martin S. (1998). *It was a very good year: Extraordinary moments in stock market history*. New York: John Wiley & Sons.
[16] FSA. (2008). Stress test. http://www.fme.is/?PageID=168.
[17] FSA. (2009). Annual report. http://fme.is/?PageID=531.
[18] Galbraith, J. K. (1997). *The Great Crash*. New York: Mariner Books.
[19] Gylfason, T. (2011). Events in Iceland: skating on thin ice? In Aliber R.Z. & Zoega, G. (Ed.), *Preludes to the Icelandic financial crisis* (pp. 290-295). London: Palgrave Macmillan.
[20] Halldorsson, O. G. & Zoega, G. (2010) Iceland's Financial Crisis in an International Perspective. http://www.hi.is/files/skjol/felagsvisindasvid/ deildir/hagfraedi/2010/GZ_OGH_iceland-paper-10october2010x.pdf
[21] Honkapohja, S., & Koskela, E. (2000). *The economic crisis of the 1990s in Finland*. Helsinki: University of Helsinki and CEPR.
[22] Honkapohja, S. (2009). The 1990's financial crises in Nordic countries. *Bank of Finland Research Discussion Papers, 5*, 7-26.
[23] Icelandic Property Registry. (2009). Vísitala íbúðaverðs [Real Estate Index] http://www3.fmr.is/Markadurinn/Visitala-ibudaverds.

[24] Ilmanen, A. (2011). *Expected return: An investor's guide to harvesting market rewards*. Chichester: John Wiley & Sons Inc.

[25] IMF (International Monetary Fund). (2012). World Economic Outlook Database. http://www.imf.org/external/pubs/ft/weo/2011/01/weodata/ index.aspx.

[26] Jannari, K. (2009). Report on Banking Regulation and Supervision in Iceland: past, present and future. http://eng.forsaetisraduneyti.is /media/frettir/KaarloJannari__2009.pdf

[27] Jonung, L. (2008). Lessons from financial liberalisation in Scandinavia. *Comparative Economic Studies, 50*, 564-598.

[28] Jonung, L., Kiander J., & Vartia P. (2008). The great financial crisis in Finland and Sweden: The dynamics of boom, bust and recovery, 1985-2000. *European Economy Economic Papers 350*, 1-70.

[29] Kindleberger, C. P. (1996). *Manias, panics, and crashes: A history of financial crises*. New York: John Wiley & Sons.

[30] Loftsdottir, K. (2010). The loss of innocence: the Icelandic financial crisis and colonial past (pp. 9-13). *Anthropology Today 26*(6), 9-13.

[31] McLean, B., & Elkind, P. (2003). *The smartest guys in the room: The amazing rise and scandalous Fall of Enron*. New York: Penguin Group.

[32] Mixa, M. W. (2009). Once in khaki suits - Socioeconomical Features of the Icelandic Collapse. Ingjaldur Hannibalsson (Ed.), *Rannsóknir í Félagsvísindum X* [*Research in Social Sciences X*], 435-447. Reykjavík: Félagsvísindastofnun Háskóla Ísland.

[33] Mixa, M. W. (2010). Verdtrygging fjarskuldbindinga: Verdtryggdir eda overdtryggdir vextir [Indexation of monetary obligations: Indexed or non-indexed interest rates]. http://www.vr.is/Uploads/VR /utgefid_efni_vr/Verdtrygging%20fjarskuldbindinga.pdf.

[34] Mixa, M. W. (2011). Hrun, íbúðarhúsnæði og Facebook [Crash, private property and facebook]. http://www.ru.is/media/hr/skjol/ Frettatiminn_03_tbl_2011_LR.pdf.

[35] Morgunbladid. (2009). Yfirlýsingin kom frá forstjóra Kaupþings. http://www.mbl.is/mm/vidskipti/frettir/2008/11/05/yfirlysingin_kom_fra_forstjora_kaupthings/.

[36] Olafsson, S. (2003). The identity of Icelanders: Scandinavian or American? Scandinavian Review. Https://borg.hi.is/IcelandID.pdf.

[37] Olafsson, S. (2011). Level of living consequences of Iceland's financial crisis: What do the social indicators tell us. http://www.imf.org /external/np/seminars/eng/2011/isl/.

[38] Portes, R. & Baldursson F.M. (2007). *The Internationalization of Iceland's Financial Sector*. Reykjavik: Iceland Chamber of Commerce.

[39] Rappoport, P. & White, E. N. (1994). Was the Crash of 1929 Expected? *The American Economic Review, 84*(1), 272–282.

[40] Reinhart, C. M. and Rogoff, K. S. (2009). *This time is different. Eight Centuries of Financial Folly*. New Jersey: Princeton University Press.

[41] Reinhart, C., & Rogoff, K. (2008). *Is the 2007 U.S. Sub-Prime Crisis So Different? An International Historical Comparison*. Massachusetts: University of Maryland and Harvard University.

[42] Sigurjonsson, T.O. (2010a) Privatization and Deregulation: A Chronology of Events. In *Documents on the Asset Price bubble in Iceland*, R. Aliber (Ed). Hampshire: Palgrave.

[43] Sigurjonsson, T.O. (2010b). The Icelandic bank collapse: challenges to governances and risk management. *Corporate Governance, the international journal of business in society, 10*(1), 33-45.

[44] Special Investigation Commission (2010). Skýrsla rannsóknarnefndar Alþingis [Report of the Special Investigation Commission]. Http://sic.althingi.is/.

[45] Statistics Denmark (2011). Http://www.statbank.dk/statbank5a/ default.asp?w=1366.

[46] Statistics Finland (2011). http://www.stat.fi/til/kihi/yht_en.html.

[47] Statistics Iceland (2013). http://www.statice.is/?PageID=2932&src=/temp_en/Dialog/varval.asp?ma=VIS01002%26ti=Consumer+price+index+from+1939%26path=../Database/visitolur/neysluverd/%26lang=1%26units=Indices.

[48] Statistics Norway (2011). Hhttp://statbank.ssb.no/statistikkbanken/Default_FR.asp?PXSid=0&nvl=true&PLanguage=1&tilside=selecttable/hovedtabellHjem.asp&KortnavnWeb=bpi.

[49] Statistics Sweden (2011). Http://statbank.ssb.no/statistikkbanken/Default_FR.asp?PXSid=0&nvl=true&PLanguage=1&tilside=selecttable/hovedtabellHjem.asp&KortnavnWeb=bpi.

[50] Valgreen, C. (2006). *Iceland: Geyser crisis.* Copenhagen: Danske Bank.

In: Financial Crises
Editor: Cooper A. Hawthorne

ISBN: 978-1-62808-293-7

Chapter 8

An Empirical Exploration of the Causes of the 2008 Financial Crisis

***Eduardo Acosta-González*[1], *Fernando Fernández-Rodríguez*[1,*] *and Simón Sosvilla-Rivero Fernando*[2]**

[1]Department of Quantitative Methods, University of Las Palmas de Gran Canaria, Campus de Tafira, Facultad de Ciencias Económicas y Empresariales, Spain

[2]Department of Quantitative Economics, Complutense University of Madrid, Campus de Somosagua, Facultad de Ciencias Económicas y Empresariales, Spain

Abstract

Starting with a large number of potential causes and indicators of the 2008 crisis (over sixty possible explanatory factors considered in the literature), the best econometric model for explaining the severity of the crisis is selected using a statistical methodology only guided by data via a Genetic Algorithm. Our results show that the best econometric model contains only one factor: 'percentage of bank claims in the year 2006'. Besides, this model is very robust after a sensitivity analysis is carried out. When lower penalty is considered for the introduction of factors in the model, the severity of the crisis is robustly explained by just two financial factors: 'percentage of bank claims in the year 2006', and 'percentage in GDP of Domestic Private Credit Sector in the year 2006'. Finally, in order to find out if all countries have the same behaviour during the crisis or if there are geographical differences in their response, we test for the presence of structural permanence of the coefficients of the main explanatory factors selected by the Genetic Algorithm. In this sense, after considering several dummy variables for different groups of countries, the existence of structural change has been rejected. Therefore, we find evidence of a uniform response on the severity of the crisis in the different countries, to changes in the factors explaining the crisis.

Keywords: Financial Crises, Genetic Algorithms

---

* Corresponding Author: Telefone: +0034928451802. Fax: +0034928451829, Email: ffernandez@dmc.ulpgc.es

Classification JEL codes: E32, E44, E51

1. INTRODUCTION

There is an increasing literature concerning potential factors determining the relative performance during the 2008 global financial crisis. So, numerous theories of the crisis′ origin have emerged. Following Rose and Spiegel (2009) the following factors stand out from others:

Factors associated with size and income of the countries, by Reinhart and Reinhart (2009). Other works place the potential causes of the crisis in the set of weaknesses exposed in national and international financial regulatory frameworks, supervision practices [Bernanke, 2009], excessive securitization and too much faith in the opinion of private rating agencies [Buiter, 2007], excessive leverage and underestimation of systemic risk [Spencer, 2008], excessively high rating received by structured instruments by rating agencies [Coval et al., 2009], pro-cyclical behaviour encouraged by the existing regulatory structures [Demirguc-Kunt and Serven, 2009]. Other authors focus on precarious financial conditions and fragility in the United States financial system [De Gregorio, 2009], risky financial market practices which exposed the banking sector to financial distress [Ceccheti, 2009, Feldstein, 2009, and White, 2008]. The bubble in real estate values and a rapid increase in other prices, especially in equity, fuelled by easy monetary policy are also considered an important cause of the crisis [Feldstein, 2009, and Reinhart and Rogoff, 2008]. Other theories concentrate attention on the international imbalances and in the precarious international financial position over the boom years [Buiter, 2009]. Also lax macroeconomic policies have been blamed for the crisis by exacerbating current account imbalances [Hall and Woodward, 2009, De Long, 2009 and Buiter, 2009]. Other works consider institutional features across countries as potential factors explaining the crisis severity [Acemoglu, et al., 2003]. Finally, geographic considerations have also been bore in mind [Danielsson, 2008].

In order to study the feasibility of an early warning system in order to predict the timing of the crises, Rose and Spiegel (2009) have studied the feasibility of modelling the causes of the financial crisis and why its severity differs across countries. Their approach attempts to model empirically the cross-country incidence of the 2008 financial crisis using a MIMIC (Multiple-Indicator Multiple Cause) model. This methodology treats the severity of the crisis as a latent variable, observed only imperfectly, and which is linked to four observable indicators of the crisis: the real GDP growth over 2008, the declines in the perception of a country's creditworthiness, equity market collapses and exchange rate depreciations. In order to combine appropriately these four factors, a common component is extracted using conventional factor analysis. Besides, with the end of carrying out sensitivity analysis, three additional variants of this common component are produced, replacing the four observable indicators of the crisis with others obtained with similar, but alternative, methodologies. So, four different variables measuring the severity of the crisis, which are strongly positively correlated, are considered.

The objective of our paper is to contribute to the debate about if the shocks that precipitated the crisis were common, and if national fundamentals may help to determine the actual incidence of the crisis across countries.

Our contribution consists of selecting the best econometric model for explaining the severity of the 2008 financial crisis from the potential factors frequently considered in the literature. In order to select the factors in the final model, we employ a purely statistical methodology that has nothing to do with the theoretical models in Macroeconomics or Finance. The purpose of it is two-fold.

On the one hand, due to redundancy of the information provided by the over sixty factors explaining the 2008 crisis employed by Rose and Spiegel (2009), the correlation between them can produce multicolineality problems in the estimations. So, it could be better to construct an econometric model just having a reduced number of factors which contains as much information as possible. Nevertheless, it is a very complex task because dismissing relevant variables conduces to model inconsistency. Besides, no logical procedure exists which is capable of identifying the factors containing the most complete information, avoiding at the same time its duplication. However, we provide a new methodology for doing this.

On the other hand, a parsimonious model of the severity of the crisis, containing few factors with as much information as possible, may give tracks to the main reasons explaining the crisis. In this case it is very important to consider the statistical significance of the variables selected in that model. Only the factors having significance may have an impact on the crisis incidence.

The crucial part of our methodology is an automatic selection of variables in the model, only guided by the data, which is carried out using a Genetic Algorithm where the lost function is the Schwartz Information Criterion (SIC, henceforth).

Our starting point is the previous paper by Rose and Spiegel (2009). They treat the severity of the crisis as a latent variable, observed only imperfectly, and which is linked to four observable indicators of it: changes in the real GDP, the stock market, country credit rating, and the exchange rate. As explanatory factors of the 2008 crisis, over sixty potential factors considered in the literature, have been included. It covers such categories as: financial system policies and conditions, asset price appreciation in real estate and equity markets, international imbalances and foreign reserve adequacy, macroeconomic policies, and institutional and geographic features.

The main contribution of this paper is to provide an algorithm for selecting the best econometric model explaining the severity of the crisis regressing it on over sixty potential factors, and getting rid off the irrelevant variables in order to find a parsimonious model explaining the manifestations of the crisis.

The final model depends on a parameter which is associated with the strength of SIC for avoiding over-parameterized models. The higher the value of this parameter, the higher is the penalty for the introduction of more factors in the model.

Employing a high penalty against over-parametrization, we get an econometric model which contains just one factor that is statistically significant: the financial variable "percentage of bank claims in the year 2006". In order to explain the severity of the 2008 crisis, this factor summarizes the effect of the other extremely correlated sixty plus factors. Besides, this model is very robust after sensitivity analysis is carried out.

Employing a lower penalty against over-parametrization, the results show that there is also a predominance of financial factors describing the severity of the crisis. It is robustly explained by two financial factors: "percentage of bank claims in the year 2006", and "percentage of GDP of the Domestic Credit Private Sector in the year 2006". Besides, the appearance in the model of the factor "Central/Eastern European or Central Asian" which is a statistically significant, geographical and non financial factor, means that these countries have received special impact during the crisis.

The remainder of this paper is structured as follows. Section 2 describes the econometric methodology adopted in this study. In Section 3 we report the empirical result. Section 4 explores the possibility of geographical differences in the severity of the crisis. Finally, Section 5 summarizes the findings and offers some concluding remarks.

2. Our Methodology

As Rose and Spiegel (2009) point out, there are doubts about the significance of the factors explaining the severity of the 2008 crisis. Starting with over sixty potential variables (with a lot of very redundant information), which are frequently considered in the literature as factors of the 2008 crisis, the main contribution of our paper is to provide an automatic procedure for selecting the final parsimonious econometric model (with a reduced amount of factors) for predicting the severity of the 2008 crisis.

Our methodology doesn't start from any set of variables prior considered as part of the final model. As Lovell (1983) pointed out the data mining activities consisting of sequentially introducing new factors to the model guided by t and R^2 considerations erode the levels of significance in hypothesis tests. So, when the new factor added to the model is highly correlated to the existing ones, the lack of statistical significance of the new factor introduced in the model doesn't mean that this factor doesn't have explanatory power over the severity of the crisis. It may just mean that its information is redundant when combined with the information of previous factors in the model. For this reason, and following the London School of Economics approach based on the theory of reduction [Hendry, 1995, ch. 9], in order to construct the best econometric model for the crisis we proceed from the general to specific. It means that we initially start with a model containing all the sixty-plus factors.

So, given a dependent variable Y, which represents the severity of the 2008 crisis, and a set $X_1,....,X_K$ of potential factors explaining it, the problem that we face is to find the best submodel of the form:

$$Y = \beta_0 + \beta_1 X_{i_1} + ... + \beta_k X_{i_k} + \varepsilon \ ,$$

$$\text{where } \{i_1, i_2 ...., i_k\} \subseteq \{1, 2, ..., K\},\ k < K \simeq 60 \ ...... \qquad (1)$$

In building this multiple regression model, due to the multicolineality produced by the redundancy of the information provided by the complete set of factors and the correlation between them, a crucial problem is the selection of regressors that should be included. If a lower amount of regressors are selected in the model, the estimate of the parameters will not be consistent and if a higher amount is selected, its variance will increase.

Given a set of potential factors, the econometric theory has developed numerous criteria for selecting the best submodel. The problem is that the number of submodels where these criteria have to be considered may be enormous. If we call the number of initial factors N, there are 2^N possible submodels. For $N = 60$, the number of possible models is higher than 10^{18}. So, the explicit computation of each model is prohibitively expensive. In order to resolve this intractable problem, several heuristic methods addressed to restrict attention to a smaller number of potential subsets of regressors are usually employed by practitioners. Some of the most popular are the stepwise procedures, such as forward selection or backward elimination, which sequentially include or exclude variables based on t-ratio statistic considerations [see Miller (2002) as a review of subset selection in regression]. However, stepwise tends to over-identify models. The probability of introducing false significant variables in the model is very high [Lovell (1983)]. In this context a recently developed methodology in Acosta-González and Fernández-Rodríguez (2007) is employed. This procedure is based on Genetic Algorithms (GA henceforth) guided by the SIC. It explores the most promising areas in the space of the 2^{60} econometric models, and is able to find the best model for explaining the 2008 crisis in a reasonable time. This methodology was employed originally by its authors for identifying the factors explaining the differences in growth rates of the countries.

A GA is a class of optimization technique, based on principles of natural evolution developed by Holland (1975) which tries to overcome problems of traditional optimization algorithms, such as an absence of continuity or differentiability of the loss function. A GA starts with a population of randomly generated solution candidates, which apply the principle of fitness to produce better approximations to optimal solution. Promising solutions, as represented by relatively better performing solutions, are selected and breeding them together through a process of binary recombination referred to as crossover inspired by Mendel's natural genetics.

The objective of this process is to generate successive populations solutions that are better fitted to the optimization problem than the solutions from which they were created. Finally, random mutations are introduced in order to avoid local optima.

The sensitivity of the GA procedure towards the multicolineality presents good behaviour as demonstrated in Acosta-González and Fernández-Rodríguez (2007). So, this methodology could be ideal concerning the problem of selecting factors explaining financial crises where the universe of available financial ratios presents high multicolineality.

The use of the SIC is crucial in our methodology. When looking for an econometric model using maximum likelihood estimation, it is possible to increase the likelihood by adding additional factors, which may result in overfitting. The SIC advises choosing the econometric model which minimizes the expression

$$SIC(m) = \log \hat{\sigma}^2 + c\frac{k}{N}\log(N) \tag{2}$$

where $\hat{\sigma}^2 = \frac{e'e}{N}$ is the variance of the residuals e, N is the sample size, k is the number of factors in the model.

The correcting factor c avoids the possibility of over-parameterized models. The higher the value of c, the higher is the penalty for the introduction of more factors in the model.

Schwarz (1978) shows that SIC is asymptotically consistent as a selection criterion; it means that given a family of models where the true model is included, the probability that SIC selects the true model tends to one, as the sample size tends to infinity. So, SIC avoids over-parametrization and resolves the trade-off between the in sample goodness of fit and the out of sample forecasting ability.

Another problem that Rose and Spiegel (2009) had to deal with in their study was missing data. Although their data base had initially 107 countries, because of missing data, the Rose and Spiegel´s estimates were actually derived from 85 countries. So, they have to eliminate a carefully chosen set of observations (countries) and variables (factors) in order to produce a data matrix without missing values. This procedure leads to a sample selection bias. The solution to the problem of missing data that we propose in this paper is to employ a technique of multiple imputation developed by King et al. (2001) which permits the approximation of missing data and allows us to obtain better estimations.

3. Empirical Results

Given an estimate of the incidence of the crisis across countries, our econometric methodology permits to link crisis incidence to a set of potential causes that are automatically selected in a process only guided by data.

Our data series, the same as employed by Rose and Spiegel (2009), were extracted from the World Bank's *World Development Indicators,* the International Monetary Fund's *International Financial Statistics*, and other key data sets. The entire (STATA 10.0) data set is available at http://faculty.haas.berkeley.edu/arose/MIMICData.zip.

We have considered two different values for the parameter c in SIC controlling the over-parameterization in the model. The case $c=2$ corresponds to a high reluctance to introduce many explicative factors. The case $c=1$ corresponds to more flexibility for introducing explicative factors.

Our main result is that the intensity of the crisis seems to be strongly linked to financial factors which in 2006 had been warning about the possibility of a financial crisis.

Depending on the value of parameter c, the number of factors explaining the crisis is different. In the case $c=2$, starting with a large number of potential causes and indicators (over sixty possible explanatory factors) of the severity of the crisis considered in the literature, the best econometric model, in the sense of the SIC, contains a constant and the statistically significant financial factor "percentage of bank claims in the year 2006". Besides this model is very robust after sensitivity analysis is carried out.

Our finding could be consistent with Eichengreen and Mitchener (2003) who conclude that financial crises throughout modern history can be viewed as "credit booms gone wrong".

Moreover, our results suggest that valuable information about macroeconomic and financial stability would be missed if central banks chose to ignore the behavior of credit aggregates and confine themselves to following inflation targeting rules. Indeed, policymakers are now taking a harder look at how to regulate credit and the procylicality of the financial system (e.g., Turner 2009).

Table 1. Estimation results for a correcting factor c=2

Severity of the crisis 1 (R2=0.2437)			
Factor name	coefficient	t-student	p-value
Constant	0.77060	3.76750	0.00010
Bank Claims, % Deposits 2006	-0.76380	-4.62860	0.00000
Severity of the crisis 2 (R2=0.3595)			
Factor name	coefficient	t-student	p-value
Constant	0.22840	1.05550	0.14680
Bank Claims, % Deposits 2006	-0.60240	-4.44190	0.00000
Civil Liberties, 2006	0.15070	3.93110	0.00010
Severity of the crisis 3 (R2=0.2268)			
Factor name	coefficient	t-student	p-value
Constant	0.67480	3.36560	0.00050
Bank Claims, % Deposits 2006	-0.66430	-4.23130	0.00000
Severity of the crisis 4 (R2=0.1995)			
Factor name	coefficient	t-student	p-value
Constant	0.88290	4.26380	0.00000
Bank Claims, % Deposits 2006	-0.85190	-4.86820	0.00000

In Table 1 we present the results of applying our genetic algorithm in order to search for the best set of factors explaining the four versions of the severity of the crisis considered by Rose and Spiegel (2009).

In three out of four cases the best econometric model contains just one factor, "percentage of bank claims in the year 2006", which is statistically significant. This variable is a typical financial factor that was signalling the 2008 financial crisis since 2006, being consistent with many theories on the sources of financial crises that highlight the importance of credit markets conditions (see, e. g., Claessen and Kose, 2013) When the second version of the severity of the crisis is considered, the best econometric model contains just two factors, the "percentage of bank claims in the year 2006" and "civil liberties in the year 2006". Both variables are statistically significant.

The relevant role we have found for "civil liberties in the year 2006" could be related to the fact that this variable could be capturing government effectiveness, and is consistent to a bourgeoning literature stressing that the influence of the political context on economic performance is paramount (see, e. g. Commander and Nikoloski, 2010). Well-institutionalized democracies are more likely to produce, over the long run, effective, efficient and sustainable economic and social policies, because they provide effective and stable institutional and procedural mechanisms to represent interests, arbitrate disputes, provide checks and balances, and negotiate change (see, e. g. Isham, Kaufmann and Pritchett, 1997, and. Kaufmann, Kraay and Zoido-Lobaton 1999).

Table 2. Estimation results for a correcting factor c=1

Severity of the crisis 1 (R2=0.4646)			
Factor name	coefficient	t-student	p-value
Constant	0.4245	0.7813	0.2182
Official Supervisory Power, 2003	0.0368	1.8709	0.0321
Domestic Credit Private Sector, %GDP 2006	-0.0064	-3.3033	0.0007
Private Sector Credit Access, 2006	0.1303	1.6968	0.0463
Bank Liquid Reserves, %Assets 2006	-0.0068	-1.5687	0.0599
Bank Capital, %Assets 2006	-0.0413	-1.0293	0.1528
Bank Claims, %Deposits 2006	-0.6718	-3.283	0.0007
CPI Inflation, 2006	-0.0389	-1.4273	0.0782
Central/Eastern European or Central Asian	-0.5003	-2.5317	0.0064
Severity of the crisis 2 (R2=0.3930)			
Factor name	coefficient	t-student	p-value
Constant	0.3914	1.7198	0.0442
Domestic Credit Private Sector, %GDP 2006	-0.0030	-2.1998	0.0150
Bank Claims, %Deposits 2006	-0.4693	-3.2717	0.0007
Civil Liberties, 2006	0.1231	3.1611	0.0010
Severity of the crisis 3 (R2=0.4033)			
Factor name	coefficient	t-student	p-value
Constant	3.4799	2.7759	0.0033
Domestic Credit Private Sector, %GDP 2006	-0.0056	-3.7641	0.0001
Bank Claims, %Deposits 2006	-0.4683	-2.4470	0.0080
Control of Corruption	0.2920	2.3781	0.0096
Central/Eastern European or Central Asian	-0.3678	-1.9292	0.0282
Log(2006 Real GDP per capita)	-0.2762	-2.1542	0.0167
Severity of the crisis 4 (R2=0.3677)			
Factor name	coefficient	t-student	p-value
Constant	0.8078	2.8442	0.0027
Declaring Insolvency Power, 2003	0.2334	1.6306	0.0530
Domestic Credit Private Sector, %GDP 2006	-0.0070	-3.2547	0.0008
Bank Claims, %Deposits 2006	-0.6467	-3.4435	0.0004
Regulatory Quality	0.3318	2.0794	0.0200
Central/Eastern European or Central Asian	-0.5500	-2.4697	0.0076

In addition, well-institutionalized democracies are more likely to rapidly activate automatic stabilizers to dampen fluctuations in real Gross Domestic Product using government budget policies, particularly income taxes and welfare spending.

Paying attention to R^2 , the explanatory power of our model is limited and the variability of the endogenous variable is explained over the 20%. Nevertheless, considering that our model has just one factor, its explanatory power is acceptable.

The variables size of the country and its income, which have been considered as basic factors for explaining the severity of the 2008 crisis by Rose and Spiegel (2009), were not selected by our algorithm. It doesn't mean that their explanatory power is null. It just means that the model we got is better in the SIC sense, and the relevant information of both factors, in order to explain the severity of the crisis, is summarized by our financial variable "percentage of bank claims in the year 2006".

In the case $c = 1$, where SIC permits more explanatory factors, starting with over sixty possible explanatory factors of the severity of the crisis, the best econometric model depends on the endogenous variable representing the severity of the crisis. The results are presented in Table 2.

As we can see in Table 2, all variables in the four models are significant with the exception of Bank Capital, % Assets 2006 for the severity variable 1.

It is also important to observe that there is a predominance of financial factors describing the severity of the crisis, in the four cases. So, there are two financial factors which were selected in each of the four models associated with the four severity measures: (i) Bank Claims, % Deposits 2006 and (ii) Domestic Credit Private Sector, %GDP 2006. Therefore, our findings offer further support for the crucial role of credit in the business cycle (see, Jordá and Schularick, 2011, among others).

A non financial factor given by the variable Central/Eastern European or Central Asian was also selected in three out of four endogenous variables describing the severity of the 2008 crisis. The appearance of this geographical and non financial factor (which is statistically significant in all of the cases) means that these European central Eastern countries and Central Asian Countries have received special impact during the crisis. Its negative sign reveals that this impact has been especially negative, and the magnitude of its coefficient measures, in any sense, the severity of the crisis.

The non financial variable Log(2006 Real GDP per capita) is only selected in the severity of the crisis measure 3. The factor associated with the size of the country was never selected in any model. The fact that the factors of size and income of the countries don't appear in the optimal econometric model doesn't mean that these variables don't have an influence on the severity of the crisis, but other variables in the model summarize the information which they provide.

Structural Permanence of the Model

The previous results can be refined by allowing for the possibility of different responses in different groups of countries. In particular, we study to find out if all countries have the same behaviour during the crisis or if there are geographical differences in their responses. So, in order to find out if all countries have the same behaviour during the crisis or if there are some groups of them which respond differently, we test for the presence of structural permanence of the coefficients of the explanatory factors selected by the Genetic Algorithm.

Table 3. Structural change test for estimation in Table 1

Severity Of The Crisis 1						
Dummy Coefficients From Equation (1)	$\hat{\alpha}_1$	$\hat{\alpha}_2$	$\hat{\alpha}_3$	$\hat{\alpha}_4$	$\hat{\alpha}_5$	$\hat{\alpha}_6$
Constant	-0.174 (0.348)	-0.053 (0.450)	0.185 (0.275)	0.123 (0.389)	-0.335 (0.324)	-0.366 (0.310)
Dummy Coefficients From Equation (2)	$\hat{\lambda}_1$	$\hat{\lambda}_2$	$\hat{\lambda}_3$	$\hat{\lambda}_4$	$\hat{\lambda}_5$	$\hat{\lambda}_6$
Slope Of Bank Claims, % Deposits 2006	-0.004 (0.493)	0.176 (0.226)	0.092 (0.267)	0.088 (0.427)	-0.423 (0.312)	-0.728 (0.299)
Severity Of The Crisis 2						
Dummy Coefficients From Equation (1)	$\hat{\alpha}_1$	$\hat{\alpha}_2$	$\hat{\alpha}_3$	$\hat{\alpha}_4$	$\hat{\alpha}_5$	$\hat{\alpha}_6$
Constant	-0.190 (0.320)	-0.114 (0.383)	-0.107 (0.359)	0.334 (0.206)	-0.218 (0.373)	-0.664 (0.163)
Dummy Coefficients From Equation (2)	$\hat{\lambda}_1$	$\hat{\lambda}_2$	$\hat{\lambda}_3$	$\hat{\lambda}_4$	$\hat{\lambda}_5$	$\hat{\lambda}_6$
Bank Claims, % Deposits 2006	0.092 (0.383)	0.214 (0.251)	-0.306 (0.119)	0.354 (0.213)	-0.280 (0.364)	-1.287 (0.159)
Civil Liberties, 2006	-0.096 (0.395)	-0.082 (0.411)	-0.100 (0.366)	0.075 (0.203)	-0.215 (0.375)	-0.332 (0.162)
Severity Of The Crisis 3						
Dummy Coefficients From Equation (1)	$\hat{\alpha}_1$	$\hat{\alpha}_2$	$\hat{\alpha}_3$	$\hat{\alpha}_4$	$\hat{\alpha}_5$	$\hat{\alpha}_6$
Constant	-0.217 (0.295)	-0.049 (0.448)	-0.079 (0.390)	0.123 (0.376)	-0.519 (0.217)	-0.892 (0.092)
Dummy Coefficients From Equation (2)	$\hat{\lambda}_1$	$\hat{\lambda}_2$	$\hat{\lambda}_3$	$\hat{\lambda}_4$	$\hat{\lambda}_5$	$\hat{\lambda}_6$
Bank Claims, % Deposits 2006	-0.030 (0.461)	0.141 (0.328)	-0.164 (0.256)	0.078 (0.428)	-0.627 (0.216)	-1.708 (0.092)
Severity Of The Crisis 4						
Dummy Coefficients From Equation (1)	$\hat{\alpha}_1$	$\hat{\alpha}_2$	$\hat{\alpha}_3$	$\hat{\alpha}_4$	$\hat{\alpha}_5$	$\hat{\alpha}_6$
Constant	-0.283 (0.305)	-0.020 (0.485)	0.344 (0.188)	0.269 (0.312)	-0.691 (0.225)	-0.933 (0.155)
Dummy Coefficients From Equation (2)	$\hat{\lambda}_1$	$\hat{\lambda}_2$	$\hat{\lambda}_3$	$\hat{\lambda}_4$	$\hat{\lambda}_5$	$\hat{\lambda}_6$
Bank Claims, % Deposits 2006	-0.149 (0.363)	0.120 (0.393)	0.203 (0.279)	0.189 (0.376)	-0.846 (0.222)	-1.821 (0.151)
P-Values Are In Parenthesis						

Instead of using the more common test of structural change, known as Chow test, [Chow(1969)] a structural change test based on dummy variables is applied. So, it may be possible to test, in an individual way, the structural change in the constant and in the coefficient of the variables. We consider several groups of countries which we wanted to test if they had the same behaviour during the crisis. To take into account these groups of countries the following dummy variables were created:

$D_{1,i} \rightarrow$ The variable is assigned a value of 1 for countries with special economic problems inside the EU (Greece, Ireland, Italy, Portugal and Spain), zero otherwise.

$D_{2,i} \rightarrow$ The variable is assigned a value of 1 for countries in the EU with triple A sovereign credit rating at the end of 2011 by Standard and Poor's, zero otherwise.

$D_{3,i} \rightarrow$ The variable is assigned a value of 1 for Euro Zone countries, zero otherwise.

$D_{4,i} \rightarrow$ The variable is assigned a value of 1 for developing countries (Brazil, China, Russia)

$D_{5,i} \rightarrow$ The variable is assigned a value of 1 for USA, zero otherwise.

$D_{6,i} \rightarrow$ The variable is assigned a value of 1 for Japan, zero otherwise.

Table 4. Structural change test for estimation in Table 2

Severity of the crisis 1						
Dummy coefficients from equation (1)	$\hat{\alpha}_1$	$\hat{\alpha}_2$	$\hat{\alpha}_3$	$\hat{\alpha}_4$	$\hat{\alpha}_5$	$\hat{\alpha}_6$
Constant	-0.117 (0.387)	-0.092 (0.406)	0.196 (0.263)	0.299 (0.227)	0.086 (0.453)	-0.023 (0.487)
Dummy coefficients from equation (2)	$\hat{\lambda}_1$	$\hat{\lambda}_2$	$\hat{\lambda}_3$	$\hat{\lambda}_4$	$\hat{\lambda}_5$	$\hat{\lambda}_6$
Official Supervisory Power, 2003	-0.008 (0.421)	-0.019 (0.317)	0.015 (0.263)	0.027 (0.251)	0.006 (0.457)	-0.004 (0.471)
Domestic Credit Private Sector, %GDP 2006	-0.001 (0.338)	-0.001 (0.351)	0.003 (0.163)	0.005 (0.199)	0.001 (0.405)	0.000 (0.462)
Private Sector Credit Access, 2006	-0.009 (0.425)	-0.008 (0.432)	0.021 (0.284)	0.036 (0.238)	0.009 (0.451)	-0.004 (0.484)
Bank Liquid Reserves, %Assets 2006	-0.052 (0.419)	-0.007 (0.486)	0.016 (0.357)	0.022 (0.239)	0.078 (0.470)	-0.043 (0.453)
Bank Capital, %Assets 2006	-0.012 (0.427)	-0.014 (0.413)	0.026 (0.268)	0.025 (0.263)	0.008 (0.455)	-0.008 (0.476)
Bank Claims, %Deposits 2006	0.019 (0.475)	0.058 (0.430)	0.051 (0.425)	0.288 (0.258)	0.056 (0.474)	-0.145 (0.458)
CPI Inflation, 2006	-0.045 (0.363)	-0.046 (0.399)	0.064 (0.248)	0.028 (0.328)	0.025 (0.456)	-0.197 (0.474)
Central/Eastern European or Central Asian 8	Exact Multicollinearity					
Severity of the crisis 2						
Dummy coefficients from equation (1)	$\hat{\alpha}_1$	$\hat{\alpha}_2$	$\hat{\alpha}_3$	$\hat{\alpha}_4$	$\hat{\alpha}_5$	$\hat{\alpha}_6$
Constant	-0.150 (0.354)	-0.074 (0.422)	-0.045 (0.439)	0.366 (0.178)	0.156 (0.411)	-0.295 (0.335)
Dummy coefficients from equation (2)	$\hat{\lambda}_1$	$\hat{\lambda}_2$	$\hat{\lambda}_3$	$\hat{\lambda}_4$	$\hat{\lambda}_5$	$\hat{\lambda}_6$
Domestic Credit Private Sector, %GDP 2006	-0.001 (0.321)	-0.001 (0.371)	0.000 (0.468)	0.007 (0.122)	0.001 (0.397)	-0.002 (0.350)
Bank Claims, % Deposits 2006	0.133 (0.332)	0.237 (0.226)	-0.282 (0.134)	0.370 (0.202)	0.160 (0.423)	-0.596 (0.325)
Civil Liberties, 2006	-0.092 (0.398)	-0.064 (0.429)	-0.044 (0.440)	0.088 (0.155)	0.165 (0.406)	-0.144 (0.338)

Table 4. (Continued)

Severity of the crisis 3

Dummy coefficients from equation (1)	$\hat{\alpha}_1$	$\hat{\alpha}_2$	$\hat{\alpha}_3$	$\hat{\alpha}_4$	$\hat{\alpha}_5$	$\hat{\alpha}_6$
Constant	-0.270 (0.236)	-0.283 (0.212)	0.158 (0.282)	0.282 (0.213)	0.098 (0.441)	-0.257 (0.349)
Dummy coefficients from equation (2)	$\hat{\lambda}_1$	$\hat{\lambda}_2$	$\hat{\lambda}_3$	$\hat{\lambda}_4$	$\hat{\lambda}_5$	$\hat{\lambda}_6$
Domestic Credit Private Sector, %GDP 2006	-0.002 (0.208)	-0.002 (0.197)	0.002 (0.206)	0.004 (0.227)	0.001 (0.410)	-0.001 (0.380)
Bank Claims, %Deposits 2006	-0.096 (0.370)	-0.101 (0.367)	0.017 (0.471)	0.289 (0.234)	0.096 (0.452)	-0.527 (0.337)
Control of Corruption	-0.040 (0.455)	-0.037 (0.451)	-0.043 (0.441)	-0.361 (0.283)	0.029 (0.469)	-0.252 (0.324)
Central/Eastern European or Central Asian	Exact Multicollinearity					
Log(2006 Real GDP per capita)	-0.027 (0.236)	-0.027 (0.213)	0.015 (0.290)	0.031 (0.215)	0.009 (0.443)	-0.025 (0.347)

Severity of the crisis 4

Dummy coefficients from equation (1)	$\hat{\alpha}_1$	$\hat{\alpha}_2$	$\hat{\alpha}_3$	$\hat{\alpha}_4$	$\hat{\alpha}_5$	$\hat{\alpha}_6$
Constant	-0.311 (0.273)	-0.118 (0.405)	0.355 (0.169)	0.421 (0.206)	-0.333 (0.355)	-0.492 (0.290)
Dummy coefficients from equation (2)	$\hat{\lambda}_1$	$\hat{\lambda}_2$	$\hat{\lambda}_3$	$\hat{\lambda}_4$	$\hat{\lambda}_5$	$\hat{\lambda}_6$
Declaring Insolvency Power, 2003	-0.292 (0.185)	-0.292 (0.189)	0.219 (0.148)	0.191 (0.247)	-0.189 (0.337)	-0.262 (0.279)
Domestic Credit Private Sector, %GDP 2006	-0.003 (0.201)	-0.002 (0.304)	0.005 (0.067)	0.007 (0.173)	-0.001 (0.425)	-0.002 (0.354)
Bank Claims, %Deposits 2006	-0.105 (0.397)	0.050 (0.453)	0.168 (0.306)	0.382 (0.250)	-0.473 (0.330)	-1.064 (0.266)
Severity of the crisis 1						
Regulatory Quality	-0.165 (0.345)	-0.092 (0.402)	0.214 (0.255)	-0.389 (0.404)	-0.248 (0.338)	-0.551 (0.275)
Central/Eastern European or Central Asian	Exact Multicollinearity					

p-values are in parenthesis

In order to carry out this test we estimate the following equations:

$$Y_i = \beta_0 + \sum_{j=1}^{6} \alpha_j D_{j,i} + \sum_{j=1}^{q} \beta_j X_{j,i} + \varepsilon_i \tag{3}$$

$$Y_i = \beta_0 + \sum_{j=1}^{q} \beta_j X_{j,i} + \sum_{j=1}^{6} \lambda_j D_{j,i} X_{p,i} \qquad p = 1, \ldots, q \tag{4}$$

In these equations the X variables represent the exogenous variables which explain the crisis and Y corresponds to one of the endogenous variables which represents the severity of the crisis. The parameter q represents the number of explanatory variables selected by the GA as the best model. For instances, q=1 when the GA has selected a model with one explanatory variable, for instances, *Bank claims, % deposits*. These equations are estimated for each one of the severity crisis measures considered and for the case where c takes the value 1 or 2 in the Schwartz criterion represented in equation (2), respectively. Besides, the equation (4) is estimated for each one of the explanatory variables selected by GASIC in each model.

The first equation permits the testing for the possibility that the constant in the model is different for each one of the diverse groups of countries considered. In the second equation we contrast the possibility that the slope of the different variables selected by GASIC may be different in each particular group of countries.

In Table 3 and Table 4 the results of the different estimation carried out are shown. So, for instance, in the case of using as endogenous variable the first version of the severity of the crisis and c=1 in the equation (2), in Table 4 it is possible to find nine estimations. The first one corresponds to the estimation of the coefficients of dichotomous variables $\alpha_j \left(j=1,\ldots 6\right)$ in the equation (3).

The rest of the estimations correspond to the coefficients of the dichotomous variables in the equation (4) $\lambda_j \left(j=1,\ldots 6\right)$. In this case the equation (4) is estimated eight times, one for each of the explanatory variables selected by GASIC in the former paragraph

As it is possible to observe in Tables 3 and 4, in practically all cases the hypothesis of structural permanence is hold. Only in the case of Japan, the model where the endogenous variable corresponds to the Severity 3 of the crisis and c=2, it may be a structural change, as much for the constant as for the slope of the variable *Bank Claims, % Deposits 2006*, with a significance level of 10%.

The same might happen in the model where the endogenous is the Severity of the crisis 4 and c=1. In this case, the slope of the variable *Domestic Credit Private Sector, %GDP 2006* may represent the structural change for the Euro countries, equally for a significance level of 10%. These results are little robust because, as it is easy to observe, when we change the measure of severity of the crisis it doesn't hold up.

This finding, that can be taken as evidence against the decoupling hypothesis, that is, the idea that business cycles in emerging market economies have become more independent of business cycles in advanced economies in recent years, and would suggest a phenomenon of re-coupling which has been consistent with the fact that the increasing globalization and interconnectedness that characterises the current world has rapidly spread and amplified economic and the financial crisis since 2008, making it a truly global crisis (see, e. g. Kim, Lee Park 2011).

CONCLUDING REMARKS

Following a previous paper by Rose and Spiegel (2009) we treat the severity of the crisis as a latent variable, observed only imperfectly, and which is linked to four observable indicators of the crisis: changes in the real GDP, the stock market, country credit rating, and the exchange rate. Over sixty potential factors considered in the literature have been included as explanatory variables. It covers such categories as: financial system policies and conditions, asset price appreciation in real estate and equity markets, international imbalances and foreign reserve adequacy, macroeconomic policies, and institutional and geographical features.

The general objective of our paper is to contribute to the debate about if the shocks that precipitated the crisis were common, and if national fundamentals may help to determine the actual incidence of the crisis across countries.

Specifically this paper has empirically tested the financial origins of the 2008 crisis. Our main result is that the intensity of the crisis seems to be strongly linked to financial factors which in 2006 had been warning about the possibility of a financial crisis. This would suggest that the current crisis could have been anticipated by avoiding the strong increase in credit, revaluating the role of credit quantities and factors affecting the supply of credit in the conduct of monetary policy.

Our main contribution consists of selecting the best econometric model for explaining the severity of the 2008 financial crisis from the potential factors frequently considered in the literature using a statistical methodology only guided by data. The factor selection procedure which we employ is an automatic method that is carried out using a Genetic Algorithm where the lost function is the Schwarz Information Criterion.

Starting with a large number of potential causes and indicators of the 2008 crisis (over sixty possible explanatory factors considered in the literature), the best econometric model for explaining the severity of the crisis is selected. Our results show that this best econometric model just contains one factor "percentage of bank claims in the year 2006".

Besides this model is very robust after sensitivity analysis is carried out. When lower penalty for the introduction of factors in the model is considered, the severity of the crisis is robustly explained by two financial factors: "percentage of bank claims in the year 2006", and "percentage in GDP of Domestic Credit Private Sector in the year 2006". Besides, the appearance in the model of the geographical and non financial factor "Central/Eastern European or Central Asian" means that these countries have received special impact during the crisis.

Finally, those results have been refined by allowing for the possibility of different responses in different groups of countries. In particular, we have studied to find out if all countries have the same behaviour during the crisis or if there are geographical differences in their response.

To that end, and as a sensitivity analysis, we test for the presence of structural permanence of the coefficients of the main explanatory factors selected by the Genetic Algorithm.

The methodology employed is called 'test of structural permanence' of the coefficient of a variable in a model; it is based on studding the permanence of the variables of the model when a change in the slope of the regressors is produced.

In our study, after considering several dummy variables for different groups of countries, the existence of structural change has been rejected. Therefore, we find evidence of a uniform response on the severity of the crisis in the different countries, to changes in the factors explaining the crisis; that is, if a country had presented a deep indebtedness, it would have to face the same severe crisis as the others.

Our findings are in line with the conclusion of a sizable body of empirical literature stating that recessions caused by financial crises have a history of being long, deep and difficult to fully escape from (e.g., Reinhart and Rogoff, 2009b), implying jobless recovery or persistently low real wages ("wageless" recovery) (e. g. Calvo, Coricelli and Ottonello, 2012).

REFERENCES

Acemoglu, D., Johnson, S., Robinson, J. and Thaicharoen Y. (2003). Institutional Causes, Macroecononomic Symptoms: Volatility, Crisis and Growth. *Journal of Monetary Economics,* 50, 49-123.

Acosta-González, E., Fernández-Rodríguez, F., 2007, Model selection via genetic algorithms illustrated with cross-country growth data. *Empirical Economics,* 33, 313-337.

Bernanke, B. S. (2009.) Lessons of the Financial Crisis of Banking Supervision. Speech at the Federal Reserve Bank of Chicago Conference on Bank Structure and Competition. Chicago, Illinois, May 7, 2009.

Buiter, W. (2007). Lessons form the 2007 Financial Crisis. Background Paper Submitted to the UK Treasury Selected Committee, December 11, 2007.

Buiter, W. (2009). Fiscal Expansion in Submerging Markets; the case of the USA and the UK. Ft.com/maverecom, February 5, 2009.

Ceccheti, S. G. (2009). Crisis and Responses: The Federal Reserve in the Early Stages of the Financial Crisis. *Journal of Economic Perspectives,* 23(1), Winter, 51-76.

Chow G. (1969). Test of Equality Between Sets of Coefficients in Two Linear Regressions. *Econometrica,* 28, 591-605.

Claessens, S., and Kose, M. (2013): Financial Crises Explanations, Types, and Implications, Working Paper No. 13/28, International Monetary Fund.

Calvo, G., Coricelli, F. and Ottonello, P. (2012): The Labor Market Consequences of Financial Crises with or Without Inflation: Jobless and Wageless Recoveries, Working Paper 18480, National Bureau of Economic Research.

Commander, S. and Nikoloski, Z. (2010): Institutions and economic performance: What can be explained?, Working Paper No. 121 European Bank for Reconstruction and Development.

Coval, J., Jurek, J. and Stafford E. (2009) The Economics of Structured Finance. *Journal of Economic Perspectives,* 23(1), Winter, 3-25.

Danielsson, J. (2008). The First Causalty of the Crisis: Iceland. In Andrew Felton and Carmen M. Reinhart, eds. The First Global Financial Crisis of the 21st Century, Part II, June-December 2008, VoxEU.org, 9-13.

De Gregorio, J. (2009). Chile and the Global Recession of 2009. Speech at the seminar Los temas del 2009, organized by the Institutode Políticas Públicas Expansivas – UDP and Libertad y Desarrollo, Santiago, Chile, March 20, 2009.

De Long, J. B. (2009). The Financial Crisis of 2007-2009: Understanding its Causes, Consequences and its Possible Cures. MTI-CSC Economics Speaker Series Lecture, Singapore, January5, 2009, htt://www.scribd. com/doc/9719227/null.

Demirguc-Kunt, A. and Serven L. (2009). Are the Sacred Cows Dead?: Implications of the Financial Crisis for Macro and Financial Policies. World Bank Policy Research Working Paper no. 4807, January. [DKL]

Eichengreen, B., Mitchener, K.J., 2003. The Great Depression as a Credit Boom Gone Wrong. Working Paper No. 137, Bank for International Settlements, September.

Feldstein, M. (2009). The Economics Stimulus and Sustained Economic Growth. Full Statement for the House Democratic Steering and Policy Committee, January7, 2009.

Hall, R. E. and Woodward S. E. (2009). The Financial Crisis and the Recession: What is happening and what the Government Should do. Financial Crisis and Recession. January 1, 2009, http:// woodwardhall.wordpress.com/.

Hendry, D.F., 1995. Dynamic Econometrics, Oxford: Oxford University Press.

Hoover, K.D., Perez, 1999, S.J., 1999. Data mining reconsidered: encompassing and the general- to-specific approach to specification search. *Econometrics Journal,* 2, 167-191.

Isham, J., Kaufmann, D. and. Pritchett, L. H. (1997): Civil Liberties, Democracy, and the Performance of Government Projects, World Bank Economic Reveview 11 (2): 219-242.

Jordá, O. and Schularick, M. (2011): "When Credit Bites Back: Leverage, Business Cycles, and Crises", Working Paper 2011-27, Federal Reserve Bank of San Francisco.

Kaufmann, D. Kraay, A. and Zoido-Lobaton. P (1999): Governance Matters, Policy Research Working Paper 2196, The World Bank.

Kim, S., Lee, J.-W. and Park, C.-Y. (2011), Emerging Asia: Decoupling or Recoupling. *World Economy,* 34: 23–53.

King G, Honaker J, Joseph A, Scheve K (2001) Analyzing incomplete political science data: an alternative algorithm for multiple imputation. *American Political Science Review,* 95:49–69.

Lovell, M.C., 1983. Data mining, *Review of Economics and Statistics,* 65, 1-12.

Reinhart, C. and Reinhart, V. (2009). From Capital Flow Bonanza to Financial Crash. In Andrew Felton and Carmen M. Reinhart, eds. The First Global Financial Crisis of the 21st Century, Part II, June-December 2008, VoxEU.org, 31-37.

Reinhart, C. and Rogoff, K.S. (2008). Is the 2007 US Sub-Prime Crisis so Different? An International Historical Comparison. American Economic Review: *Papers and Proceedings,* 98:2, 339-344.

Rose, A.K. Spiegel, M.M., 2009. Cross-Country Causes and Consequences of the 2008 Crisis: Early Warning. Federal Reserve Bank of San Francisco. Working Paper 2009-17. Available at http://www.frbsf.org/publications/economics/papers/2009/wp09-17bk.pdf.

Spencer, M. (2008) Balance Sheets and Income Statements: Breaking the Downward Spiral. Ft.com/economists forum. November 24, 2009.

White, L. (2008). How did we get into this Financial Mess?. CATO Institute Briefing Paper no. 110, November 18, 2009.

Schwarz, G. 1978. Estimating the dimension of a model. *Annals of Statistics,* 6, 461-464.

Turner, A., 2009. The Turner Review: A Regulatory Response to the Global Banking Crisis. London: Financial Services Authority. Available at http://www.fsa.gov. uk/pubs/other/turner_review.pdf.

In: Financial Crises
Editor: Cooper A. Hawthorne
ISBN: 978-1-62808-293-7

Chapter 9

SEEING LIKE A CREDIT RATING AGENCY: THE CONSTITUTION OF FINANCIAL UNCERTAINTIES DURING THE GREEK SOVEREIGN DEBT CRISIS

Grégoire Mallard[1,*] and Pierre Pénet[2,*]
[1]Department of Sociology, Northwestern University, Evanston, Illinois, US
[2]Department of Sociology, Northwestern University, Evanston, Illinois, US & SciencesPo Paris/OSC, Paris, France

ABSTRACT

Building on a relatively new literature in the sociology of knowledge and science studies, this paper analyzes how financial actors minimized the uncertainties arising in the recent European sovereign debt crisis by resorting to non-linear practices of risk valuation by which they "constituted" the reality of those same financial uncertainties. Centering on the Greek sovereign debt crisis, we explain why credit rating agencies (CRAs), specifically Moody's, failed to recognize early signs of trouble in Greece, and displayed rating inertia before issuing multi-notch downgrades. Using ratings reports and press releases published by Moody's, we first show that CRAs used ratings they had already assigned to constitute the new threats they were tasked with predicting, a technique we call "backward reasoning." Second, we show that market regulators also made constitutive use of ratings' forecasting capacities to carry out their tasks of market surveillance and monitoring, forcing CRAs to anticipate the potentially destabilizing effects that further downgrades would have on Greece's borrowing costs. Such non-linear risk valuation practices created several inconsistencies in CRAs' predictions about Greece's ability to meet its financial commitment. We additionally show how these inconsistencies played out in the unfolding Greek sovereign debt crisis.

For many, the 2008 financial crisis demonstrated the colossal failure of credit rating agencies (CRAs) to predict risk events. This was especially true of their ability to predict the prospect that sovereign (country) issuers would default on their debt. Until 2008, investors

* Corresponding author: g-mallard@northwestern.edu and pierrepenet2013@u.northwestern.edu, or to Pierre Pénet, Department of Sociology, Northwestern University, 1810 Chicago Avenue, Evanston 60208 IL, USA.

and CRAs considered the sovereign bond market a safe haven for a wide range of reasons. From the years following World War II until the late-1990s, sovereign debt rescheduling and defaults remained quite low (Reinhart and Rogoff 2009). And, although most advanced economies saw their credit positions erode in the 2000s due to a conjunction of factors (including higher public spending, lower capacity to tax, and low GDP growth), investors assumed the trend of trustworthiness would last. But the European sovereign debt crisis beginning in 2009 proved everyone wrong: sovereign defaults could still trigger devastating financial and economic consequences, even at the heart of the Western world. The 2012 Greek default—the largest sovereign default in recent history and the epicenter of the European debt crisis—spurred controversies about the role of CRAs and led investors, regulators, and public officials to blame CRAs for their lack of foresight in the months leading up to the Greek sovereign crisis.

In financial markets, as in any market environment, competing and often contradictory forms of knowledge circulate. In global credit markets, risk knowledge essentially comes from two sources: (1) Market-based risk information embedded in market prices (yields, spreads), that provides an aggregated snapshot of the millions of risk pricing transactions at any given time, and (2) Expert judgment in a standardized (ratings, rankings), written (reports, policy briefs), or oral (press conferences) form, which reflects the particular risk views of their originators, whether governmental organizations, private agencies or international institutions.

In the months leading up to the Greek sovereign crisis, risk perceptions expressed in market prices and expert assessments significantly diverged. Credit default swap (CDS) and government bond spreads suggested a much higher probability of Greek default than was encoded in the ratings of the three main CRAs, notably Moody's. Converting CDSs into CDS-implied ratings (CDS-IRs), Gaillard (2012) finds that investors had already begun to price Greek government debt in the speculative-grade category as early as December 2009, well before CRAs aggressively downgraded Greek bonds to junk status after months of rating inertia. As the market's risk perceptions diverged from those of CRAs, the ratings of the three main CRAs also varied substantially from one another. All three major CRAs had more optimistic risk views than the market-based perceptions embedded in market prices, notably CDS spreads. Standard & Poor's (S&P) and Fitch, however, still perceived Greece as more risky than did Moody's,[44] until Moody's finally issued a four-notch downgrade on Greek sovereign ratings in June 2010.

Between September 2008 and June 2010, CRAs failed to recognize early signs of trouble in Greece and displayed rating inertia before issuing multi-notch downgrades. This pattern of rating migration poses a problem of valuation and begs the question of how CRAs "see" risk and produce risk knowledge. Greece is not an isolated case, as evidenced by the similar problem of valuation of risky credit derivatives in the U.S. subprime market. Upon realizing that they had bestowed generous ratings to debt instruments that were defaulting at a much higher rate than anticipated, CRAs aggressively downgraded the ratings of billions of dollars' worth of securities. This wave of downgrades prompted global panic across capital markets,

[44] From 2008 to mid-2010, Moodys' ratings sharply contrasted from the ratings of S&P and Fitch as well as from market indicators: until the first European bailout of Greece in May 2010, Moody's proceeded to only two rating changes (downgrades) against 4 and 5 for Fitch and S&P, respectively. Moody's finally issued a four-notch downgrade of Greek bonds on 14 June 2010, almost 2 years after the collapse of Lehman Brothers.

an event widely cited as one of the main causes of the subprime mortgage crisis and the 2008 financial meltdown (Carruthers 2010; Rona-Tas and Hiss 2011).

Such a dramatic rating migration pattern arouses suspicion and seems to indicate that ratings were too high in the first place. In this spirit, economists have pursued studies of rating criteria and ratings' informational content which seek to explain CRAs' poor predictive performance, thereby lending credence to the notion that CRAs "missed" the crisis (Bhatia 2002; Cantor et al. 1996; Ferri et al. 1999). Their informational approach suggests that CRAs' poor track record in predicting future outcomes originates in the failure to "discover" market information, which results in inaccurate predictions. However, this purely informational approach to rating failure has limited explanatory value for the sovereign debt market because financial parties (including investors and CRAs) typically rely on similar credit information from public sources or governmental agencies. Therefore, information issues pertaining to access, quality or asymmetry—to pick just a few—cannot alone explain the gap between ratings and market perceptions. Nor can an informational approach explain why CRAs maintained their ratings in spite of conspicuous evidence of a rapidly changing market environment. And finally, such an approach cannot properly explain why Moody's downgraded Greek government bonds by six notches in just six months between December 2009 and June 2010, a rating pattern unprecedented in the recent history of sovereign ratings.

In this article we argue that CRAs' failure was not merely informational but also socio-cognitive. We do so by pointing to several inconsistencies at the level of the *evaluative practices* that CRAs use to produce anticipatory knowledge under high uncertainty. In the face of ambiguous, contradictory or fragmented information—such as in contexts of financial innovation or rapidly changing market environments typical of times of crisis—anticipatory knowledge producers like CRAs do more than simply collect additional information when they are unsure about their ratings. Knowledge producers also engage in a cognitive effort to reengineer evaluative practices so as to minimize uncertainty.

Sociologists of knowledge and science studies scholars have only recently begun to focus on those practical dimensions of anticipatory knowledge which determine its ability to predict likely outcomes. Their work includes studies in banking and high finance (Knorr Cetina 2011; Muniesa and Callon 2007; Stark 2009, MacKenzie 2011), environmental policy (Dalmedico and Guillemot 2008), and food safety (Borraz and Besançon 2008). No research has yet focused on sovereign ratings, partly because the latter do not mobilize the highly formalized models that CRAs use to rate other classes of assets, most notably structured financial instruments. Indeed, CRAs use more qualitative analytical techniques to formalize sovereign risk and arrive at a judgment about the *willingness* of a country to repay its debt on time and in full.

In this chapter, we argue that the specific socio-cognitive problems associated with the calculation of sovereign risks by CRAs originate from the non-linear aspect of anticipatory knowledge practices at play in their valuation processes. Most studies of risk valuation adhere to a conventional—linear—framework in which time flows from the past to the future. From this perspective, producers of anticipatory knowledge analyze past and present information in order to assign a single distribution of probabilities to future outcomes. Moreover, under a linear approach to temporality, producers of anticipatory knowledge work in the isolation of the laboratory, never having to acknowledge the consequences their predictions may bear on a future course of events. Departing from this linear narrative, we suggest a more complex vision of how anticipatory knowledge producers articulate the past, present, and future. In doing so, we claim that social scientists should study anticipatory knowledge not only for its predictive purpose (whether it produces accurate or inaccurate predictions about the future likelihood of specific events), but also for its "constitutive purpose" (Mallard and Lakoff 2011), e.g. the use of some knowledge of the future (anticipatory knowledge) to constitute present uncertainties. We pay particular attention to the constitutive use of ratings first, by CRAs, and second, by market regulators.

First, as we show in our preliminary investigation of the Greek sovereign debt crisis, CRAs adapted strategically to cognitive inconsistencies and credibility concerns by using ratings they have already assigned to constitute the new threats they were tasked with predicting. In doing so, CRAs used a technique we call "backward reasoning." This appeal to the future to make sense of present threats also guarantees that new risk threats will acquire meaning in ways that vindicate their previous views, because the terms of meaning are generated by their own previously-assigned ratings. Therefore backward reasoning helps CRAs maintain continuity between ratings, thereby preserving the consistency of opinion that marks CRAs as credible producers of valid anticipatory knowledge. However, while their non-linear technique of rating production mitigated their most immediate concerns about uncertainty and credibility, we show that it also resulted in rating path dependency and informational diminishing returns, two inconsistencies which are highlighted in Moody's' unusual pattern of rating migration.

Second, our preliminary investigation of the Greek sovereign debt crisis shows how knowledge producers may have to anticipate the likely consequences of their predictions as they are *used* in the financial world, especially by market regulators. Indeed, since the 1990s it has become common practice for market regulators to make constitutive use of ratings' forecasting capacities to carry out their tasks of market surveillance and monitoring (Partnoy 1999).[45] When regulators appeal to ratings for "governmentality" purposes (Foucault 2009) such as defining acceptable investing practices, credit standards, and accounting norms, they inevitably alter the rules governing the market reception of ratings. When ratings are extended legal influence, they cease simply to be fluctuating opinions about the future. Instead, they function as fixed market rules, and the mechanisms governing their reception become no longer deliberative but legally binding because investors and other financial parties must comply with the enforceable standards which regulators have developed in reference to ratings. As a result, CRAs no longer produce ratings in isolation from their predicted outcomes. Rather, they must anticipate how their predictions about long-term future risks will affect their environment – what Espeland and Saunder (2007) define as "reactivity." With specific reference to Moody's, we will show that CRAs account for the potentially destabilizing consequences of their predictions on issuers when assessing new threats. In light of this evidence, we show that the constitutive use of ratings by market regulators can strongly influence the rating process, as evidenced by Moody's' inertia during the Greek debt crisis.

The main data sources for this chapter are ratings reports and press releases published by Moody's between October 2009 and September 2010 (available on the agency's website).[46] Since the motivations behind rating actions are not always clear, especially in time of acute

[45] Ratings are now routinely used in bank capital requirements and in SEC and Basel prudential regulations in the U.S. and Europe. Rating-based regulations can take many other forms. See: Bank for International Settlements (2009) and Cantor et al. (2007) for an overview.

[46] Pierre Pénet has conducted the analysis of the primary material.

financial stress, these materials deserve careful attention.[47] In the event of a rating action, CRAs typically issue a rating report to subscribers via a press release. In these, they establish a dialogue with investors and provide explanatory guidance that can be difficult to pass along in ratings alone. Weaving together various threads of meaning and context, these reports thus provide insight into the considerations CRAs undertake and the choices they make when reflecting on the relevance of a rating action. If reports give prime access to the rationale behind rating actions, they also reflect on the messy and highly ambiguous nature of the rating process by displaying the doubts, hesitations, and occasional contradictions that rating activity invariably entails. Overall, these documents offer a key perspective on the processes of risk assessment and reality construction that underwrite any rating process.

In the first section, we cover CRAs' views on the Greek economy during the period of September 2008 through December 2009. We show that their initially contrarian risk predictions were not inaccurate but instead reflected a highly plausible rating scenario among other equally plausible scenarios. However, as our inspection of rating reports reveals, Moody's continued to use investment-grade ratings they had previously assigned while the Greek crisis amplified, simultaneously making sense of Greece's developing threats and "constituting" the list of events to which they assigned probabilities. By doing so, Moody's sought to minimize the uncertainties which the European sovereign debt crisis posed to their valuation of risk while maximizing the continuity between ratings and thereby appease concerns about their credibility. In the second section, and focusing on the period of January through June 2010, we investigate how the ECB's constitutive use of ratings in defining market regulations changed the market reception of ratings and forced Moody's to anticipate the potentially destabilizing consequences that further downgrades would have on Greece's borrowing costs. In both cases, we argue, the constitutive use of ratings by regulators and CRAs themselves greatly affected the rating process and contributed strongly to the problem of valuation described above.

1. Backward Reasoning and Rating Inertia

Backward reasoning is a non-linear process by which a producer of anticipatory knowledge infers the meaning of new information in a way that vindicates former views, which are themselves embedded in the producer's present anticipations of a future outcome. We suggest that Moody's employed backward reasoning as an adaptive strategy, on the one hand, to minimize the political uncertainties that emerged from the valuation of new risk threats in the Eurozone sovereign debt market, and, on the other, to maximize stability between ratings in order to maintain their overall rating credibility.

Our examination of the press release (Moody's 2008) and two rating reports (Moody's 2009a; Moody's 2009b) published by Moody's between September 2008 and October 2009 suggests four persistent and complementary views supporting Moody's initial "A" investment-grade rating for Greek government bonds.

[47] The rating industry is notoriously secretive and resistant to investigation by social scientists. As a result, little is known about the ways in which CRAs compute risk.

Greek fundamentals and government resolve and credibility: Moody's emphasize the potentially destabilizing effect of Greece's poor economic performance, weakening competitiveness, and growing debt levels in both the public and private sectors. At the same time, however, they note their intention to monitor deteriorating fundamentals in relation to other risk factors, including political ones. At the national level, Moody's state their plan to assess the Greek government's resolve to shore up creditworthiness, as well as its margin for maneuver and capacity to implement efficient reform.

External support: The prospect of a sovereign debt crisis involving a Eurozone member had little precedent and did not lend itself to easy calculation. A member of the European currency zone, Greece did not control exchange rate or monetary policy. The ECB's decision to extend external support was thus crucial, especially given Greece's soon-to-be non-existent access to capital markets. Since the legal rules and procedures contained in the European Stability and Growth Pact had made external support from the ECB conditional (see: section 2), Moody's had to issue a judgment about the Greek government's willingness to repay its debt in time and in full, but they also had to imagine and evaluate the probability of another element in this scenario: the willingness of the ECB to assume its role of lender of last resort, should Greece need them to do so. For CRAs and specifically Moody's, the prevailing belief that the ECB would not let a member default made the prospect of a Greek default highly unlikely. According to Moody's rationale, liquidity risk could only materialize if the ECB refused to approve external support for a Eurozone member, a possibility Moody's considered extremely unlikely.

Market prices: Moody's also acknowledged the significance of market price fluctuation on Greek government borrowing costs. Moody's did not expect a direct causal relationship between higher borrowing costs and liquidity crisis, as long as the Greek government sustained credibility and foreign support remained plausible. This is why, despite soaring prices and increasing risk fears expressed in CDS spreads, Moody's did not downgrade Greek sovereign bonds in the fall of 2008.

Equivalent ratings: Finally, rating all 16 country members of the Eurozone, Moody's sought to contextualize the Greek economic situation relative to countries with comparable fundamentals. They did so for the purpose of commensuration, in order to ensure that they applied similar ratings to equivalent levels of trustworthiness. Until October 2009, Moody's justified its "A" investment-grade rating for Greece by arguing that its financial situation was not materially different from that faced by other equivalent European countries.

After the collapse of Lehman Brothers in September 2008, fears that the American financial meltdown would spill over into Europe began to damage market perceptions of Greek economic trustworthiness. Although sovereign CDS and bond spreads were on the rise, CRAs did not change their ratings of Greek government bonds until the end of 2009, with the exception of S&P, who downgraded Greek bonds by one notch in January 2009. For instance, Moody's maintained its "A1" rating for Greece from November 2002 until December 2009. Until October 2009, Moody's' projected scenario was eminently plausible and, in fact, accurate: market fears had eased and Greek bond and CDS spreads declined to almost pre-crisis levels, thus confirming the relatively optimistic scenarios CRAs had predicted. For weeks, Greek officials used Moody's contrarian views to convince financial parties to invest more heavily in its debt. Their appeal was predicated on the logic that Moody's' countercyclical perception of future events was more rewarding for all parties than the "consensual" market perception reflected in sovereign bond and CDS spreads.

However, Greece's unexpected revision of its 2009 deficit projection from 3.7% of GDP to 12.5% on October 20 stunned markets. As a result, Greek sovereign CDS and government bond spreads begun to widen again in October 2009, signaling deteriorating perceptions of Greece's creditworthiness. By December, markets were already pricing Greek sovereign bonds in the speculative-grade debt category and Greek sovereign CDS spreads had risen well above those of Ireland, Portugal, and Spain (Gaillard 2012). The deficit revision significantly undermined the risk scenario that Moody's had predicted for Greece: only one item of Moody's rationale (external support) could be said to remain unchanged.

In spite of these developments, Moody's did not downgrade Greek government bonds, but continued, instead, to use their existing rationale for investment grade rating to make sense of the uncertainties arising from increasingly negative perceptions of Greek sovereign risk. In the rest of this section we show how they did so, even as the limits of plausibility of their investment-grade rating were being tested from October 2009 onward.

Moody's press releases published in December 2009 (2009c; 2009d) justify (albeit somewhat warily) an investment-rating for Greece that challenges market fears that Greece's deteriorating economic situation could materialize in a significant liquidity risk. In the note, "Investor Fears of Liquidity Risks in Greece are Overdone," Moody's reaffirms its prevailing confidence in the ECB and calls the prospect of a Greek default "extremely unlikely." Only in the highly remote case that Greek government debt became ineligible as collateral, the note claims, would liquidity risk become a possibility.

Moody's deep-seated expectation of ECB support constituted their evaluation of Greece's new risks. Beginning in October 2009, Moody's relied on this expectation as a cognitive antecedent that conferred meaning on any new risk information pertaining to Greece's deteriorating economic situation. Thus, despite Greek government's weakening fundamentals, declining financial maneuver, lowered credibility, and borrowing costs that had risen above those of any other European country they had previously deemed comparable, Moody's reaffirmed its investment-grade rating. The single-notch downgrade issued by Moody's on December 22 still maintained Greece in the "A" investment-grade range and was widely viewed by market actors as "softer" than expected.[48]

Moody's decision to maintain its investment-grade rating for Greece even when its initial rationale was no longer (as a whole) valid has several implications. First, by calling investor fears over Greek government liquidity "misplaced" and "exaggerated," Moody's seemed to hope it could once again shape investors' perceptions about the Greek government's ability to repay its debt and encourage market parties to bring about the conditions that would justify an "A" investment-grade scenario. After all, between January and October 2009, CRAs' (and specifically Moody's') rating inertia seemed to have achieved precisely that goal, with CDS and sovereign bond spreads returning to their pre-crisis levels after a temporary surge in the fall of 2008. Until 2009, the initial gap between CRAs' perception of Greece's trustworthiness and the more conservative views embedded in market prices essentially

[48] *The Financial Times*, "Moody's gives Greece breathing space on debts," 23 December 2009.

expressed a conflict between *equally plausible* risk scenarios that had been resolved in favor of CRAs.

Second, after Greece's October deficit revision announcement and its destabilizing consequences for the Greek government's fundamentals, borrowing costs, and overall credibility, Moody's rationale for its investment-grade became significantly more contrarian and the possibility that market actors would bring their predictions to pass more remote. That Moody's refrained from downgrading Greece to the "B" range suggests a path dependency of ratings we interpret as a manifestation of backward reasoning. Moody's consistently made constitutive use of the prospect of external ECB support to restrict the range of meaning that information could acquire, even under markedly different conditions. Moody's were embroiled in a dynamic cognitive process whereby constitutive use of rating models created diminishing informational returns for every piece of new information collected. Thus, rating inertia appears to be the path-dependent outcome of a non-linear process of knowledge production and credibility assurance: so long as CRAs can use existing risk rationales, in whole or in part, to make sense of new risk information, CRAs have an incentive to uphold ratings. Therefore, non-linear rating practices and backward reasoning creates an interesting paradox where, over time, the *predictive* capacities of existing rating scenarios increase the *uncertainties* of present threats.

Moody's expectation that the ECB—or, for that matter, the Eurozone stakeholders—would assume of the responsibilities of lender of last resort was considerably challenged in January. This political decision brought about the considerable amount of uncertainty to which we turn in the following section.

2. Market Monitoring and Rating Standoff

Since the creation of the European and Monetary Union in 1994, European financial institutions have routinely used ratings to define the risk weight of their financial exposure. Under the Capital Requirement Directive, the ECB applies a rating threshold to define the acceptable quality of collateral for refinancing purposes. In October 2008, the ECB lowered the normal "A3/A-" threshold to a more relaxed "Baa3/BBB-" to enhance provisions of liquidity to the Eurozone. However, the ECB announced in January 2011 that they would revert to their usual, tighter collateral framework. As explained above, financial parties (most notably CRAs) expected the ECB to provide strong institutional commitment and to agree to step in as lender of last resort, should the need arise. Therefore, financial parties, and especially Moody's, anticipated further amendments to the ECB's collateral framework rating threshold, to accommodate the rapidly changing Greek economic situation. Instead, the contrary happened: on January 14, 2010, the ECB President Jean-Claude Trichet reaffirmed its intention to let its "Baa3/BBB-" threshold expire in January 2011.[49] This decision increased fears that liquidity risk could materialize if CRAs lowered ratings, which would bring Greek bonds closer to ineligibility for refunding purposes. The ECB's decision thus changed the meaning that further downgrades would have on Greece's ability to borrow.

[49] "We will not change our collateral framework for the sake of any particular country. Our collateral framework applies to all countries concerned. And that has been said already by the Vice-President, by me and by colleagues. That is crystal clear." (ECB 2010a).

Indeed, having faced prohibitive borrowing costs since January 2010, the Greek government was left with little means to propose a financial support package of its own and was effectively squeezed out of capital markets. It was therefore critical to Greece's ability to fund itself that its sovereign bonds remain eligible as collateral in exchange for low-interest loans from the ECB.

The ECB's constitutive use of ratings in defining its threshold for collateral eligibility produced a rating standoff in which a downgrade was as undesirable for Moody's as it was for Greece. Fitch and S&P issued multi-notch downgrades in March and April 2010 respectively, with S&P relegating Greece to junk-bond status on April 22. With its rating well-anchored in the investment grade category, Moody's remained the only strong holdout, effectively serving with Fitch as a buffer against the prospect of Greek speculative status. Because the ECB determines the eligibility of collateral by applying the higher of the lowest two ratings,[50] the ECB thus used Fitch's "BBB-" rating, the lowest within the investment-grade category, only because Moody's were still rating Greece in the investment-grade category.

Moody's were thus operating under a strong and ever-increasing incentive not to translate its pessimism about Greece's financial future into a downgraded rating. Had it matched S&P's speculative rating, Moody's would have rendered Greek government bonds ineligible as ECB collateral. A downgrade into the junk status would almost certainly catalyze a significant liquidity crisis, which in turn would force Moody's—and other CRAs—to issue another downgrade (which itself would have to take into account the consequences of its own downgrade on Greek finances). Like a receding horizon, rating accuracy became moved ever-more out of reach; no matter what considerations Moody's took, the prospect of downgrading Greek sovereign bonds in an orderly fashion was no longer a possibility.

The ECB's May 3rd announcement to suspend its minimum credit rating threshold for Greece (ECB 2010b) was widely interpreted as a strategic attempt to diffuse the risk of a potential Moody's downgrade. Crucially and ironically, however, the decision also removed the incentive for Moody's not to downgrade. A month later on June 14, Moody's issued the most severe downgrade of sovereign bonds in recent history, knocking it down four-notches, to speculative status. Ultimately, the timing of Moody's multi-notch downgrade was not motivated by a change in Greek fundamentals, but by the ECB's modification of its collateral framework, a change that essentially "liberated" Moody's to downgrade Greece's government without jeopardizing the country's ability to qualify for low-interest loans. Past studies have concluded that regulatory reliance on CRA predictions favors high ratings (Gaillard 2012). We propose that this is the case because high ratings create incentives for ratings inertia. They can only do so temporarily, however, ultimately giving way to more dramatic patterns of rating change.

CONCLUSION

This chapter yields several findings. First, we challenge the common view that CRAs merely "misread" the Greek crisis. The examination of rating reports shows that Moody's' rationale for its investment-grade rating of Greece was initially highly plausible. We then

[50] See Committee of European Banking Supervisors (2006), (clause 178) p.35.

show that CRAs adapted strategically to cognitive inconsistencies and credibility concerns by making constitutive use of the ratings they had already assigned to constitute the new threats they were tasked with predicting. As such, CRAs resorted to a technique we call "backward reasoning" that mitigated their most immediate concerns about uncertainty and credibility but also resulted in rating path dependency and informational diminishing returns: so long as CRAs could use existing risk rationales, in whole or in part, to make sense of new risk information, CRAs had an incentive to uphold ratings. Our preliminary study of the Greek debt crisis shows that backward reasoning creates an interesting paradox where, over time, the *predictive* capacities of existing rating scenarios increase the *uncertainties* of present threats. Finally, we indicate that the ECB's constitutive use of ratings in defining market regulations also greatly affected the rating process by forcing CRAs to anticipate the potentially destabilizing consequences that further downgrades would have on Greece's borrowing costs.

We believe that this analysis of the non-linear dimensions of risk evaluation practices opens interesting avenues for the sociology of knowledge and social studies of finance. Our preliminary analysis of the Greek sovereign debt crisis points to a non-linear, complex web of cognitive, legal, and political transactions, that complicate previous understandings of the market infusion of ratings (most notably those produced by theories of performativity). A future article will provide analyses of additional concrete cases and develop more refined typologies of these forms of anticipatory knowledge. In this chapter and future work, we aim to develop a better understanding of how constitutive knowledge is used and produced in financial worlds.

References

Bank for International Settlements. (2009). *Stocktaking on the use of credit ratings*: Basel Committee on Banking Supervision – The Joint Forum, June.

Bhatia, Ashok V. (2002). *Sovereign credit ratings methodology: an evaluation*: International Monetary Fund.

Borraz, Olivier., and Julien Besançon. (2008). "Uncertainties in regulating food safety in France." 49-67 in *Uncertain Risks Regulated*, Edited by Ellen Vos, and Michelle Everson: Routledge.

Cantor, Richard., Frank Packer, and Federal Reserve Bank of New York. (1996). *Determinants and impacts of sovereign credit ratings*, Public Information Department: Federal Reserve Bank of New York.

Cantor, Richard., Owain Ap Gwilym, and Stephen Thomas. (2007). "*The use of credit ratings in investment management in the US and Europe*." Available at SSRN 996133.

Carruthers, Bruce G. (2010). "Knowledge and liquidity: Institutional and cognitive foundations of the subprime crisis." *Research in the Sociology of Organizations*, *30*, 157-82.

Commitee of European Banking Supervisors. (2006). "Guidelines on the recognition of External Credit Assessment Institutions."

Dalmedico, Amy., and Hélène Guillemot. (2008). "Climate Change: Scientific Dynamics, Expertise and Geopolitical Challenges." 195–221 in *Global Science and National*

Sovereignty: Studies in Historical Sociology of Science, Edited by Grégoire Mallard, Catherine Paradeise, and Ashveen Peerbaye. New York: Routledge.

ECB. (2010a). "Press Conference, Introductory statement with Q&A." 14 January 2010.

—. (2010b). "Press Release: 'ECB announces change in eligibility of debt instruments issued or guaranteed by the Greek government.'" 3 May 2010.

Espeland, Wendy N., and Michael Sauder. (2007). "Rankings and Reactivity: How Public Measures Recreate Social Worlds." *American Journal of Sociology*, *113(1)*, 1-40.

Ferri, Giovanni., Li-Gang Liu, and Joseph E. Stiglitz. (1999). "The procyclical role of rating agencies: Evidence from the East Asian crisis." *Economic Notes*, *28*(3), 335-55.

Foucault, Michel. (2009). *Security, Territory, Population: Lectures at the College de France 1977—1978*. Paris: Seuil.

Gaillard, Norbert. (2012). "The Limits of Sovereign Ratings in Light of the Greek Debt Crisis of 2009–2010." 171-87 in *A Century of Sovereign Ratings*: Springer.

Knorr Cetina, Karin. (2011). "Thirteen / Financial Analysis: Epistemic Profile of an Evaluative Science." 405-441 in *Social Knowledge in the Making*, Edited by Charles Camic, Neil Gross, and Michèle Lamont: University of Chicago Press.

MacKenzie, Donald. (2011). "The Credit Crisis as a Problem in the Sociology of Knowledge." *American Journal of Sociology*, *116(6)*, 1778-1841.

Mallard, Grégoire., and Andrew Lakoff. (2011). "How Claims to Know the Future Are Used to Understand the Present." 339-377 in *Social Knowledge in the Making*, Edited by Charles Camic, Neil Gross, and Michèle Lamont: Chicago University Press.

Moody's. (2008). "Greece's political unrest exposes constraints reflected in A1 rating." Announcement: Moody's Investors Service.

—. (2009a). "*Moody's changes the outlook for Greece's A1 rating to stable*." Rating Action: Moody's Investors Service.

—. (2009b). "*Moody's places Greece's ratings on review for possible downgrade*." Rating Action: Moody's Investors Service.

—. (2009c). "*Moody's: Investor Fears Over Greek Government Liquidity Misplaced*." Announcement: Moody's Investors Service.

—. (2009d). "*Moody's downgrades Greece to A2 from A1*." Rating Action: Moody's Investors Service.

Muniesa, Fabian., and Michel Callon. (2007). "Economic experiments and the construction of markets." 163-189 in *Do economists make markets? On the performativity of economics*, Edited by Donald MacKenzie, Fabian Muniesa, and Lucia Siu: Princeton University Press

Partnoy, Frank. (1999). "The Siskel and Ebert of financial markets: Two thumbs down for the credit rating agencies." *Washington University Law Quartely*, *77(3)*, 619-714.

Reinhart, Carmen M., and Kenneth S. Rogoff. (2009). *This time is different: Eight centuries of financial folly*: Princeton University Press.

Rona-Tas, Akos., and Stefanie Hiss. (2011). "Forecast as Valuation: The Role of Ratings and Predictions in the Subprime Mortgage Crisis in the US." 223-246 in *Worth of Goods. Valuation and Pricing in the Economy*, Edited by Jens Becker and Patrick Aspers: Princeton University Press.

Stark, David. (2009). *The sense of dissonance: accounts of worth in economic life*: Princeton University Press.

In: Financial Crises
Editor: Cooper A. Hawthorne

ISBN: 978-1-62808-293-7

Chapter 10

CORRELATION AND NETWORK STRUCTURE OF INTERNATIONAL FINANCIAL MARKETS IN TIMES OF CRISIS

Leonidas Sandoval Junior*
Insper, Instituto de Ensino e Pesquisa

Abstract

The chapter considers the correlation, volatility, and clustering structure of the benchmark indices of the main stock exchanges in the world. The importance of understanding how stock markets relate to each other, and which ones are the most connected, is of paramount importance to the study of how crises develop and propagate. We focus on the largest worldwide crisis in the last two decades, which started with the USA subprime mortgage crisis of 2008, and continued to the Credit Crisis in Europe (2009-2012). The data consists on 79 benchmark indices of stock exchanges across the world, from 2003 to 2012. We start by studying how the use of Random Matrix Theory helps identify a market mode that varies in intensity across the years, in particular in years of crises, and a structure that is typical of markets operating at different time zones. Then, the average correlation between indices and a global measure of volatility are compared, showing that in times of high volatility the international financial market indices are more correlated between themselves. We finally analyze the clustering of those indices, using tools from Network Theory. By doing so, it becomes clear that the correlations between international financial market indices depend very much on the geographical position of their markets, and on the operating times of those markets.

1. Introduction

The last two largest global economic crises have their origins in the financial markets: the first one, which reached its peak in 2008, originated from the so-called suprime mortgages. This crisis was triggered by the default of a large number of mortgages in the USA. Subprimes are loans to borrowers who have low credit scores. Most of them had a small initial

*E-mail address: leonidassj@insper.org.br

interest rate, adjustable for future payments, which led to many home foreclosures after the rates climbed substantially. Meanwhile, the loans were transformed in pools that were then resold to interested investors. Since the returns of such investments were high, a financial bubble was created, inflating the subprime mortgage market until the defaults started to pop up.

Because of their underestimation of risk, financial institutions worldwide lost trillions of dollars, and many of them declared bankruptcy, and credit lines tightened around the world, taking the financial crisis to the so-called real economy and hitting many countries in Europe with devastating effects. The so-called Credit Crisis is an ongoing one, and no one knows how much damage to the world economies it is yet to cause.

Other global financial crises that happened fairly recently were the Black Monday (1987), the Asian Crisis (1997), the Russian Crisis (1998), the burst of the dot.com bubble (2000 and 2001), and many minor crises. All of them should not have happened in all of the age of the Universe (about 13 billion years), according to the mainstream financial theory and practice.

Economists have been studying the reasons why markets crash, and why there is propagation of volatility from one market to another, since a long time. After the crash of 1987, many studies have been published on transmission of volatility (contagion) between markets using econometric models [1]- [8], on how the correlation between world markets change with time [9]- [11], and how correlation tends to increase in times of high volatility [12]- [24]. This issue is of particular importance if one wishes to build portfolios of international assets which can withstand times of crisis [25]- [31].

One tool that was first developed in nuclear physics for studying complex systems with unknown correlation structure is random matrix theory [32]- [35], which confronts the results obtained for the eigenvalues of the correlation matrix of a real system with those of the correlation matrix obtained from a pure random matrix. This approach has been successfully applied to a large number of financial markets [36]- [59], and also to the relation between world markets [60]. This approach has also been used in the construction of hierarchical structures between different assets of financial markets [61]- [73].

In this chapter, we shall focus on the time series of 79 benchmark indices across the world during the 10 years from the beginning of 2003 to the end of 2012. The indices and the countries they belong to are described in Section 2. The other crises listed above have been analyzed in [74], using basically the same tools as here, and their network structure was studied in [75] (as Minimum Spanning Trees) and in [76] (as Asset Graphs). Section 3 explains how Random Matrix Theory is applied to the data; Section 4 deals with the connection between the correlation of indices and the volatility of the world market; Section 5 uses the correlation between indices in order to build networks based on asset graphs. Section 6 offers some final conclusions.

2. The Data

The data consists on the time series of the closing values of the benchmark indices of 79 stock exchanges across the globe, collected from the beginning of 2003 to end of 2012. The indices and the countries to which they belong are: S&P 500 (United States of America), S&P/TSX Composite (Canada), IPC (Mexico), Bermuda SX Index (Bermuda), Jamaica

SX Market Index (Jamaica), BCT Corp Costa Rica (Costa Rica), Bolsa de Panama General (Panama), Merval (Argentina), Ibovespa (Brazil), IPSA (Chile), IGBC (Colombia), IGBVL (Peru), IBC (Venezuela), FTSE 100 (United Kingdom), ISEQ (Ireland), CAC 40 (France), DAX (Germany), ATX (Austria), SMI (Switzerland), BEL 20 (Belgium), AEX (Netherlands), OMX Stockholm 30 (Sweden), OMX Copenhagen 20 (Denmark), OMX Helsinki (Finland), OBX (Norway), OMX Iceland All-Share Index (Iceland), MIB-30 (Italy), IBEX 35 (Spain), PSI 20 (Portugal), Athens SX General Index (Greece), WIG (Poland), PX 50 (Czech Republic), SAX (Slovakia), CROBEX (Croatia), OMXT (Estonia), OMXR (Latvia), Budapest SX Index (Hungary), SOFIX (Bulgaria), PFTS (Ukraine), MICEX (Russia), ISE National 100 (Turkey), KASE (Kazakhstan), Malta SX Index (Malta), Tel Aviv 25 (Israel), Al Quds (Palestine), ASE General Index (Jordan), BLOM (Lebanon), TASI (Saudi Arabia), MSM 30 (Oman), DSM 20 (Qatar), ADX General Index (United Arab Emirates), Karachi 100 (Pakistan), SENSEX 30 (India), DSE General Index (Bangladesh), Colombo All-Share Index (Sri Lanka), Nikkei 25 (Japan), Hang Seng (Hong Kong), Shangai SE Composite (China), TAIEX (Taiwan), KOSPI (South Korea), MSE TOP 20 (Mongolia), Straits Times (Singapore), Jakarta Composite Index (Indonesia), KLCI (Malaysia), SET (Thailand), PSEI (Philippines), VN-Index (Vietnam), S&P/ASX 200 (Australia), NZX 50 (New Zealand), CFG 25 (Morocco), TUNINDEX (Tunisia), EGX 30 (Egypt), Nigeria SX All Share Index (Nigeria), Gaborone (Botswana), Ghana All Share Index (Ghana), NSE 20 (Kenya), SEMDEX (Mauritius), and FTSE/JSE Africa All Share (South Africa). The data were collected from a Bloomberg terminal.

Since we are dealing with countries that have different holidays and, in some cases, different weekends, we fixed the dates in which the New York Stock Exchange, by far the most important in terms of volume of negotiations and in influence, operated. If an index was not computed in one of the same dates, its value of the previous working day was repeated; in case one index operated in a day the New York Stock Exchange did not, then the index for that date was deleted. This contrasts with the common method used, which is to delete all days to which one of the time series had no data assigned; that would lead to the deletion of too many days, and we then would have returns that were not true to the real variations of the indices. Indices that were most affected by our method were the ones from Israel, Jordan, Saudi Arabia, Oman, Qatar, the United Arab Emirates, and Egypt, where weekends are not on Saturdays and Sundays. Nevertheless, we think that our choice preserves best the real returns in the major stock markets.

The data were used in order to calculate log-returns, defined as

$$S_t = \ln(P_t) - \ln(P_{t-1}) \approx \frac{P_t - P_{t-1}}{P_t} , \qquad (1)$$

where P_t is the value of an index on day t and P_{t-1} is the value of the same index on the previous day. Such measure is often used in order to avoid non-stationarity of data.

The log-returns are then used in order to calculate the Spearman rank correlation between each index, and the results are ordered in a correlation matrix. The reason for using the Spearman rank correlation and not the usual Pearson correlation is because the former is better at measuring nonlinear correlations, although both correlation measures yield very similar results [76].

In order to study the effects of the crisis of 2008 and onwards, we divide the data into two blocks, the first pertaining the 5 years from 2003 to 2007, and the other containing the years from 2008 to 2012. Then, Random Matrix Theory is used in order to find correlations that seem not to be random. This is explained in the next section.

3. Random Matrix Theory

Random matrix theory had its origins in 1953, in the work of the Hungarian physicist Eugene Wigner [32] [33]. He was studying the energy levels of complex atomic nuclei, such as uranium, and had no means of calculating the distance between those levels. He then assumed that those distances were random, and arranged the random number in a matrix which expressed the connections between the many energy levels. Surprisingly, he could then be able to make sensible predictions about how the energy levels related to one another.

This method also found connections with the study of the Riemann zeta function, which is of primordial importance to the study of prime numbers, used for coding and decoding information, for example. The theory was later developed, with many and surprising results arising. Today, random matrix theory is applied to quantum physics, nanotechnology, quantum gravity, the study of the structure of crystals, and may have applications in ecology, linguistics, and many other fields where a large amount of apparently unrelated information may be understood as being somehow connected (for a recent book on the subject, see [34]). The theory has also been applied to finance in a series of works dealing with the correlation matrices of stock prices, and also to risk management in portfolios [35]- [41].

The first result of the theory that we shall mention is that, given an $L\times N$ matrix with random numbers built on a Gaussian distribution with average zero and standard deviation σ, then, in the limit $L\longrightarrow\infty$ and $N\longrightarrow\infty$ such that $Q=L/N$ remains finite and greater than 1, the eigenvalues λ of such a matrix will have the following probability density function, called a Marčenku-Pastur distribution [44]:

$$\rho(\lambda)=\frac{Q}{2\pi\sigma^2}\frac{\sqrt{(\lambda_+-\lambda)(\lambda-\lambda_-)}}{\lambda}\ , \tag{2}$$

where

$$\lambda_-=\sigma^2\left(1+\frac{1}{Q}-2\sqrt{\frac{1}{Q}}\right)\ ,\ \lambda_+=\sigma^2\left(1+\frac{1}{Q}+2\sqrt{\frac{1}{Q}}\right)\ , \tag{3}$$

and λ is restricted to the interval $[\lambda_-,\lambda_+]$.

Figure 1 shows some Marčenku-Pastur distributions for some values of Q and σ. Since the distribution (2)is only valid for the limit $L\longrightarrow\infty$ and $N\longrightarrow\infty$, finite distributions will present differences from this behavior. Another source of deviations is the fact that financial time series are better described by non-Gaussian distributions, such as t Student or Tsallis distribution. Biroli, Bouchaud, and Potters calculated a probability density function analogous to the Marčenku-Pastur distribution, but based on a t Student distribution for the randomized data [77]. Their results show that there is a longer tale towards higher eigenvalues which decays as a power law.

In Figure 2, we compare the theoretical distribution for $Q=10$ and $\sigma=1$ to distributions of the eigenvalues of three correlation matrices generated from finite $L\times N$ matrices such that $Q=L/M=10$, and the elements of the matrices are random numbers with mean zero and standard deviation 1. Real data will deviate from the theoretical probability distribution.

This may be taken into account by randomizing the order of data in each of the time series used so as to preserve its mean and standard deviation, but destroy any correlation between the time series. The result of a large enough number of such simulations may then be compared with the results obtained with the original data instead of comparing the latter with the theoretical Marčenku-Pastur distribution.

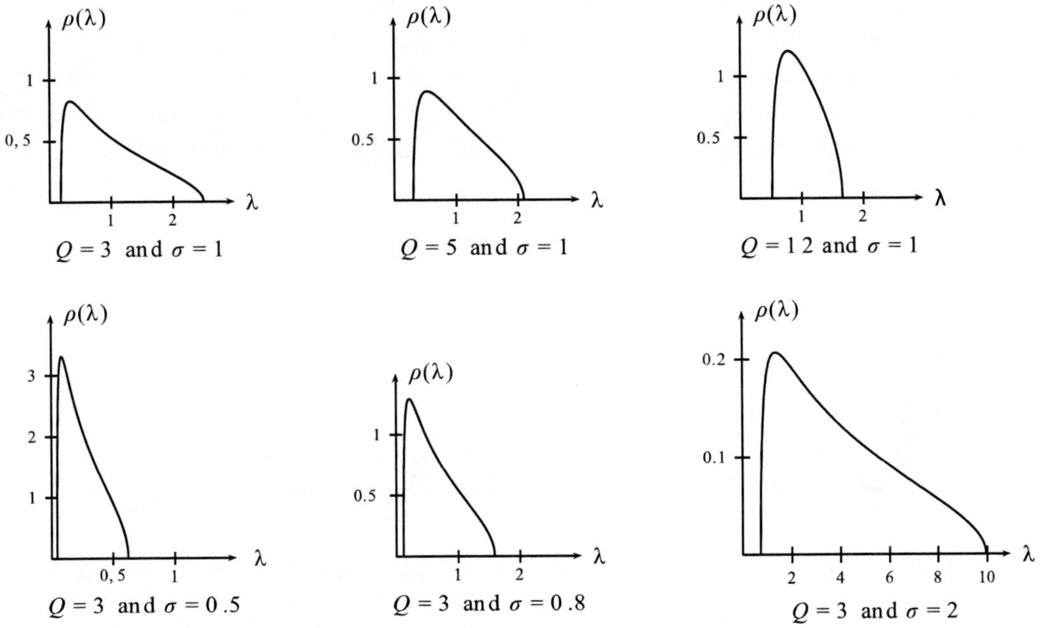

Figure 1. Marčenku-Pastur distribution for fixed values of Q and σ

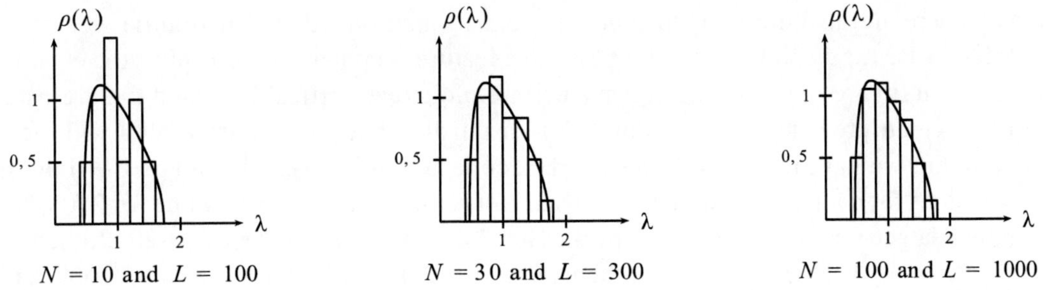

Figure 2. Histograms of eigenvalues for generated correlation matrix and Marčenku-Pastur distribution (solid line) for $Q = 10$ and $\sigma = 1$.

In order to apply Random Matrix Theory to the 79 stock exchanges, we divide their time series into two blocks: the first ranging from the beginning of 2003 to the end of 2007, so pre-crisis, and the second encompassing the years from 2008 to 2012 (post-crisis).

The first block of time series is formed by 1258 observations (days), so that $Q = L/M = 1258/79 \approx 15,92$; the second block of time series is formed by 1259 observations (days), so that $Q = L/M = 1259/79 \approx 15,94$. For these values, we have $\lambda_- \approx 0.56$ and $\lambda_+ \approx 1.56$ for both blocks of time series.

The two blocks of log-returns are used in order to build correlation matrices (using the Spearman rank correlation) and then to calculate the eigenvalues and eigenvectors of both matrices. The two graphs of Figure 3 show histograms for the eigenvalues of the correlation matrices for 2003-2007 (left graph) and for 2008-2012 (right graph). Together with the graphs are plotted as solid lines the probability distributions of the eigenvalues for 10,000 simulations with randomized data for each block of observations. The results of the simulations are very similar to the theoretical Marčenku-Pastur distributions.

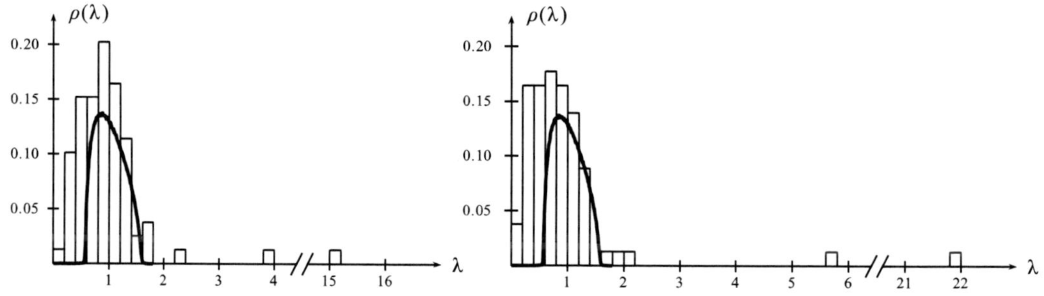

Figure 3. Histograms of the eigenvalues of the correlation matrices obtained from the log-return series for 2003-2007 (left graph) and for 2008-2012 (right graph), in block graphs. The probability distributions of the eigenvalues for 10,000 simulations with randomized data for each block of observations are shown as solid lines.

The first striking feature is that the largest eigenvalue for each block of data is much larger than the maximum limit expected from a distribution obtained from random data. There are also other eigenvalues that are located outside the region defined by the Marčenku-Pastur theoretical distribution. This feature is enhanced if one plots the eigenvalues, like in Figure 4, where the eigenvalues are plotted as vertical lines and the gray areas are the region predicted for the Marčenku-Pastur distribution, and associated with noise. On the left, we have the eigenvalues for data collected in 2003-2007, and on the right, the eigenvalues for data collected in 2008-2012. Note that the largest eigenvalue for 2008-2012 is rather larger than the largest eigenvalue for 2003-2007. Also, for 2008-2012, there are three other eigenvalues that detach themselves from the bulk, while for 2003-2007, there are two of them. Besides the eigenvalues that are above the values predicted for a random collection of data, there are many eigenvalues bellow the same prediction. This happens in both periods being analyzed.

More information on the meaning of the largest eigenvalues may be obtained if one plots the eigenvectors associated with them. Figure 5 shows the components of the eigenvectors, plotted as column bars, associated with the three largest eigenvalues for the data collected

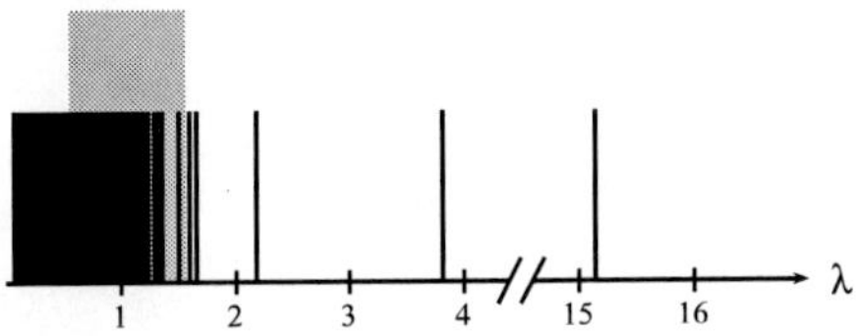

Figure 4. Eigenvalues of the correlation matrices for the log-returns of 2003-2007 (left) and 2008-2012 (right), represented as vertical lines. The gray areas are the regions predicted for the Marčenku-Pastur distribution, and associated with noise.

in 2003-2007. The eigenvalue associated with the largest eigenvalue (e_1) has a very distinct structure, as nearly all indices appear with positive values. The exceptions are indices from stock markets that are very small in terms of number of stocks and of volume of negotiations. This eigenvector is often associated with a *market mode*, and a portfolio built by taking the value of each index as its weight would follow very closely the general movements of the international stock market. In fact, when compared with an index of the global stock market, like the MSCI World Index, the portfolio built in terms of eigenvector e_1 has Pearson correlation 0.77.

Eigenvector e_2, related with the second largest eigenvalue, has a structure that is typical of stock markets that do not operate at the same time [78] [74]. It generally shows positive values for Western countries and negative values for Eastern ones, defining two basic blocks. Eigenvector e_3, associated with the third largest eigenvalue, shows strong positive peaks in North America and South America, and negative peaks in Europe. Eigenvalue e_4, associated with the fourth largest eigenvalue, has strong positive peaks in Arab countries in the Middle East and North Africa, and smaller negative ones for Pacific Asian countries. Other eigenvectors also show some structure, but it is quickly lost as their associated eigenvalues approach the region where noise dominates.

Figure 6 shows similar results for the eigenvectors associated with the four largest eigenvalues of the correlation matrix obtained from the log-returns of data in 2008-2012.

Eigenvector e_1 still represents a market mode, with all significant indices appearing with positive values, and eigenvector e_2 shows two blocks, a Western and an Eastern one. Eigenvector e_3 shows a block formed by North and South American indices, a block of European indices, probably joined by the African indices that operate at the same hours as the Central European markets, and a third block, of Pacific Asian indices, and it is probably connected with a fine tuning of the difference in operation hours of markets. Eigenvector e_4 separates indices from the Americas, from Europe, Arab countries, and Pacific Asian ones.

Comparing the eigenvectors in figures 5 and 6, one may also notice that there were no substantial changes to the structure shown by them from the period 2003-2007 to the period 2008-2012, leading to the belief that there is some stability on the world stock market structure, even during periods of crises.

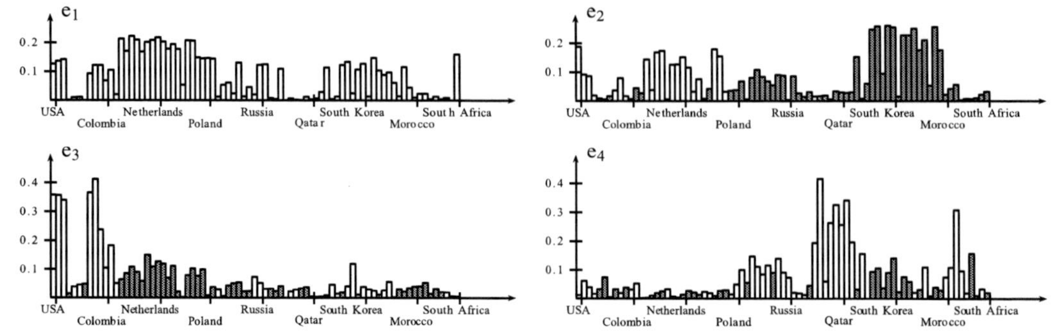

Figure 5. Components of the eigenvectors of the four largest eigenvalues of the correlation matrix of the log-returns of indices collected in 2003 - 2007. White bars mean positive values and gray bars, negative ones. The order of indices is the following: **USA**, Canada, Mexico, Bermuda, Jamaica, Costa Rica, Panama, Argentina, Brazil, Chile, **Colombia**, Peru, Venezuela, UK, Ireland, France, Germany, Austria, Switzerland, Belgium, **Netherlands**, Sweden, Denmark, Finland, Norway, Iceland, Italy, Spain, Portugal, Greece, **Poland**, Czech Republic, Slovakia, Croatia, Estonia, Latvia, Hungary, Bulgaria, Romania, Ukraine, **Russia**, Turkey, Kazakhstan, Malta, Israel, Palestine, Jordan, Lebanon, Saudi Arabia, Oman, **Qatar**, United Arab Emirates, Pakistan, India, Bangladesh, Sri Lanka, Japan, Hong Kong, China, Taiwan, **South Korea**, Mongolia, Singapore, Indonesia, Malaysia, Thailand, Philippines, Vietnam, Australia, New Zealand, **Morocco**, Tunisia, Egypt, Nigeria, Botswana, Ghana, Kenya, Mauritius, and **South Africa**.

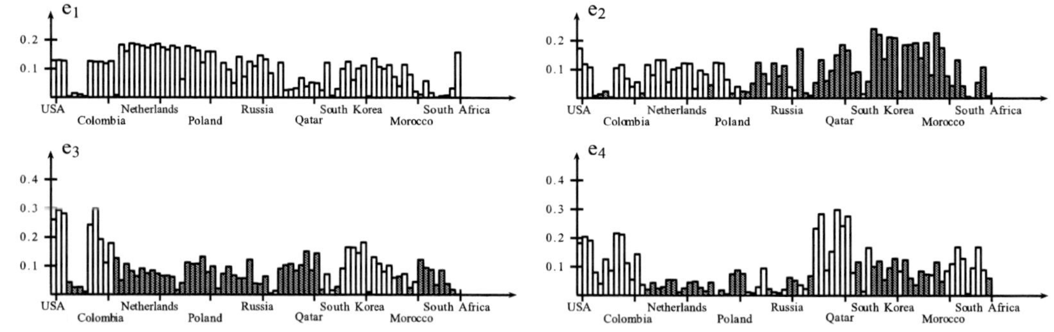

Figure 6. Components of the eigenvectors of the four largest eigenvalues of the correlation matrix of the log-returns of indices collected in 2003 - 2007. White bars mean positive values and gray bars, negative ones. The order of indices is the same as in Figure 5.

4. Correlation and Volatility of the Market

It is a general consensus [12]- [24] that, when markets are more volatile, they tend to behave more similarly, so that volatility and correlation of assets or indices should move relatively together. In [74], we made calculations of the average value of correlation matrices and of the volatilities of the market mode for running windows during the periods of some of the major financial crises of the past decades. Here, we come back to that study, but now using our data of 79 indices for the years from 2003 to 2012. The approach is a little different than what has been done before, as we shall compare the average correlation of indices with the volatility of the MSCI World Index, which is a stock market index of over 6,000 stocks of companies in different stock markets across the globe, and is often used as a benchmark for the global financial market.

The calculations are done in running windows of 100 days each, moving one day at a time. This gives us a total of 2415 windows running from 2003 to 2012. The average correlation is calculated as the mean of the elements of the correlation matrix obtained from each window, and it is assigned to the last day of the window (so, results start from 100 days after the beginning of 2003). We also calculate the standard deviation of the elements of the correlation matrix for each window. The volatility of the MSCI World Index is also calculated in moving windows of 100 days, with steps of one day, and it is computed as the standard deviation of the log-returns of the index for each window. This volatility is also assigned to the last day of the window.

The results are plotted in Figure 7. The graph on the left is the evolution in time of the average of the elements of the correlation matrix of the log-returns (black line) and of the average of the volatility of the MSCI World Index (gray line). In order to best compare both measures, they are both normalized so as to have standard deviation one. The graph on the right is the dispersion graph of the average correlation and of the average volatility, not normalized. The Pearson correlation between both measures is 0.84.

Note that, when volatility rises, mainly during and after the subprime crisis of 2008, the correlation between the indices also rises. This is evidence that correlation and volatility go hand in hand when it concerns world financial markets. This effect is bad news for investors who wish to avoid risk in times of crisis by diversifying their portfolios using assets from different countries.

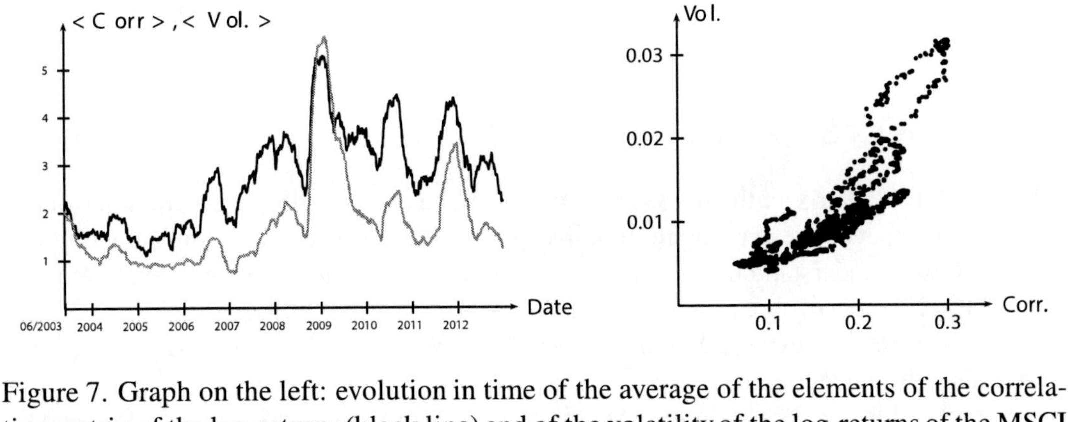

Figure 7. Graph on the left: evolution in time of the average of the elements of the correlation matrix of the log-returns (black line) and of the volatility of the log-returns of the MSCI World Index (gray line), both normalized so as to have standard deviation one. The graph on the right is the dispersion graph of the average correlation and of the average volatility, not normalized.

Another measure that is very much correlated with both the average of the elements of the correlation matrix and the volatility of the MSCI World Index is the largest eigenvalue of the correlation matrix. Figure 8 shows the first three largest eigenvalues of correlation matrices calculated in running windows of 100 days with steps of one day from 2003 to 2012. The first and the second largest eigenvalues are more sensitive to periods of high volatility.

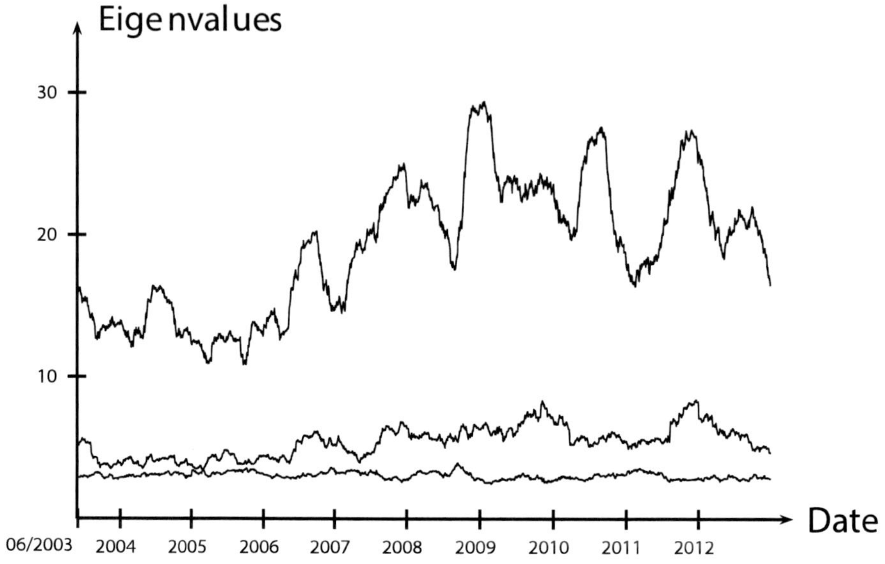

Figure 8. Three largest eigenvalues of the correlation matrix of the log-returns of the indices, calculated in running windows of 100 days with a step of one day.

Next, we shall focus on the network structure of the stock market indices that can be derived from their correlations.

5. Network Structure

The correlation matrix of the time series of financial data encodes a large amount of information, and an even greater amount of noise. That information and noise must be filtered if one is to try to understand how the elements (in our case, indices) relate to each other and how that relation evolves in time. One of the most common filtering procedures is to represent those relations using a *Minimum Spanning Tree* (MST) [79]- [91], which is a graph containing all indices, connected by at least one edge, so that the sum of the edges is minimum, and which presents no loops. Another type of representation is that of a *Planar Maximally Filtered Graph* (PMFG) [92]- [98], which admits loops but must be representable in two-dimensional graphs without crossings.

Yet another type of representation is obtained by establishing a number which defines how many connections (edges) are to be represented in a graph of the correlations between nodes. There is no limitation with respect to the crossing of edges or to the formation of loops, and if the number is high enough, then one has a graph where all nodes are connected to one another. These are usually called *Asset Trees*, or *Asset Graphs* [99]- [106], since they are not trees in the network sense. Another way to build asset graphs is to establish a value (threshold) such that distances above it are not considered. This eliminates connections (edges) as well as indices (nodes), but also makes the diagrams more understandable by filtering both information and noise. Some previous works using graphic representations of correlations between international assets (indices or otherwise) can be found in [83], [96], [105], and [107].

We shall then represent the indices as asset graphs built from the correlation matrices obtained from their log-returns. Given a correlation coefficient c_{ij} in a correlation matrix of all indices, a distance measure [79] may be defined as

$$d_{ij} = \sqrt{2\,(1-c_{ij})}\ . \tag{4}$$

As correlations between indices vary from -1 (anticorrelated) to 1 (completely correlated), the distance between them vary from 0 (totally correlated) to 2 (completely anticorrelated). Totally uncorrelated indices would have distance 1 between them.

Based on the distance measures, two-dimensional coordinates are assigned to each index using an algorithm called Classical Multidimensional Scaling [108], which is based on minimizing the stress function

$$S = \left[\frac{\sum_{i=1}^{n}\sum_{j>i}^{n}\left(\delta_{ij}-\bar{d}_{ij}\right)^2}{\sum_{i=1}^{n}\sum_{j>i}^{n} d_{ij}^2}\right]^{1/2}, \tag{5}$$

where δ_{ij} is 1 for $i=j$ and zero otherwise, n is the number of rows of the correlation matrix, and $\bar{d}_{ij}$ is an m-dimensional Euclidean distance (which may be another type of distance for other types of multidimensional scaling) given by

$$\bar{d}_{ij} = \left[\sum_{a=1}^{m}\left(x_{ia}-x_{ja}\right)^2\right]^{1/2}. \tag{6}$$

The outputs of this optimization problem are the coordinates x_{ij} of each of the nodes, where $i=1,\cdots,n$ is the number of nodes and $j=1,\cdots,m$ is the number of each dimension in an m-dimensional space. It is customary for the representation of the network to be well represented in smaller dimensions than m, and in the case of this article we shall consider $m=2$ for a 2-dimensional visualization of the network. The choice is a compromise between fidelity to the original distances and the easiness of representing the networks.

As some correlations may be the result of random noise, we ran some simulations based on randomized data, consisting on randomly reordering the time series of each index so as to destroy any true correlations between them but maintain each frequency distribution intact. The result of 1000 simulations is a distance value above which correlations are probably due to random noise, which, in our case, is $d=1.36$.

Our asset graphs are built using distance measures as thresholds. As an example, for threshold $T=0.5$, one builds an asset graph where all distances bellow 0.5 are represented as edges (connections) between nodes (indices). All distances above this threshold are removed, and all indices that do not connect to any other index bellow this threshold are also removed.

Before drawing them, there is a further innovation that must be discussed. The particular nature of stock markets that operate at different time zones makes it difficult to make a representation of them that shows the cyclical nature of the rotation of the planet, with markets from the East being more connected with their counterparts in the West from the previous day. A solution to that [78] is to build a network based on the stock market indices and also on their lagged values of the previous day. So, one now has, instead of the 79 original indices, 79 more indices associated with their lagged values, for a total of 158 indices. Since it has already been shown [74] that the asset graphs of the stock market indices do not change much in time, we shall consider the asset graphs based on the whole period, from 2003 to 2012.

In Figure 9, we plot all indices on their coordinates. The indices are represented by the four first letters of each country, with the exception of Austria, which is written *Autr* so as to differentiate it from Australia, and by three or fours letters in case of countries with multiple words, like CzRe for the Czech Republic or USA for the United States of America. Lagged indices are represented by black boxes and the original ones are represented in white boxes. Note that there is a clear distinction between original and lagged indices, forming two separate clusters with some interaction occurring for indices which are not very correlated to any other indices in the network, like some Arab and African indices. There is also a clear clustering of indices according to geography (or by time zones), particularly for Western European indices, American, and Pacific Asian ones.

Figure 10 shows the asset graphs for the world stock market indices, displaying only the indices that are connected bellow certain distance thresholds ($T = 0.5$, $T = 0.7$, $T = 0.9$, and $T = 1.1$) and their connections. For $T = 0.5$, the only countries that are connected are France, Germany, the Netherlands, and Italy, original and lagged ones, forming the core of the Central European countries. For $T = 0.7$, the UK, Switzerland, Belgium, Sweden, Finland, and Spain join the European cluster, which is represented in its two versions (original and lagged).

At $T = 0.9$, two more clusters are formed: one of American indices, made by the USA, Canada, Mexico, and Brazil, and one of Pacific Asian indices, made by Japan, Hong Kong, South Korea, Singapore, and Taiwan. For $T = 1.1$, the clusters join and add to themselves many more indices. Something to be noticed is that Israel and South Africa are part of the European cluster, and that Australia and New Zealand join the Pacific Asian cluster. Most important, there are now connections between lagged and original indices, with the lagged indices of the USA, Canada, Mexico, and Brazil forming connections with the next day indices of Japan, Hong Kong, the Philippines, Australia, and New Zealand. If one makes asset graphs including indices that are lagged by two and three days, a similar structure appears, with American indices being correlated with Pacific Asian and Oceanian ones.

The structure of the network of stock market indices may be used to study the propagation of crises. There is a vast literature on contagion between banks or other markets via networks [110]- [152]. In the majority of these works, the interbank loans and liabilities are used in order to build networks of financial institutions. A general result is that contagion

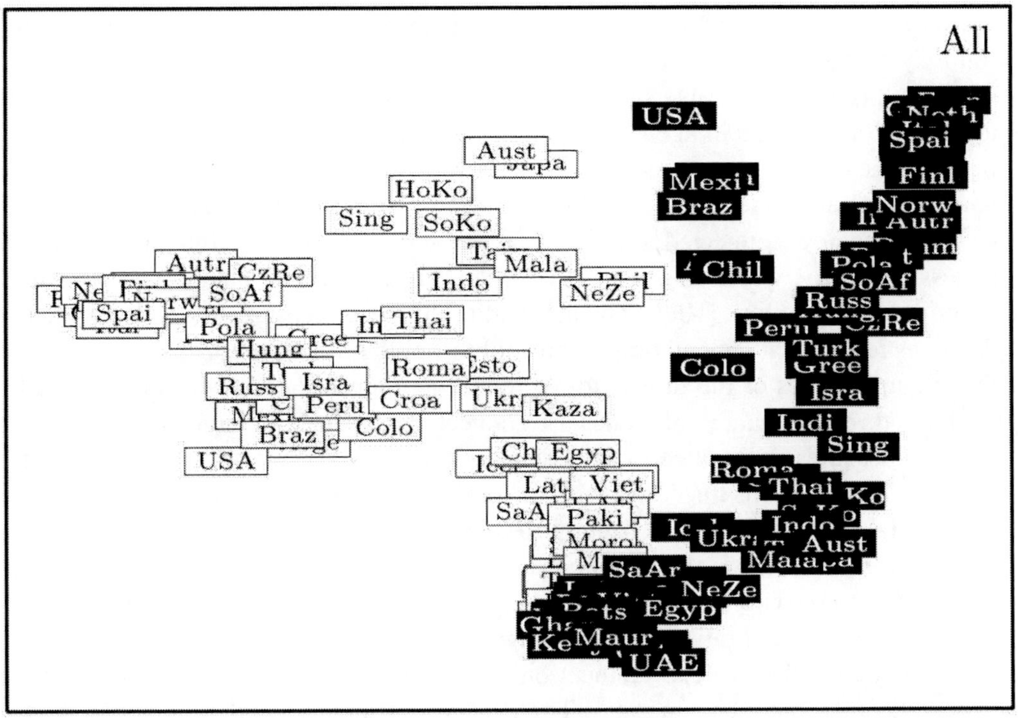

Figure 9. Two-dimensional representation of the node structure (without the connections) of the world stock market indices. White boxes represent the original indices and black boxes represent the lagged indices.

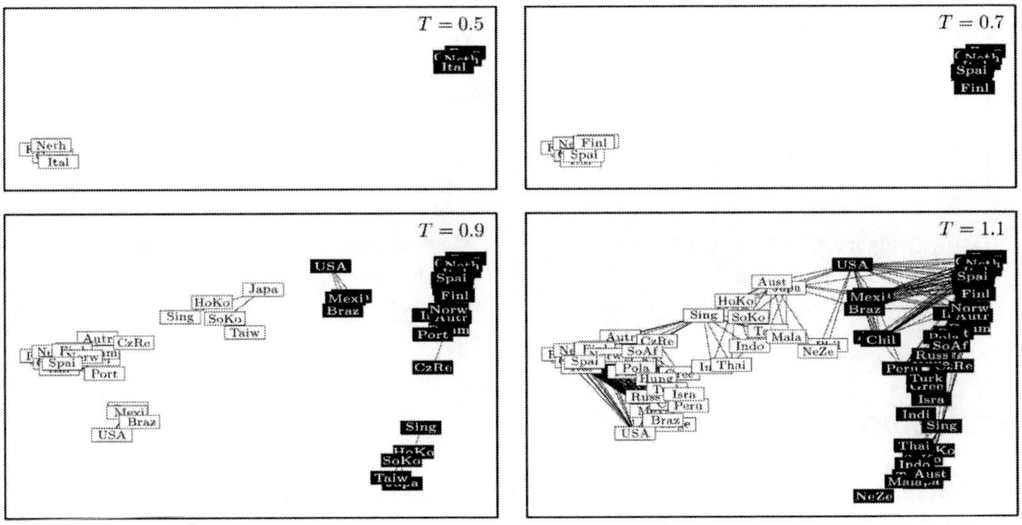

Figure 10. Asset graphs of the world market indices for distance threshold values $T = 0.5$, $T = 0.7$, $T = 0.9$, and $T = 1.1$. White boxes represent the original indices and black boxes represent the lagged indices.

may occur for a certain critical level of integration between institutions, and that high integration may be both a curse and a blessing for the propagation of crises. This will not be discussed in this chapter, but we stress that certain measures of centrality may be useful in the identification of the main agents in the propagation of a crisis.

Some of the main centrality measures used in the theory of Complex Networks are *node centrality*, which measures the number of connections a node has, *eigenvector centrality*, which measures how connected a node is, and how connected its neighbors are, and *betweenness centrality*, which measures if a node is in the shortest path connecting all the other nodes in the network [109]. The application of these measures of centrality to asset graphs gives results that depend on the threshold level that is chosen [74]. As an example, for low enough values of the threshold, there are no connections between nodes, and for high enough threshold values, all nodes are connected to every other node in the network.

If these measures are applied to the asset graph for $T = 1.1$, we obtain the results listed in Table 1, which contains the nodes with the ten best scores in each of the centrality measures. Central European indices occupy the first positions both for node centrality and eigenvector centrality, since they are very connected and in a region of highly connected nodes. So, Europe would be a center for the propagation of crises in a variety of models. Now for betweenness centrality, we have Singapore and Japan occupying the first two positions, mainly due to their role as connections between Pacific Asian and European indices to the next day indices of the Americas. The USA also occupies a high rank due to the same reason.

Table 1. Highest ranking stock market indices according to node centrality, eigenvector centrality, and betweenness centrality

Node Degree	Eigenvector Centrality	Betweenness Centrality
France	UK, France	Singapore
UK	Netherlands	Japan
Netherlands	Belgium, Italy, Germany	USA
Finland, Italy, Belgium, Germany, Norway	Finland	France
Sweden, Spain	Sweden, Spain	Australia
Australia	Norway	Netherlands
Switzerland	Austria	Finland
Denmark, Czech Republic, USA	Switzerland	Hong Kong
Poland	Czech Republic	Austria
South Africa, Hungary, Ireland	Denmark, Poland	Denmark

Conclusion

Based on the time series of 79 stock indices taken from a variety of countries from 2003 to 2012, we built correlation matrices based on the log-returns of those indices, first comparing the results of 2003-2007 (a period of low volatility) with the ones of 2008-2012 (a time of high volatility) under the light of Random Matrix Theory. We identified a large eigenvalue which represents a market mode, which conveys the general behavior of the world stock market, and a second largest one, which highlights the differences between stock markets operating in different time zones. We also use correlation matrices calculated in running windows of 100 days with time step of one day in order to compare the average correlation of stock markets with the volatility of the world stock markets represented by the MSCI World Index, showing there is a strong correlation between them so that, in times of high volatility, stock markets tend to behave in the same way. Next, we built networks of the stock market indices, as represented by asset graphs, in which a structure highly dependent on geographical position and/or on operation hours is clear. We could see that some Central European markets are highly correlated, and that two other cluster, one of American markets, and another of Pacific Asian ones, forms under lower correlation values. We could also see that stock market indices in Pacific Asia are correlated with the previous day's indices of America, and that Central European indices occupy a position of high centrality in a network of stock market indices, and that Singapore and Japan present a high number of betweennness centrality, being the main channels between Eastern and Western indices.

Acknowledgments

The author acknowledges the support of this work by a grant from Insper, Instituto de Ensino e Pesquisa. This chapter was written using LaTeX, all figures were made using PSTricks, and the calculations were made using Matlab, Excel, and Ucinet. All data and algorithms used are freely available upon request to the author at leonidassj@insper.edu.br.

References

[1] King, M.; Wadhwani, S. *Transmission of volatility between stock markets*, (1989) National Bureau of Economic Research working paper series, number 2910.

[2] King, M.; Sentana, E.; Wadhwani, S. *Volatility and links between national stock markets*, (1990) National Bureau of Economic Research working paper series, number 3357.

[3] Ammer, J.; Mei, J. *Measuring international economic linkages with stock market data*, (1993) Board of Governors of the Federal Reserve System, International finance discussion papers, number 449.

[4] Lin, W-L; Engle, R.F.; Ito, T. *Do bulls and bears move across borders? International transmission of stock returns and volatility as the world turns*, Review of Financial Studies 7 (1994) 507-538.

[5] Erb, C.B.; Harvey, C.R.; Viskanta, T.E. *Forecasting internationsl equity correlations*, Financial Analyst Journal (November-December) (1994) 32-45.

[6] Baig, T.; Goldfajn, I. *Financial market contagion in the Asian Crisis*, (1999) IMF Staff Papers 46.

[7] Forbes, K.; Rigobon, R. *No contagion, only interdependence: measuring stock market co-movements*, Journal of Finance 57 (2002) 2223-2261.

[8] Corsetti, G.; Pericoli, M.; Sbracia, M. *Some contagion, some interdependence. More pitfalls in tests of financial contagion*, (2003).

[9] Longin, F.; Solnik, B. *Is the correlation in international equity returns constant: 1960-1990?*, J. of Int. Money and Finance 14 (1995) 3-26.

[10] Bekaert, G.; Harvey, C.R. *Time-varying world market integration*, The Journal of Finance 1 (1995) 403-444.

[11] Santis, G.; Gerard, B. *International asset pricing and portfolio diversification with time-varying risk*, The Journal of Finance 52 (1997) 1881-1912.

[12] Solnik, B.; Boucrelle, C.; Le Fur, Y. *International market correlation and volatility*, Financial Analysts Journal 52 (1996) 17-34.

[13] Meric, I.; Meric, G. *Co-movements of European equity markets before and after the 1987 crash*, Multinational Finance Journal 1 (1997) 137-152.

[14] Longin, F.; Solnik, B. *Correlation structure of international equity markets during extremely volatile periods*, Le Cashiers de Reserche, HEC Paris 646 (1999).

[15] Hartmann, P.; Straetmans, S.; de Vries, C.G. *Asset market linkages in crisis periods*, (2001) Tinbergen Institute Discussion Paper, TI 2001-71/2.

[16] Lillo, F.; Bonanno, G.; Mantegna, R.N. *Variety of stock returns in normal and extreme market days: the August 1998 crisis*, Proceedings of Empirical Science of Financial Fluctuations, Econophysics on the Horizon, Edited by H. Takayasu (2001).

[17] Ang, A.; Chen, J. *Asymmetric correlations of equity portfolios*, Journal of Financial Economics 63 (2002) 443-494.

[18] Longin, F.; Solnik, B. *Extreme correlation of international equity markets*, The Journal of Finance 56 (2001) 649-675.

[19] Meric, I.; Kim, S.; Kim, J.H.; Meric, G. *Co-movements of U.S., U.K., and Asian stock markets before and after September 11, 2001*, Journal of Money, Investiment and Banking 3 (2008) 47-57.

[20] Cizeau, P.; Potters, Potters; Bouchaud, J-P. *Correlation structure of extreme stock returns*, Quantitative Finance 1 (2001) 217-222.

[21] Malevergne, Y.; Sornette, D. *Investigating extreme dependences: concepts and tools*, Extreme Financial Risks (From dependence to risk management) (2006) Springer, Heidelberg.

[22] Marshal, R.; Zeevi, A. *Beyond correlation: extreme co-movements between financial assets*, Working Paper, Columbia Business School (2002).

[23] Bartram, S.M.; Wang, Y-H. *Another look at the relationship between cross-market correlation and volatility*, Finance Research Letters 2 (2005) 75-88.

[24] Knif, J.; Kolari, J.; Pynnönen, S. *What drives correlation between stock market returns?*, IMF Working Paper WP/07/157 (2007).

[25] Campbell, R.; Koedijk, K. *Covariance and correlation in international equity returns: a value-at-risk approach*, (2000).

[26] Pafka, S.; Kondor, I. *Noisy covariance matrices and portfolio optimization*, Eur. Phys. J. B 27 (2002) 277-280.

[27] Rosenow, B.; Plerou, V.; Gopikrishnan, P.; Stanley, H.E. *Portfolio optimization and the random magnet problem*, Europhys. Lett. 59 (2002) 500.

[28] Ang, A.; Bekaert, G. *International asset allocation with regime shifts*, The Review of Financial Studies 15 (2002) 1137-1187.

[29] Onnela, J-P; Chakraborti, A.; Kaski, K. *Dynamics of market correlations: taxonomy and portfolio analysis*, Phys. Rev. E 68 (2003) 056110.

[30] Tola, V.; Lillo, F.; Gallegati, M.; Mantegna, R.N. *Cluster analysis for portfolio optimization*, Journal of Economic Dynamics and Control 32 (2008) 235-258.

[31] Pantaleo, E.; Tumminello, M.; Lillo, F.; Mantegna, R.N. *When do improved covariance matrix estimators enhance portfolio optimization? An empirical comparative study of nine estimators*, Working paper (2010) arXiv:1004.4272v1.

[32] Wigner, E. P. *Characteristic vectors of bordered matrices with infinite dimensions*, Ann. Math. 62 (1955), 548-564.

[33] Wigner, E. P. *On the distribution of the roots of certain symmetric matrices*, Ann. Math. 67 (1958), 325-327.

[34] Marĕnko, V.A.; Pastur, L.A. USSR-Sb 1 (1967) 457-483.

[35] Mehta, M. L. *Random Matrices*, (2004) Academic Press.

[36] Laloux, L.; Cizeau, P.; Bouchaud, J-P; Potters, M. *Noise dressing of financial correlation matrices*, Phys. Rev. Letters 83 (1999) 1467-1470.

[37] Laloux, L.; Cizeau, P.; Bouchaud, J-P; Potters, M. *Random matrix theory and financial correlations*, Mathematical Models and Methods in Applied Sciences (2000).

[38] Plerou, V.; Gopikrishman, P.; Rosenow, B.; Amaral, L.A.N.; Stanley, H. E. *A random matrix theory approach to financial cross-correlations*, Physica A 287 (2000) 374-382.

[39] Plerou, V.; Gopikrishman, P.; Rosenow, B.; Amaral, L.A.N.; Guhr, T.; Stanley, H. E. *Application of random matrix theory to study cross-correlations of stock prices*, Int. J. of Theoret. and Appl. Finance 3 (2002) 399-403.

[40] Plerou, V.; Gopikrishman, P.; Rosenow, B.; Amaral, L.A.N.; Guhr, T.; Stanley, H. E. *Random matrix approach to cross-correlations in financial data*, Phys. Rev. E 65 (2002) 066126.

[41] Kulkarni, V.; Deo, N. *Correlation and volatility of an Indian stock market: a random matrix approach*, Eur. Phys. J. B 60 (2007) 101-109.

[42] Kwapièn, J.; Drożdż, S.; Oświęcimka, P. *The bulk of the stock market correlation matrix is not pure noise*, Physica A 359 (2006) 589-606.

[43] Kwapièn, J.; Drożdż, S.; Oświęcimka, P. *Asymmetric matrices in an analysis of financial correlations*, Acta Physica Polonica B 37 (2006) 3039-3048.

[44] Potters, M.; Bouchaud, J-P; Laloux, L. *Financial applications of random matrix theory: old laces and new pieces*, Proceedings of the Cracow conference on "Applications of random matrix theory to economy and other complex systems" (2005).

[45] Bouchaud, J-P; Laloux, L.; Miceli, M.A.; Potters, M. *Large dimension forecasting models and random singular value spectra*, European Physical Journal B 2 (2007) 201-207.

[46] Rak, R.; Drożdż, S.; Kwapien, J.; Oświęcimka, P. *Correlation matrix decomposition of WIG20 intraday fluctuations*, Acta Physica Polonica B 37 (2006) 3123-3132.

[47] Birolli, G.; Bouchaud, J-P; Potters, M. *On the top eigenvalue of heavy-tailed random matrices*, Europhysics Letters 78 (2007) 10001.1-10001.5.

[48] Chakraborti, A. *An outlook on correlations in stock prices*, Econophysics of Stock and other Markets - Proceedings of the Econophys-Kolkata II (2007) Springer Milan.

[49] Martins, A.C.R. *Non-stationary correlation matrices and noise*, Physica A 379 (2007) 552-558.

[50] Martins, A.C.R. *Random but not so much. A parametrization for the returns and correlation matrix of financial time series*, Physica A 383 (2007) 527-532.

[51] Pan, R.K.; Sinha, S. *Collective behavior of stock price movements in an emerging market*, Phys. Rev. E 76 (2007) 1-9.

[52] Chakraborti, A.; Patriarca, M.; Santhanam, M.S. *Financial time-series analysis: a brief overview*, Proceedings of the International Workshop "Econophys-Kolkata III" (2007) Springer, Milan.

[53] Dimov, I.I.; Kolm, P.N.; Maclin, L.; Shiber, D.Y.C. *Hidden noise structure and random matrix models of stock correlations*, (2009) arXiv:0909.1383v3.

[54] Chakraborti, A.; Toke, I.M.; Patriarca, M.; Abergel, F. *Econophysics: empirical facts and agent-based models*, submitted to Quantitative Finance.

[55] Bouchaud, J-P; Potters, M. *Financial applications of random matrix theory: a short review*, to appear in the "Handbook on random matrix theory", Oxford University Press.

[56] Noh, J.D. *A model of correlations in stock markets*, Phys. Rev. E 61 (2000) 5981.

[57] Rak, R.; Kwapień, J.; Droźdź, S.; Oświęcimka, P. *Cross-correlations in Warsaw Stock Exchange*, Acta Physica Polonica A 114 (2008) 561-568.

[58] Conlon, T.; Ruskin, H.J.; Crane, M. *Cross-correlations dynamics in financial time series*, Physica A 388 (2009) 705-714.

[59] Münnix, M.C.; Schäfer, R.; Guhr, T. *Compensating asynchrony effects in the calculation of financial correlations*, Physica A 389 (2010) 767-779.

[60] Maslov, S. *Measures of globalization based on cross-correlations of world financial indices*, Physica A 301 (2001) 397-406.

[61] Mantegna, R.N. *Hierarchical structure in financial markets*, The European Phys. J. B 11 (1999) 193.

[62] Bonanno, G.; Lillo, F.; Mantegna, R.N. *High-frequency cross-correlation in a set of stocks*, Quantitative Finance 1 (2001) 96-104.

[63] Gopikrishnan, P.; Rosenow, B.; Plerou, V.; Stanley, H.E. *Identifying business sectors from stock price flutuations*, Phys. Rev E 64 (2001) 35106.

[64] Micchichè, S.; Bonanno, G.; Lillo, F.; Mantegna, R.N. *Degree stability of a minimum spanning tree of price return and volatility*, Physica A 324 (2003) 66-73.

[65] Coronnello, C.; Tumminello, M.; Lillo, F.; Micchichè, S.; Mantegna, R.N. *Sector identification in a set of stock return time series traded at the London Stock Exchange*, Acta Phys. Pol. B 36 (2005) 2653-2679.

[66] Sinha, S.; Pan, R.K. *Uncovering the internal structure of the Indian financial market: cross-correlation behavior in the NSE*, in "Econophysics of markets and business networks", Springer (2007) 215-226.

[67] Coronnello, C.; Tumminello, M.; Lillo, F.; Micchichè, S.; Mantegna, R.N. *Economic sector identification in a set of stocks traded at the New York Stock Exchange: a comparative analysis*, Proceedings of the SPIE, vol. 6601, 66010T (2007).

[68] Winston, W.L. *Operations Research, applications and algorithms*, fourth edition, (2004) Thomson Learning.

[69] Aste, T.; Di Matteo, T. *Correlation filtering in financial time series, Noise and Fluctuations in Econophysics and Finance*, Proceedings of the SPIE 5848 (2005) 100-109.

[70] Tumminello, M.; Di Matteo, T.; Aste, T.; Mantegna, R.N. *Correlation based networks of equity returns sampled at different time horizons*, Eur. Phys. J. B 55 (2007) 209Ű217.

[71] Tumminello, M.; Liloo, F.; Mantegna, R.N. *Kullback-Leiber distance as a measure of the information filtered from multivariate data*, Phys. Rev. E 76 (2007) 031123.

[72] Tumminello, M.; Liloo, F.; Mantegna, R.N. *Shrinkage and spectral filtering of correlation matrices: a comparison via the Kullback-Leiber distance*, Acta Physica Polonica B 38 (2007) 4079-4088.

[73] Tumminello, M.; Liloo, F.; Mantegna, R.N. *Correlation, hierarchies, and networks in financial markets*, Journal of Economic Behavior & Organizations (2010) Article in press.

[74] Sandoval Jr., L.; Franca, I.P. *Correlation of financial markets in times of crisis*, Physica A 391 (2012) 187-208.

[75] Sandoval Jr., L. *Pruning a minimum spanning tree*, Physica A 391 (2012) 2678-2711.

[76] Sandoval Jr., L. *Cluster formation and evolution in networks of financial market indices*, Algorithmic Finance, (2013) in print.

[77] Biroli, G.; Bouchaud, J-P; Potters, M. *The Student Ensemble of Correlation Matrices: Eigenvalue Spectrum and KullbackŰLeibler Entropy*, Acta Physica Polonica B 13 (2007) 4009-4026.

[78] Sandoval Jr., L. *To lag or not to lag?*, arXiv:1201.4586 (2012).

[79] Mantegna, R.N. *Hierarchical structure in financial markets*, The European Phys. J. B 11 (1999) 193.

[80] Bonanno, G.; Lillo, F.; Mantegna, R.N. *High-frequency cross-correlation in a set of stocks*, Quantitative Finance 1 (2001) 96-104.

[81] Micchichè, S.; Bonanno, G.; Lillo, F.; Mantegna, R.N. *Degree stability of a minimum spanning tree of price return and volatility*, Physica A 324 (2003) 66-73.

[82] Bonanno, G.; Caldarelli, G.; Lillo, F.; Micciché, S.; Vandewalle, N.; Mantegna, R.N. *Networks of equities in financial markets*, The European Phys. J. B 38, (2004) 363Ű371.

[83] Coelho, R.; Gilmore, C.G.; Lucey, B.; Richmond, P.; Hutzler, S. *The evolution of intcrdcpendence in world equity markets - evidence from minimum spanning trees*, Physica A 376 (2007) 455-466.

[84] Borghesi, C.; Marsili, M.; Micciché, S. *Emergence of time-horizon invariant correlation structure in financial returns by subtraction of the market mode*, Phys. Rev. E 76 (2007), 026104.

[85] Brida, J.G.; Risso, W.A. *Multidimensional minimal spanning tree: the Dow Jones case*, Physica A 387 (2008) 5205-5210.

[86] Kwapień, J.; Gworek, S.; Drożdż, S.; Górski, A. *Analysis of a network structure of the foreign currency exchange market*, J. of Economic Interaction and Coordination 4 (2009), 55-72.

[87] Kwapień, J.; Gworek, S.; Drożdż, S. *Structure and evolution of the foreign exchange networks*, Acta Physica Polonica B 40 (2009), 175-194.

[88] Drożdż, S.; Kwapień, J.; J. Speth, J. *Coherent patterns in nuclei and in financial markets*, AIP Conf. Proc. 1261 (2010), 256-264.

[89] Zhanga, Y.; Leea, G.H.T.; Wonga, J.C.; Kokb, J.L.; Prustyb, M.; Cheong, S.A. *Will the US Economy Recover in 2010? A Minimal Spanning Tree Study*, (2010) Physica A 390 (2011) 2020-2050.

[90] Keskin, M.; Deviren, B.; Kocalkaplan, Y. *Topology of the correlation networks among major currencies using hierarchical structure methods*, Physica A 390 (2011), 719-730.

[91] Sandoval Jr., L. *Pruning a minimum spanning tree*, Physica A (2012) DOI 10.1016/j.physa.2011.12.052.

[92] Tumminello, M.; Aste, T.; Di Matteo, T.; Mantegna, R.N. *A tool for filtering information in complex systems*, Proceedings of the National Academy of Sciences of the United States of America 102, (2005) 10421-10426.

[93] Coronnello, C.; Tumminello, M.; Lillo, F.; Micchichè, S.; Mantegna, R.N. *Sector identification in a set of stock return time series traded at the London Stock Exchange*, Acta Phys. Pol. B 36 (2005) 2653-2679.

[94] Aste, T.; Di Matteo, T. *Correlation filtering in financial time series, Noise and Fluctuations in Econophysics and Finance*, Proceedings of the SPIE 5848 (2005) 100-109.

[95] Tumminello, M.; Di Matteo, T.; Aste, T.; Mantegna, R.N. *Correlation based networks of equity returns sampled at different time horizons*, Eur. Phys. J. B 55 (2007) 209Ű217.

[96] Coronnello, C.; Tumminello, M.; Lillo, F.; Micchichè, S.; Mantegna, R.N. *Economic sector identification in a set of stocks traded at the New York Stock Exchange: a comparative analysis*, Proceedings of the SPIE, vol. 6601, 66010T (2007).

[97] Tumminello, M.; Lillo, F.; Mantegna, R.N. *Correlation, hierarchies, and networks in financial markets*, Journal of Economic Behavior & Organizations 75 (2010), 40-58.

[98] Kenett, D.Y.; Tumminello, M.; Madi, A.; Gur-Gershgoren, G.; Mantegna, R.N.; Ben-Jacob, E. *Dominating Clasp of the Financial Sector Revealed by Partial Correlation Analysis of the Stock Market*, PLoS ONE 5 (12) (2010) e15032.

[99] Onnela, J.-P.; Chakraborti, A.; Kaski, K.; Kertész, J. *Dynamic asset trees and portfolio analysis*, The European Phys. J. B 30 (2002) 285-288.

[100] Onnela, J.-P.; Chakraborti, A.; Kaski, K. *Dynamics of market correlations: taxonomy and portfolio analysis*, Phys. Rev. E 68 (2003) 1-12.

[101] Onnela, J.-P.; Chakraborti, A.; Kaski, K.; Kertész, J. *Dynamic asset trees and Black Monday*, Physica A 324 (2003) 247-252.

[102] Onnela, J.-P.; Chakraborti, A.; Kaski, K.; Kertész, J.; Kanto, A. *Asset trees and asset graphs in financial markets*, Phys. Scripta T 106 (2003) 48-54.

[103] Onnela, J.-P.; Kaski, K.; Kertész, J. *Clustering and information in correlation based financial networks*, Eur. Phys. J. B 38 (2004) 353-362.

[104] Sinha, S.; Pan, R.K. *Uncovering the internal structure of the Indian financial market: cross-correlation behavior in the NSE*, in "Econophysics of markets and business networks", Springer (2007) 215-226.

[105] Ausloos, M.; Lambiotte, R. *Clusters or networks of economies? A macroeconomy study through gross domestic product*, Physica A 382 (2007) 16-21.

[106] Sandoval Jr., L. *A Map of the Brazilian Stock Market*, Advances in Complex Systems 15 (2012) 1250042-1250082.

[107] Eryiğit, M.; Eryiğit, R. *Network structure of cross-correlations among the world market indices*, Physica A 388 (2009), 3551-3562.

[108] Borg, I.; Groenen, P. *Modern Multidimensional Scaling: theory and applications*, 2nd edition, (2005) Springer-Verlag.

[109] Newman, M.E.J. *Networks, and introduction*, (2010) Oxford University Press.

[110] Kirman, A. *The economy as an evolving network*, Journal of Evolutionary Economics 7 (1997) 339-353.

[111] Allen, F.; Gale, D. *Financial contagion*, Journal of Political Economy 108 (2000) 1-33.

[112] Watts, D. *A simple model of global cascades on random networks*, Proceedings of the National Academy Sciences 99 (2002) 5,766-5,771.

[113] Nagurney, A. *Financial and economic netowrks: an overview*, in Innovations in financial and economic networks (2003), Edward Elgar Publishibg, 1-25.

[114] Boss, M.; Elsinger, H.; Thurner, S.; Summer, M. *An empirical analysis of the network structure of the Austrian interbank market*, Österreichischer Nationalbank Financial Stability Report (2004) 77-87.

[115] Vivier-Lirimont, S. *Interbanking networks: towards a small financial world?*, Cahiers de la Maison des Sciences Economiques v04046 (2004), Université Panthon-Sorbonne (Paris 1).

[116] Eboli, M. *Systemic risk in financial networks: a graph theoretic approach*, Universitá di Chieti Pescara (2004).

[117] Boss, M.; Elsinger, H.; Thurner, S.; Summer, M. *The network topology of the interbank market*, Quantitative Finance 4 (2004) 677-684.

[118] Leitner, Y. *Financial networks: contagion, commitment and private sector bailouts*, Journal of Finance 60 (2005) 2,925-2,953.

[119] Iori, G.; Masi, G.; Precup, O.V.; Gabbi, G.; Caldarelli, G. *A network analysis of the Italian overnight money market*, Discussion Paper Series 05/05, City University London (2005).

[120] Leitner, Y. *Financial networks: contagion, commitment and private sector bailouts*, Journal of Finance 60 (2005) 2925-2953.

[121] Markose, S.M. *Computability and evolutionary complexity: markets as complex adpative systems (CAS)*, Economic Journal 115 (2005) F159-F192.

[122] Muller, J. *Interbank credit lines as a channel of contagion*, Journal of Financial Services Research 29 (2006) 37-60.

[123] Soramäki, K.; Bech, M.L.; Arnold, J.; Glass, R.J.; Beyeler, W.E. *The topology of interbank payment flows*, Physica A 379 (2007) 317333.

[124] Nier, E.; Yang, J.; Yorulmazer, T.; Alentorn, A. *Network models and financial stability*, Journal of Economic Dynamics and Control (2007).

[125] Kleinberg, J. *Cascading behavior in networks: algorithmic and economic issuses*, in Algorithmic Game Theory, 613-632, Cambridge University Press (2007).

[126] Castiglionesi, F.; Navarro, N. *Optimal fragile financial networks*, Tilburg University Discussion Paper no. 2007-100 (2007).

[127] Nier, E.; Yang, J.; Yorulmazer, T.; Alentorn, A. *Network models and financial stability*, Journal of Economic Dynamics and Control 31 (2007) 2,033-2060.

[128] Soramali, K.; Bech, M.L.; Arnold, J.; Glass, R.J.; Beyeler, W.E. *The topology of interbank payment flows*, Physica A 379 (2007) 317-333.

[129] Cossin, D.; Schellhorn, H. *Credit risk in a network economy*, Management Science 53 (2007) 1,604-1,617.

[130] Lorenz, J.; Battiston, S.; Schweitzer, F. *Systemin risk in a unifying framework for cascading processes on networks*, European Physics Journal B 71 (2009) 441-460.

[131] Haldane, A. *Rethinking the financial network*, speech delivered at the Financial Student Association, Amsterdam, Aprol (2009).

[132] Allen, F.; Babus, A. *Networks in finance*, in Kleindorfer, P., Wing, Y.,and Gunther, R. (eds.), *The network challenge: strategy, profit, and risk in an interlinked world*, (2009) Wharton Scool Publishing.

[133] Chan-Lau, J.; Espinosa, M.; Solé, J. *On the use of network analysis to assess systemic financial linkages*, (2009) IMF Global Financial Stability Report, Vol. 2, April 2009. Available at SSRN: http://ssrn.com/abstract=1417920.

[134] Georg, C-P; Poschmann, J. *Sistemic risk in a network model of interbank markets with central bank activity*, Jena Economic Research Papers (2010), University of Jena.

[135] Cont, R.; Moussa, A.; Santos, E.B. *Network Structure and Systemic Risk in Banking Systems* (2010). Available at SSRN: http://ssrn.com/abstract=1733528 or http://dx.doi.org/10.2139/ssrn.1733528

[136] Gai, P.; Kapadia, S. *Contagion in Financial Networks*, Proceedings of the Royal Society A 466 (2010).

[137] Canedo, J.M.D.; Martínez-Jaramillo, S. *Financial contagion: a network model for estimating the distribution of loss for the financial system*, Journal of Economic Dynamics and Control 34 (2010) 2358-2374.

[138] Cohen-Cole, E.; Patacchini, E.; Zenou, Y. *Systemic risk and network formation in the interbank market*, (2010) CAREFIN Research Paper No. 25/2010, University of Stockholm. Available at SSRN: http://ssrn.com/abstract=1799925.

[139] Dette, T.; Pauls, S.; Rockmore, D.N. *Robustness and contagion in the international financial network* (2010) arXiv:1104.4249v2.

[140] Georg, C-P *The Effect of the Interbank Network Structure on Contagion and Financial Stability*, Working Papers on Global Financial Markets, No. 12 (2010).

[141] Markose, S.; Giansante, S.; Gatkowski, M.; Shaghaghi, A.R. *Too Interconnected To Fail: Financial Contagion and Systemic Risk In Network Model of CDS and Other Credit Enhancement Obligations of US Banks*, COMISEF Working Papers Series WPS-033 21/04/2010 (2010).

[142] European Central bank Report, *Recent advances in modelling systemic risk using network analysis*, (2010), in http://www.ecb.int/pub/pdf/other/modellingsystemicrisk012010en.pdf.

[143] Billio, M.; Getmansky, A.; Lo, W.; Pelizzon, L. *Econometric measures of connectedness and systemic risk in the finance and insurance sectors*, (2011) Journal of Financial Economics, forthcoming.

[144] Larry, D.; Easley, J.; Kleinberg, R.; Tardos, E. *Network formation in the presence of contagious risk*, in Proceedings of the 12th ACM Conference on Electronic Commerce (2011), 1-10.

[145] Diebold, F.X.; Yilmaz, K. *On the network topology of variance decompositions: measuring the connectedness of financial firms* (2011) PIER Working Paper 11-031.

[146] Amini, H.; Cont, R.; Minca, A. *Resilience to contagion in financial networks*, (2012) arXiv:1112.5687v1.

[147] Babus, A. *The formation of financial networks*, (2012) Discussion Paper 06-093, Tinbergen Institute.

[148] Baral, P. *Strategic Behavior and endogenous risk of contagion in a financial network: a network financial game* (2012) Discussion Paper, Indiana University.

[149] Cabrales, A.; Gottardi, P.; Vega-Redondo, F. *Risk-sharing and contagion in networks* (2013) Economics Working Papers, http://EconPapers.repec.org/RePEc:cte:werepe:we1301.

[150] Elliott, M.; Golub, B.; Jackson, M.O. *Financial Networks and Contagion* (2013). Available at SSRN: http://ssrn.com/abstract=2175056.

[151] Acemoglu, D.; Ozdaglar, A.; Tahbaz-Salehi, A. *Systemic Risk and Stability in Financial Networks* (2013) NBER Working Paper No. 18727.

[152] Glasserman, P.; Young, H.P. *How likely is contagion in financial networks?* (2013) Oxford University - Department of Economics Discussion Paper Series.

INDEX

A

B

C

D

E

F

G

H

I

J

K

L

M

N

R

S

T

U

V

W

Y